INSTRUCTIONAL
COACHING

For Jenny—without your unwavering love and support this book never would have been written.

INSTRUCTIONAL COACHING

A Partnership Approach to Improving Instruction

JIM KNIGHT

A Joint Publication

CORWIN PRESS
A SAGE Publications Company
Thousand Oaks, CA 91320

For information:

Corwin Press
A Sage Publications Company
2455 Teller Road
Thousand Oaks, California 91320
www.corwinpress.com

Sage Publications Ltd.
1 Oliver's Yard
55 City Road
London EC1Y 1SP
United Kingdom

Sage Publications India Pvt. Ltd.
B 1/I 1 Mohan Cooperative Industrial Area
Mathura Road, New Delhi
India 110 044

Sage Publications Asia-Pacific Pte. Ltd.
33 Pekin Street #02-01
Far East Square
Singapore 048763

Printed in the United States of America

Library of Congress Cataloging-in-Publication Data

Knight, Jim.
Instructional coaching: A partnership approach to improving instruction / Jim Knight.
    p. cm.
Includes bibliographical references and index.
ISBN-13: 978-1-4129-2723-9 (cloth)
ISBN-13: 978-1-4129-2724-6 (pbk.)
    1. Teachers—Inservice training—United States. 2. Teacher effectiveness—United States. I. Title.
LB1731.K573 2007
370.71′5-dc22   2006030810

This book is printed on acid-free paper.

07 08 09 10 11   10 9 8 7 6 5 4

Acquisitions Editor:	Rachel Livsey
Editorial Assistant:	Phyllis Cappello
Production Editor:	Beth A. Bernstein
Copy Editor:	Jennifer Withers
Typesetter:	C&M Digitals (P) Ltd.
Proofreader:	Penny Sippel
Indexer:	John Hulse
Cover Designer:	Scott Van Atta
Graphic Designer:	Lisa Miller

Contents

Preface   ix

Acknowledgments   xi

About the Author   xv

1. Why Coaching?   **1**
    Chapter Overview   1
    The Failure of Traditional Professional Development   1
    So Why Doesn't Traditional Professional
       Development Work?   4
    The October Session: One Experience With
       One-Shot Sessions   5
    What Are Some Common Forms of Coaching?   9
    What's in the Book?   14
    A Final Word About Coaches   15
    Going Deeper   16
    To Sum Up   17

2. What Does Coaching Look Like?   **19**
    Chapter Overview   19
    What Does Coaching Look Like?   19
    Overcoming the Biggest Fear at the Start   20
    Finding the Right Starting Point   22
    The Big Four   23
    Building an Emotional Connection   24
    Encouraging Implementation   26
    Collaboration   27
    Modeling: You Watch Me   29
    Observing and Providing Feedback   29
    Support   31
    Partnering With the Principal   32
    Going Deeper   33
    To Sum Up   33
    Notes   33

3. What Is the Partnership Philosophy?   **37**
    Chapter Overview   37
    What Is the Partnership Philosophy?   37
    Going Deeper   52
    To Sum Up   53

4. **Partnership Communication: Creating Learning Conversations**   **57**

    Chapter Overview   57

    Creating Learning Conversations   57

    The Communication Process   59

    Employing Authentic Listening   60

    Understanding Our Audience   65

    Recognizing and Overcoming Interference   69

    Just Talking Together   73

    The Subtle Language of Communication: Facial Expressions and Emotional Connections   73

    Building an Emotional Connection   75

    How It All Fits Together, Sort Of   78

    Going Deeper   78

    To Sum Up   79

5. **Getting Teachers on Board and Finding a Starting Point**   **81**

    Chapter Overview   81

    Getting Teachers on Board   81

    Stages of Change: Prochaska, Norcross, and DiClemente   85

    The Stages of Change and Professional Learning in Schools   87

    Sourpuss   89

    The Components of Coaching: Enroll, Identify, and Explain   89

    How to Build Relationships During Interviews   94

    Going Deeper   106

    To Sum Up   107

6. **Modeling, Observing, and Collaboratively Exploring Data**   **109**

    Chapter Overview   109

    Empowering Teachers to Master New Teaching Practices   110

    Model: You Watch Me   111

    The Light Just Went On   118

    Model Lessons and Tacit Knowledge   119

    Observe: I Watch You   120

    Explore: The Collaborative Exploration of Data   122

    Core Concerns   132

    Going Deeper   135

    To Sum Up   136

7. **Focusing on the Big Four: Behavior, Content Knowledge, Direct Instruction, and Formative Assessment**   **139**

    Chapter Overview   139

    The Power of Focus   139

    Two Disclaimers Before We Begin   140

The Big Four   141
Developing and Teaching Expectations   143
Content Coaching   151
Coaching Instruction   162
Instructional Coaching and Formative Assessment   170
Going Deeper   176
To Sum Up   177
Note   177

8. How Coaches Can Spread Knowledge   **179**
Chapter Overview   179
How Ideas Spread   179
Understanding Memes   181
Resilient Viruses   182
Born Again   183
Ensuring That Practices Shared Are Easy and Powerful   184
Employing Self-Organization and Coherence-Building
     Practices to Go School wide With Instructional Coaching   185
Having an Infectious Personality   187
Partnering With the Principal   189
Following the Law of the Few   191
Going Deeper   194
To Sum Up   195
Note   195

9. Coaches as Leaders of Change   **197**
Coaches as Leaders of Change   197
Tactic 1: Stay Detached   198
Tactic 2: Walk on Solid Ground   203
Tactic 3: Clarifying Your Message   204
Tactic 4: Managing Change Effectively   205
Tactic 5: Confronting Reality   208
Tactic 6: Understanding School Culture   210
Tactic 7: Being Ambitious and Humble   211
Tactic 8: Taking Care of Yourself   213
Faith   215
The Final Word on Jean Clark and Bohemia Manor
     Middle School   216
Going Deeper   217
To Sum Up   218
Note   218

Resource: Instructional Coach's Tool Kit   **219**

References   **225**

Index   **233**

My interest in instructional coaching has been percolating ever since I first began leading professional development sessions more than 15 years ago. In my early days, when I was facilitating one-day inservice sessions on the scientifically proven writing strategies from the Strategic Instruction Model, I would give each participant a stamped postcard, explaining that I really wanted to hear their success stories. "When you try these strategies out," I'd say, "be sure to send me a quick note to let me know how things went." At the end of 2 years, I had not received one postcard! The reality was, I suspected, that inservice sessions just did not provide enough support for most people to actually implement what they had learned. Some other form of professional development was needed if teachers were actually going to be able to implement new practices. What model of professional development could provide the kind of support teachers require to implement new proven practices?

After trying to answer that question for 10 years, I feel confident saying that instructional coaching is one approach that does provide the necessary support for implementation. This book describes the "nuts and bolts" of instructional coaching, the principles behind those "nuts and bolts," and the preliminary research I have conducted on coaching. This is a "how-to guide" and a description of a new model. I hope instructional coaches and anyone else interested in establishing, supporting, or learning about instructional coaching find this book to be a comprehensive and useful guide.

The book, however, has another purpose. One of my goals is to promote healthier, more respectful conversations. When people talk about learning, the experience should be exciting, energizing, and empowering. After talking together, both instructional coaches and teachers should feel more competent and committed to making a difference in children's lives. Instructional coaches, I believe, can have an unmistakable, positive impact on schools simply by having many, many healthy conversations with teachers. This book, then, is about how to improve instruction, but it is also about how to improve school culture.

The main ideas addressed by each chapter are summarized below:

- Chapter 1 includes an introduction to instructional coaching, summarizes the research I have conducted on this approach, and lays out the general plan of the book.

- Chapter 2 provides a quick overview of the typical activities completed by instructional coaches in schools.
- Chapter 3 summarizes the partnership principles, the theory behind our model of instructional coaching.
- Chapter 4 describes several communication strategies people can use to increase their ability to communicate effectively.
- Chapter 5 explains strategies instructional coaches can use to enroll teachers in coaching, to identify new teaching practices, and to explain those practices teachers will learn during instructional coaching.
- Chapter 6 explains strategies instructional coaches can use to model, observe, and provide feedback on new teaching practices.
- Chapter 7 describes many proven teaching practices instructional coaches can share, organized by a framework we refer to as the Big Four of behavior, content knowledge, direct instruction, and formative assessment.
- Chapter 8 offers suggestions on how coaches can spread ideas across schools.
- Chapter 9 describes several leadership tactics instructional coaches can use to overcome obstacles they will encounter as they lead change.

After Chapter 1, every chapter contains features that I have included to paint a more vivid picture of what instructional coaching is and what it can be. Each chapter profiles an instructional coach and includes vignettes written in the real voices of coaches, boxes highlighting especially important information or resources, a "Going Deeper" section filled with suggestions for further readings, and a short summary of the main points of each chapter.

I hope the format and content of the book prove helpful to everyone engaged in this complex and very important work of improving the lives of students by improving the ways teachers teach and interact in schools. Indeed, for those of you who do implement these ideas, I'd love to hear from you. Postcards would be especially nice.

—Jim Knight
University of Kansas Center for Research on Learning
Lawrence, Kansas

Acknowledgments

Conversation stands at the heart of instructional coaching and at the heart of my work on this book. Some conversations have been interviews, chats on the phone, or heated, joyful interactions in teachers' lounges, homes, restaurants, or hotel lobbies during conferences. I've also had many conversations with the books and articles written by authors and researchers, literally too numerous to mention. I am very thankful for the words, ideas, and insights gathered from all of these conversations, whether with people or texts.

The influence of many has been so profound that I must express my gratitude to those individuals by name. I am especially grateful to the instructional coaches featured in these chapters: Lynn Barnes, Shelly Bolejack, Jean Clark, Devona Dunekack, LaVonne Holmgren, Tricia McKale, Ric Palma, and Sue Woodruff all generously shared their time and, more important, their ideas and insights during numerous interviews over the past several years.

Other instructional coaches have taught me about the day-to-day joys and sorrows of their profession. In particular, I'm grateful to instructional coaches from the Pathways to Success Project, including Stacy Cohen, Susan Claflin, Shelly Kampshroeder, Wendy Meier, and Margo Stewart, as well as instructional coaches from Passport to Success in Maryland, including Sherry Eichinger, Dona Fava, Cheryl Malone, Monica Phelps, Lisa Sligh, and my sister (in every way except heredity) Doris Williams. Also, Project Coordinator Bill Towns and USD 501's District Liaison Jim Glass have both put innumerable hours into supporting Pathways to Success.

My thinking about what instructional coaching is and can be has also been greatly advanced by several authors who have taken time to share their insights with me as I've stumbled along this twisted road we call school improvement. I am especially grateful to Michael Fullan, who started me on this professional journey and whose ideas lie just beneath the surface of many of the words written here. Stephanie Hirsh, Joellen Killion, Wendy Reinke, Randy Sprick, and Richard Stiggins have also very generously taken time out to share their knowledge with me on many occasions. Each of these authors truly influences me and, indeed, they are shaping the way in which students are taught in schools across North America. We all owe them a great debt of gratitude.

The research and writing of this book have been especially aided by the excellent effort of my longtime coworker Carol Hatton, who has kept the wheels on every project I've led in the past 10 years.

David Gnojek is a gifted graphic artist who formatted all of the forms in this book. Soonhwa Seok has been a tireless research assistant, and Kirsten McBride's edits and comments improved the writing of every page in this book. Ethel Edward's careful reading and comments also significantly improved my text. I am grateful for each person's willingness to help with this project and more grateful for their substantial contributions. I would also like to acknowledge the U.S. Department of Education for supporting our professional development efforts and offer a special thanks to our GEAR UP program officer, Karmon Simms-Coates, for her timely, warmhearted support and advice.

I also wish to express my gratitude to my research colleagues at the Kansas University Center for Research on Learning. Better advisors than Don Deshler and Jean Schumaker do not exist. They taught me how to do research, how to write about it, and even more about how to be a decent human being. My other colleagues at CRL, Irma Brasseur, Jan Bulgren, Barb Ehren, Mike Hock, and Keith Lenz, are doing work that continually shapes my thinking, encourages me to do better, and profoundly improves the lives of children.

Finally, I am grateful to my family. My parents, Doug and Joan Knight, have always shown amazing and maybe even irrational parental faith in me. My children, Geoff, Cameron, David, Emily, Ben, and Isaiah, have patiently and graciously allowed me the freedom to work on this project at times when they could have rightfully asked for more of my time or compassion. Finally, the heroic support, patience, and encouragement of my wife, Jenny, have made it possible for me to do this work. She also happens to be an incredibly dedicated, loving, and talented teacher.

Corwin Press gratefully acknowledges the contributions of the following reviewers:

Jane Ellison
Codirector
Center for Cognitive Coaching
Centennial, CO

Cathy Collins Block
Professor of Education
Texas Christian University
Fort Worth, TX

J. Helen Perkins
Assistant Professor of Urban Literacy and Reading
College of Education, Instruction and Curriculum Leadership
University of Memphis
Memphis, TN

Dale Moxley
Principal
Round Lake Conversion Charter School
Mount Dora, FL

Laurie Crehan
Educational Consultant
San Diego, CA

Joellen Killion
Director of Special Projects
National Staff Development Council
Arvada, CO

Audrey F. Lakin
Teacher Induction and Mentoring Coordinator
Community Unit District #300
Carpentersville, IL

Mark Bower
Director of Elementary Education and Staff Development
Hilton Central School District
Hilton, NY

Kathy Kee
Leadership Coach and Consultant
Coaching School Results
Shady Shores, TX

Jim Knight, a Research Associate at the University of Kansas Center for Research on Learning, has spent the past decade studying instructional coaching. Jim directs Pathways to Success, a districtwide instructional improvement partnership between the University of Kansas and the Topeka, Kansas, School District. Jim is a coauthor of *Coaching Classroom Management* along with Randy Sprick, Wendy Reinke, and Tricia McKale, and he has published several articles on instructional coaching in publications such as *The Journal of Staff Development*, *Principal Leadership*, and *The School Administrator*. Jim is frequently asked to provide professional development on instructional coaching and has presented in more than 35 states, most of the Canadian provinces, and Japan. He has also won several university teaching and leadership awards. Having lived the majority of his life in Canada, Jim now calls Lawrence, Kansas, home.

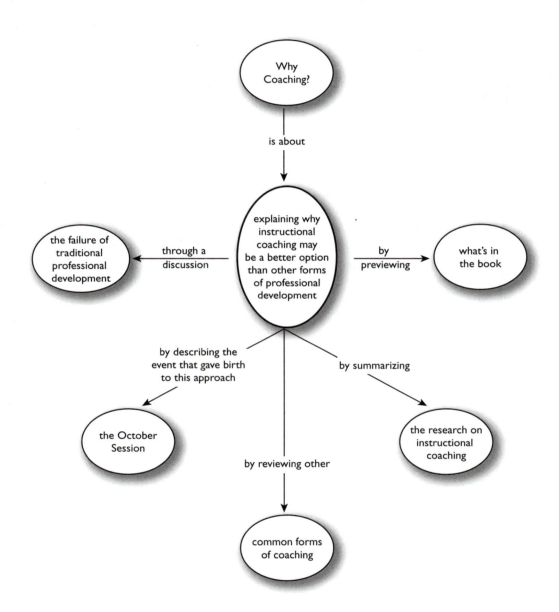

Why Coaching?

Chapter 1

Quick fixes never last and teachers resent them; they resent going to inservices where someone is going to tell them what to do but not help them follow up. Teachers want someone that's going to be there, that's going to help them for the duration, not a fly-by-night program that's here today gone tomorrow.

—Lynn Barnes, instructional coach, Pathways to Success

CHAPTER OVERVIEW

The pressure to improve instruction in schools may be greater today than at any other time in the history of American education. Instructional coaching, the topic of this book, can help schools respond to the pressure. This chapter provides an introduction to instructional coaching, discussing (a) why traditional professional development fails, (b) the session that prompted the development of this model of instructional coaching, (c) various forms of coaching, (d) the research conducted on instructional coaching, and (e) the topics that will be discussed in future chapters.

THE FAILURE OF TRADITIONAL PROFESSIONAL DEVELOPMENT

For better or worse, the No Child Left Behind (NCLB) legislation has turned the nation's attention to the way teachers teach and students learn, and schools everywhere are searching for proven ways to improve students' scores and to help their schools achieve Annual Yearly Progress (AYP). Feeling the heat of NCLB, educational leaders are paying unprecedented attention to how students and teachers learn in their schools and classrooms. With their magnifying glasses focused on instructional practices, many school leaders are discovering that traditional training methods simply do not get the job done.

The unprecedented interest in instructional improvement has also heightened decision makers' interest in effective professional development practices. As research has shown for years, traditional forms of professional development are not effective, usually getting no better than a 10% implementation rate (Bush, 1984). Teachers' stories reinforce what research suggests. During hundreds of interviews I've conducted across the United States, teachers are unanimously critical of one-shot programs that fail to address practical concerns. Teachers criticize training that lacks follow-up and that fails to recognize their expertise.

The old model of an expert talking to a room full of strangers is in some cases literally worse that nothing, leaving teachers frustrated, disappointed, insulted—feeling worse off than before the session. One teacher I interviewed a few years ago summed up the view of many teachers I've spoken with over the years: "It's not like we are undergraduates. There are many people on our staff who are bright and who do read what's going on in the field, who do take classes on their own time, not because they have to but because they love to teach. And I do think it's kind of demeaning [when a presenter appears not to] know about that."

The worst consequence of an overreliance on traditional forms of professional development may be that poorly designed training can erode teachers' willingness to embrace *any* new ideas. After attending several unsuccessful training sessions, teachers often lose their enthusiasm for new interventions, and each additional ineffective session makes it more and more difficult for them to embrace new ideas. Increasingly, as the diagram below indicates, it looks like the chances are slim that any one-shot program, no matter how well presented, will have any positive impact on teaching.

Figure 1.1 Impact of One-Shot Professional Development on Teacher Practices

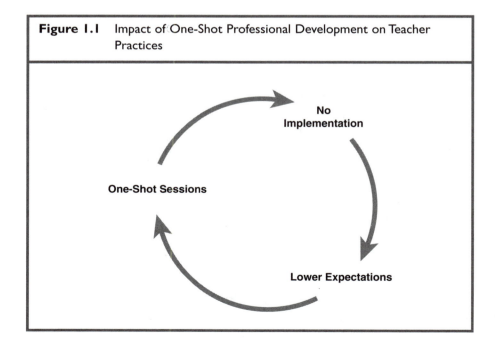

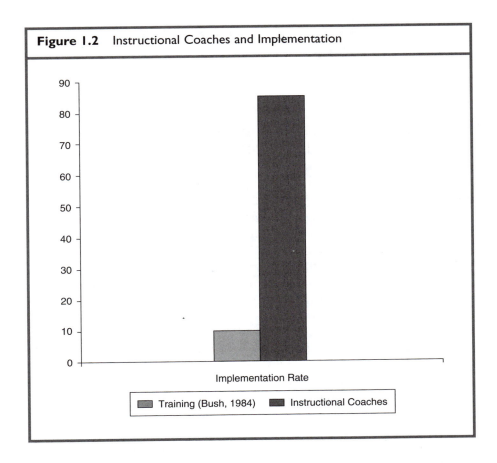

Figure 1.2 Instructional Coaches and Implementation

When educational leaders see their one-shot programs failing to catch fire, they start searching for reasons for that failure. Not surprisingly, teachers are often blamed for "resisting change." In turn, teachers, feeling slighted by their leaders, tell each other "this too will pass" whenever a new innovation is introduced. Ultimately, both educational leaders and teachers get caught in a vicious cycle of blame and resistance. That is, educational leaders increasingly express their frustration with teachers who resist change, and teachers who experience poorly designed program after program adopt apathy as a cultural norm.

After interviewing more than 150 teachers across the United States about their views on professional development, I have concluded that teachers do not resist change so much as *they resist poorly designed change initiatives.* Teachers engage in professional development every day—they just don't do it with professional developers. Teachers learn from each other all the time, sharing lesson plans, assessments, activities, and ideas about individual students. Our experience has shown that when teachers receive an appropriate amount of support for professional learning, more than 90% of them embrace and implement programs that improve students' experiences in the classroom. The challenge for educational leaders, then, is to create and deploy professional development that makes it easier for teachers to implement change initiatives.

SO WHY DOESN'T TRADITIONAL PROFESSIONAL DEVELOPMENT WORK?

There are many reasons why traditional professional development fails. First, all teachers face what Michael Fullan and Andy Hargreaves (1996) have referred to as a "pressing immediacy." "There are always things to be done, decisions to be made, children's needs to be met, not just every day, but every minute, every second" (p. 65). In a typical day, teachers have stacks of papers that need to be graded, parents who need to be called, lesson plans that need to be developed, reports that need to be completed, meetings that need to be attended, and so on. On top of that, they must complete all of these tasks while working on a job that requires a great deal of emotional fortitude. The result is that even if teachers want to implement some new program, they may not have the energy necessary to put it into practice.

But let's say a teacher does have an astonishing abundance of energy and the emotional resilience necessary to learn new things in the middle of his or her busy days. A second common barrier to implementing new programs is the sheer number of competing interventions in a district. With districts desperate to reach AYP, many leaders have decided that more is better, even if more is just more strategies without any kind of realistic implementation plan. The tendency of some districts to offer more and more new practices, without developing effective supports for those practices, reminds me of an old joke by Woody Allen. Two women are talking about the food in their retirement home. One turns to the other and says, "The food here is terrible." The other nods in agreement, frowns, and says, "Oh yes, and the portions are so small."

Like the women in the joke, many teachers face a menu of too much training, too poorly delivered. They are expected to implement Assessment for Learning, Understanding by Design, Differentiated Instruction, Dimensions of Learning, Positive Behavior Supports, Content Enhancement, and Learning Strategies Instruction all at once, usually with very little support. Each of these interventions, properly supported, could make a difference in students' lives. But when intervention upon intervention is served up with no attention to implementation planning, teachers begin to feel overwhelmed. Eric Abrahamson has rightly referred to this phenomenon as "initiative overload," "the tendency of organizations to launch more change initiatives than anyone could reasonably handle" (2004, p. 3). When faced with "initiative overload," Abrahamson says, "people . . . begin to duck and take cover whenever they see a new wave of initiatives coming" (p. 3).

Another reason why change doesn't occur is the complexity of change of any sort at the individual level. Personal change is much more complicated than most people realize. Changing the way we teach requires us to change habits of behavior, and changing habits is not easy, as anyone who has tried to quit smoking, lose weight, stop spending, or increase exercising has realized. Loehr and Schwartz's research (2003) on personal change gives us some insight into why we often find it difficult to change. The authors explain that even if we really want to change in some way, personal change only happens when we overcome our habitual way of living. Desire and willpower usually aren't enough to make real change occur. Due to our habitual nature, we are naturally inclined to protect the status quo. James Flaherty, an expert in the broader field of coaching, makes the same observation about coaching: "people generally aren't open to being coached because they already have a habitual way of accomplishing something with all the resultant components of that process, both physical and mental" (1999, p. 61).

Change is difficult because change requires us to change our habits and create new routines. If teachers are emotionally fatigued by the pressing immediacy of their professional life, overwhelmed by innovation overload, is it any surprise if they are not quick to pick up a practice and make it a routine in the classroom? Yet teachers need to keep trying to learn and implement better instructional practices if schools are going to get better at reaching all students. Instructional coaching represents one efficient method to help teachers learn better ways to teach their students.

The seeds for the particular model of instructional coaching I describe in this book ironically grew out of one of my worst experiences as a professional developer.

THE OCTOBER SESSION: ONE EXPERIENCE WITH ONE-SHOT SESSIONS

Several years ago, when I was a wet-behind-the-ears professional developer, I learned first-hand how ineffective my own traditional professional development sessions could be. Enthusiastic about sharing my experiences of teaching learning strategies from the Strategic Instruction Model developed at the Kansas University Center for Research on Learning, I found myself presenting to people I had never met before. Armed with all of my own personal success stories and a hefty stack of overhead transparencies, I was frequently disappointed to see how my audiences reacted to my presentations. During my one-shot sessions, teachers read newspapers, did crossword puzzles, graded assignments, engaged in side conversations, drew up football plays— pretty much did anything except listen to me. When I looked at the teachers in my sessions, I saw far too many people who did not look happy. "Why is everyone so angry about what I've got to say?" I wondered. Even if my postworkshop evaluations were positive, when I checked back to see what was happening in the schools, I discovered that no one was implementing what I had trained them on.

My unhappy experiences as a professional developer came to a head during a workshop I led on the Concept Mastery Routine (Bulgren, Deshler, & Schumaker, 1993) in a small urban district. During this session, teachers actually started to attack one another in a nasty argument after I asked them what barriers prevented them from implementing the routine. Some teachers said they flat-out could not see how Concept Mastery could help them in their classroom. Others said that they didn't like being taken away from their students for professional development. Some claimed they had no idea of the purpose of the session.

The discussion got more heated. Two teachers angrily argued about coordinating extracurricular tasks and schoolwork. Some teachers shushed others, while others openly criticized their peers for being rude. Teachers complained about such problems as teaching to the test, lack of time, jargon, lack of prior knowledge for the training, poor communication, class size, and a lack of motivation for change. Luckily, after everyone had expressed their opinions, I had a Jerry Seinfeld film clip to show that helped to reduce some of the tension and get the group back on track. In the workshop evaluations, however, the group's feelings still came out:

- There is so much negativity, it seems, just toward trying something new.
- I regret the less-than-warm reception you have received from our department.
- Education is in such a state of flux that we need to be tolerant of change. Clearly, we have a problem there.
- The lack of communication ended up putting you in a sticky, hostile situation.
- There is no way you can convince all of us to do this.
- Not all of us are feeling as bitchy as some of the others around us.
- The problem of education is too overwhelming; we should all be put on retirement and get a new fresh group to learn the new way to teach the kinds of students that we get today. Anyone with any prior knowledge or experience is too set in their ways, old and jaded.
- I have a really bad headache and I have to have an ulcer test Monday.

One teacher's comments about the session, reconstructed in the following vignette, convey the sentiments most people held about the session.

The October Session

I always find it embarrassing to be a part of that group. I think we [could have] treated you better. I think it was set up to fail because there was no real ... maybe there was an attempt on various parts to communicate, but communication was not clear ... what

> *our goals were and what we were doing there. I don't think anyone had a clear purpose in being there, but that kind of meeting where people are angry is pretty typical of many of our meetings. I usually go away with a stomachache because I think there is a lot of disregard for the way people are treated, and there's lack of respect for individual differences and just a lot of impracticality. I think, for me personally, I would have cut through the crap and got it done. That was not your problem, but I felt that you had to deal with the brunt of that, and I was angry at the leadership for not being more assertive and knowing, or making us know, that these weren't your issues and what we were doing there....*

Since I am both a professional developer and a researcher, I was able to put some distance between myself and the failure of my session by turning the event into a research project. I decided to interview all of the teachers to find out why they reacted as they did. After I conducted the interviews and analyzed the data, I found that the workshop was a much more complex human interaction than I had realized. In the interviews, several reasons surfaced for why teachers acted as they did, summarized in the following five themes:

1. The middle school teachers, who had been asked by the senior high teachers to attend this workshop, considered this to be one more example of the senior high teachers not valuing them as educators.

2. There were several interpersonal issues that I was unaware of. In fact, I had put two people together in a cooperative learning activity who had not talked to each other for five years.

3. Many saw the session as an attempt by the administration to tell them what to do without consulting with teachers; for some, it was just another example of the "head shed" telling the teachers what to do.

4. Teachers were overwhelmed, feeling that they did not have time to implement any new innovation. Many resented the time taken up by the session, which they thought they could have used more productively on their own.

5. There was a history of poor professional development in the district, so the teachers came in with very low expectations.

During my interviews, I listened to the teachers with a mixture of relief and sadness. On the one hand, I was relieved to find that I personally wasn't the reason why the session had failed—the Wayne Gretzky of professional developers probably couldn't have pulled off the session since there were so many negative subcurrents. On the other hand, I began to wonder how any professional development session could work. Every person I spoke with made it clear that traditional professional development was much more of a burden than a help.

Ironically, in the midst of these interviews, as I heard repeatedly about the failure of professional development, the seeds of a new approach to teacher learning began to take root. The same teachers who had read newspapers and carefully ignored my eye contact in the workshop were transformed during the interviews into engaging, warm people that I enjoyed talking with and who seemed to enjoy talking with me. Teachers were candid, open, and good-humored, and they treated me more like a colleague than an outsider. I laughed with them; I did my best to understand their way of understanding events, and I came to feel a real connection with many. After every interview, I felt that each of us left feeling respected by each other.

When I returned to lead another workshop with the same teachers, they related to me in a completely different way. Since the interviews, the teachers had come to see me as someone like them. As a result, they listened during the session, and then honestly said what they thought. Not everyone agreed that the Content Enhancement Routine I was discussing was ideal for them, but many liked it, and the others were honest and tactful about respecting their colleagues' choices.

The comments on evaluations from the second session showed how much the interviews had changed the teachers' experience of the professional development I offered:

- Session today went fine. This session let us work together. We really made some progress—it was positive.
- I'm feeling very positive about knowing exactly what I'm working towards.
- Some of the other strategies sound cool (like comparison and anchoring) and I'm anxious to learn about these as well.
- The dialogue among teachers was terrific!
- I feel up, positive, and excited about the pending changes in Eng I and Eng II. I think today went well.
- This went fantastically! This is the first time in a *long* time that I have felt upbeat and positive about approaching curriculum change—almost even about the teaching process given the challenges we will be faced with.
- There is a light at the end of the tunnel, and we're beginning to breathe fresh air.

My research on professional development for the past 15 years has largely involved a variety of attempts at trying to understand and describe why it was that I was able to get through to this group of teachers. Since that workshop, I've come to believe, and my research suggests the same (Knight, 2000), that the theory underlying a professional developer's approach is an important predictor of success or failure. I've also come to see that working one-to-one, listening, demonstrating empathy, engaging in dialogue, and communicating honestly are all a part of successful professional development. The seeds that were planted when I conducted my interviews several years ago have grown into an approach that I refer to as *instructional coaching*. This book defines what instructional coaching is, how and why instructional coaching works, and what effective instructional coaches (ICs) do. Let's begin by looking at various models of coaching in education and other fields.

WHAT ARE SOME COMMON FORMS OF COACHING?

The concept of coaching, though it has been around for decades, perhaps centuries, has been described in much greater detail over the past 20 years. Indeed, the publications from the business world, other sectors, and from education are providing a clearer picture of just what coaching is and is not.

Executive Coaching

The most comprehensive literature on coaching comes from the business world, where executive coaching has become a booming industry. Given such names as transformational coaching and process coaching, executive coaching is an increasingly popular method for helping people become more competent in one or more areas of their (usually professional) lives. As Marshall Goldsmith and his colleagues so succinctly summarize it, an executive coach "establishes and develops healthy working relationships by surfacing issues (raw data gathering), addressing issues (through feedback), solving problems (action planning), and following through (results)—and so offers a process in which people develop and through which obstacles to obtaining business results are removed" (Goldsmith, Lyons, & Freas, 2000, p. xviii).

Coactive Coaching

Whitworth, Kimsey-House, and Sandahl's *Co-active Coaching* (1998) steps beyond the traditional borders of executive coaching to assume a client-coach relationship that involves the "whole of a person's life" (p. 7). Thus coactive coaches may address issues related to their client's "career, health, finances, relationships, personal growth, spirituality, and recreation" (p. 7). Coactive coaches work in partnership with their clients so that their clients can live more fulfilled, balanced, and effective lives.

This approach to coaching is "coactive" because (a) clients work with a coach so that they can *act* on aspects of their lives and (b) the coaching relationship that is the catalyst for the learning that makes action possible is entirely a *collaborative* effort. As Whitworth and her colleagues have stated (1998), "in a coactive coaching relationship the agenda comes from the client, not the coach. The relationship is entirely focused on getting the results clients want. They set the agenda" (p. 4) and "the coach and client work together to design an alliance that meets the client's needs" (p. 7).

Coactive coaches work with clients to bring about more learning and action in three broad domains: fulfillment, balance, and process. *Fulfillment* is the goal of living a life in which we feel we are doing the most important work and action we can do. *Fulfillment* "at its deepest level is about finding and experiencing a life of purpose. It's about reaching one's full potential" (Whitworth et al., 1998, p. 7). *Balance* is the goal of living a life in which all aspects of our life are fully developed, and thus coactive coaching addresses "the whole of a person's life" (p. 11). Finally, *process* refers to the coach's role in walking through action and learning with a client, and helping the client to see beyond "trapped perspectives" that might limit learning or action. As Whitworth et al. observe, "part of the coach's job is to be with the client in the process—to be in the flow with the client" (1998, p. 144). Clients, working with coactive coaches, "realize they are not buying an off-the-shelf personal success program. They are committing themselves to an ongoing relationship" (p. 13).

To produce meaningful learning and action in so many aspects of a person's life requires a particular kind of relationship. Coactive coaching brings coach and client together to work on the agenda that has been set by the client. However, the coach often has to work hard to help clients see just what it is that they want. Coactive coaches, thus, are curious, intuitive, authentic listeners who respect their client's confidentiality. Coactive coaches create space for conversation by remaining nonjudgmental.

Cognitive Coaching

Cognitive coaching is one of the most widely used forms of coaching in American schools today. Costa and Garmston (2002), through their publications and ongoing professional development, have articulated a theory of coaching that has provided tools for working with teachers and other educators. Thus, cognitive coaching lays out an efficient process for enhancing teachers' professional learning, describes useful communication and relationship-building tools that coaches can employ, and grounds those tools and procedures in a coherent theoretical foundation.

Cognitive coaching is predicated on the assumption that behaviors change after our beliefs change. "All behavior," Costa and Garmston (2002) observe, "is determined by a person's perceptions and . . . a change in perception and thought is prerequisite to a change in behavior . . . human beings construct their own meaning through reflecting on experience and through dialogue with others" (p. 7).

Since they assume that "a change in perception and thought is prerequisite to a change in behavior" (Costa & Garmston, 2002, p. 7), cognitive coaches work together with teachers to enhance their ability to reflect in collaboration with teachers. Thus, "Cognitive Coaching is non-judgmental mediation of thinking" (p. 12), something like reflection on steroids. Cognitive coaches learn to ask questions that encourage people to think about their actions; they listen attentively, and they use a variety of communication techniques to build and sustain the kind of rapport that is necessary for meaningful conversation.

Cognitive coaching can involve planning for and reflecting on one particular event, or it can stretch over years, requiring numerous interactions between a coach and colleague who together reflect on many different activities. Whether it takes place in a week or over several years, cognitive coaching almost always involves three interrelated elements: (a) a planning conversation; (b) an event, which usually is observed by the cognitive coach; and (c) a reflecting conversation.

The planning conversation usually occurs between a coach and a colleague before an event, most frequently before a teacher teaching a lesson. Among other things, the coach and colleague together clarify what the teacher's goals will be, what success will look like, the data that will be necessary to measure success, how the data will be collected, and strategies, methods, and decisions that will be necessary for success to be achieved.

The event may be anything that the cognitive coach and colleague agree on, but most frequently it is a lesson taught by the teacher. In most cases, a teacher teaches a lesson employing the strategies, methods, and decisions identified by the coach and teacher together. During the lesson, the cognitive coach gathers the data identified as necessary to measure success. The coach's goal is to objectively gather data so that the two partners will later be able to have a reflecting conversation about the event.

The reflecting conversation occurs after the event. Here, the cognitive coach and colleague review the data that the coach gathered while observing the lesson or event, make sense of the data by uncovering cause-effect relationships, construct new learning, decide how to apply that new knowledge, and then commit to using the new knowledge. Costa and Garmston (2002) state that an additional kind of conversation, a problem-resolving conversation, may be employed "when a colleague feels stuck, helpless, unclear or lacking in resourcefulness; experiences a crisis; or requests external assistance from a mediator" (p. 34).

The cognitive coach's focus throughout all conversations and events is "on mediating a practitioner's thinking, perceptions, beliefs, and assumptions toward the goals of self-directed learning and increased complexity of cognitive processing" (Costa & Garmston, 2002, p. 5). This focus also is a part of a much larger goal of helping individuals to work more effectively within larger systems and enhancing the effectiveness of professional and personal communities. As Costa and Garmston (2002) have observed, "the mission of Cognitive Coaching is to produce self-directed persons with the cognitive capacity for high performance, both independently and as members of a community" (p. 16).

Literacy/Reading Coaching

The terms *literacy coach* and *reading coach* are being used in a variety of ways in schools to refer to educators performing many different activities.

In some schools, a literacy coach has a wide range of responsibilities, all with the goal of helping teachers better serve students. For example, a literacy coach might teach teachers about reading strategies, graphic organizers, or teaching activities that will make it easier for students to understand texts or for teachers to communicate how language functions in their particular disciplines. In other situations, a literacy coach's primary responsibility might be to help students improve their writing skills, and the coach might perform little or no coaching with teachers. Not surprisingly, the various ways in which the term has been used have led to some confusion about what a literacy coach does.

This terminological confusion is further complicated by the equally inconsistent use of the term *reading coach*. Reading coaches may work as teachers providing services directly to students, may perform assessments for student placement decisions, or may be solely responsible for providing professional development to teachers. In some schools, the terms *literacy coach* and *reading coach* are used interchangeably, while in others, the roles of reading coach and literacy coach have very specific, distinct roles and responsibilities. Elizabeth Sturtevant, who conducted a review of the literature on literacy coaches, offered the following comments:

> The position of literacy coach is, in many ways, similar to that of the 1970s and early 1980s secondary school reading specialist who worked in federally funded projects in low-income schools across the United States. Like these earlier counterparts, the twenty-first century literacy coach must be highly knowledgeable in reading and literacy. (Sturtevant, 2005, p. 19)

In time, the role and certification requirements of literacy coaches will, no doubt, be articulated much more precisely. As I write these words, I am working with a committee of educators and researchers at the International Reading Association who are developing standards for literacy/reading coaches, and I expect those standards will help clarify what literacy coaches do and do not do. At this point, we can sum up by commenting generally that literacy and reading coaches perform a wide range of valuable activities in schools, sometimes working with students and more frequently working with teachers, to increase students' literacy skills and strategies.

Instructional Coaching

The rest of this book is dedicated to explaining what ICs do. We use the term to refer to individuals who are full-time professional developers, on-site in schools. ICs work with teachers to help them incorporate research-based instructional practices. When ICs work with students, they do so with the primary goal of demonstrating new effective practices to teachers. Like executive coaches, ICs must be skilled at unpacking their clients' (collaborating teachers) goals so that they can help them create a plan for realizing their professional goals. Like coactive coaches, ICs have to have a repertoire of excellent communication skills and be able to empathize, listen, and build relationships and trust. Also, like cognitive coaches, ICs must be highly skilled at facilitating teachers' reflection about their classroom practices.

Finally, like literacy coaches, ICs have to know a large number of scientifically proven instructional practices. While the literacy coach naturally focuses on literacy issues, the IC focuses on a broader range of instructional issues, sharing a variety of effective practices that might address classroom management, content enhancement, specific teaching practices, or formative assessment. The IC, in other words, collaborates with teachers so they can choose and implement research-based interventions to help students learn more effectively.

The Research

Much of the information in this book is the result of more than 10 years of systematic study of professional development. The bulk of that content comes from studies completed during Pathways to Success, a project funded by the national GEAR UP program. Pathways to Success is a partnership between the Kansas University Center for Research on Learning, where I work, and the Topeka, Kansas, school district—the district made famous more than 50 years ago by the Brown v. Board of Education ruling (Knight, 2004). Topeka is in many ways a typical urban district, with more than 60% of its students living in poverty, a high mobility rate for both students and teachers, and many students struggling to be academically successful. Since 1999, Pathways to Success has placed full-time ICs in all middle schools, and since 2002–2003, ICs have been employed in all of the high schools.

During Pathways to Success, we have conducted an intensive study of instructional coaching that has included dozens of ethnographic interviews with coaches, teachers, administrators, district administrators, and other educators in the district, and an annual monitoring of the percentage and depth of implementation in all middle and high schools. The scope (nine schools) and length (seven years) of Pathways to Success has provided an opportunity to also study how coaches can improve student achievement by enabling what we refer to as "hi-fi" teaching," teaching that demonstrates fidelity to the scientifically proven critical teaching behaviors of the various interventions being implemented.

Further, Pathways to Success has allowed us to conduct dozens of pretest-posttest and comparative studies of the impact of particular interventions, and we have also identified and validated practices that coaches can use to lead professional learning communities. The results of those studies, along with dozens of individual studies we've conducted of teachers implementing interventions, inform this discussion.

A second project, the Maryland State Department of Special Education Departments' Passport to Success, has provided another setting for extended study of instructional coaching. Passport to Success has achieved results that are comparable to the results achieved by Pathways to Success.

Prior to Pathways and Passport to Success, several other studies were conducted to establish the research foundation for the study of instructional coaching. First, to understand how teachers experience professional development, I conducted the ethnographic study described above (Knight, 2000), along with over 150 interviews with teachers across the nation. To better understand teachers, I also conducted a study of the role of personal vision in teachers' professional lives (Knight, 1994).

To validate the theoretical foundation for the instructional coaching approach, I conducted a study comparing two different approaches to professional development: (a) a traditional, lecture-based instructional model and (b) Partnership Learning, a dialogic approach to professional development built on seven principles of human interaction: equality, choice, voice, reflection, mutual learning, dialogue, and praxis (Knight, 1998). The partnership philosophy articulated for this study has come to be the theoretical foundation for instructional coaching.

Along with Don Deshler, Jean Schumaker, Irma Brasseur, and Paula Lancaster, I began the preliminary study of instructional coaching with the Strategic Advantage project, funded by the Office of Special Education in 1996. Strategic Advantage, a partnership between the Kansas University Center for Research on Learning and the Lawrence School District in Lawrence, Kansas, was a testing ground for many of the ideas that we implemented and studied more thoroughly with the Pathways to Success project.

WHAT'S IN THE BOOK?

This book provides an explanation of what instructional coaching is and how you can make it become a reality in your school or district. Each of the following chapters will describe practical ideas, concepts, theories, and skills that all coaches can use to be more effective. Also, each chapter will profile a particular coach and use his or her comments as real-life examples of the material being discussed. The chapters are organized as follows:

- Chapter 2: "What Does Coaching Look Like?" provides an overview of a typical IC's tasks and experiences.
- Chapter 3: "What Is the Partnership Philosophy?" provides an overview of the theory, philosophy, or mind-set on which we base our approach to instructional coaching.
- Chapter 4: "Partnership Communication: Creating Learning Conversations" includes descriptions of several communication strategies that ICs can employ to build healthy, mutually humanizing relationships with their colleagues.

- Chapter 5: "Getting Teachers on Board and Finding a Starting Point" is the first of two chapters providing an overview of the components of the instructional coaching process, including explanations of how ICs can enroll teachers, identify appropriate effective practices, and explain those practices.
- Chapter 6: "Modeling, Observing, and Collaboratively Exploring Data" continues the description of the components of instructional coaching with explanations of how ICs provide model lessons, observe teachers, gather data, collaboratively explore those data with teachers, and reflect on what they've done well as coaches and what they need to improve.
- Chapter 7: "Focusing on the Big Four: Behavior, Content Knowledge, Direct Instruction, and Formative Assessment" explains how effective coaches can focus their attention on high-leverage effective practices in four areas: behavior, content knowledge, direct instruction, and formative assessment.
- Chapter 8: "How Coaches Can Spread Knowledge" summarizes theories on how ideas spread in organizations and explains how coaches should employ these ideas as they spread knowledge in their schools.
- Chapter 9: "Coaches as Leaders of Change" describes eight leadership tactics coaches can use to lead change in schools and to protect themselves as they lead change.

A FINAL WORD ABOUT COACHES

Before describing some of the specific activities that coaches commonly do, I would like to discuss the implications of the term *coach*. I use the term with some cautions. For many years, we used the term *instructional collaborator* rather than *instructional coach* in Pathways to Success. We felt that the word *collaborator* best captured the kind of interaction that took place between coaches and collaborating teachers. In coaching relationships, both parties work in partnership to identify what intervention will be implemented, they plan instruction, they observe each other, and they share ideas back and forth in collaboration.

For many on the Pathways to Success team, the term *coach* is problematic because it has become associated with TV images of belligerent coaches throwing chairs across the court after a loss, or winning-obsessed coaches verbally abusing young people who mess up during a game. We obviously have another concept of coach in mind. Many who have been involved with coaches (sports coach, drama coach, or speech coach, for example) have had the pleasure of a different experience. A good coach is an excellent teacher and is kind-hearted, respectful, patient, compassionate, and honest. A good coach has high expectations and provides the affirmative *and* honest feedback that helps people to realize those expectations. A good coach can see something special in you that you didn't know was there and help you to make that something special become a living part of you. That is the kind of coach we have in mind when we use the term *instructional coach*.

GOING DEEPER

Coaching in Schools

Several books, listed here in alphabetical order, provide valuable perspectives on the potential for coaching in schools. Bloom, Castagna, Moir, and Warren's *Blended Coaching: Skills and Strategies to Support Principal Development* (2005) draws on the literature on coaching to present a comprehensive, adaptive coaching model for principals. Costa and Garmston describe the theory and practice of cognitive coaching in *Cognitive Coaching: A Foundation for Renaissance Schools* (2002). More information may be found at their Web site, http://www.newteachercenter.org/blended_coaching. Joellen Killion and Cindy Harrison's book *Taking the Lead: New Roles for Teachers and School-Based Coaches* (2006) provides a comprehensive description of the many roles that coaches perform in schools. Jane Kise's *Differentiated Coaching: A Framework for Helping Teachers Change* (2006) provides tools and a model coaches can use to recognize and respond to the differences in adults.

Other Books on Coaching

My understanding of instructional coaching has also been enriched by authors writing primarily for a business audience. Goldsmith, Lyons, and Freas's *Coaching for Leadership* (2000), which includes the bold claim that "coaching is destined to be the leadership approach of the twenty-first century" (p. xiii), offers a compendium of articles that look at such topics as defining coaching, describing the coaching relationship, providing feedback, contracting for coaching, and coaching for outcomes. Whitworth's *Coactive Coaching* (1998), "an approach that can be broadly applied to different occupations and coaching needs" (p. xviii), provides a coherent model of coaching that responds to all aspects of a person's life. Flaherty's *Coaching: Evoking Excellence in Others* (1999) provides a phenomenological theory of coaching and offers insight into how each individual's perceptions and interpretations impact the coaching experience. Duke Corporate Education's *Coaching and Feedback for Performance* (2006) includes a short overview of the GAPS process for coaching, which involves (a) goal setting, (b) assessing current progress, (c) planning the next steps, and (d) supporting the action.

TO SUM UP

- There is unprecedented interest in improving instruction in our schools.
- Traditional one-shot professional development usually fails to have any significant positive impact on teachers' instructional practices.
- Instructional coaching, used within the Pathways to Success project, has consistently achieved a 85% implementation rate in Topeka middle and high schools.
- The primary goal of instructional coaching is to enable teachers to implement scientifically proven instructional practices that respond directly to teachers' burning issues.
- Instructional coaching involves a carefully articulated philosophy and set of actions.

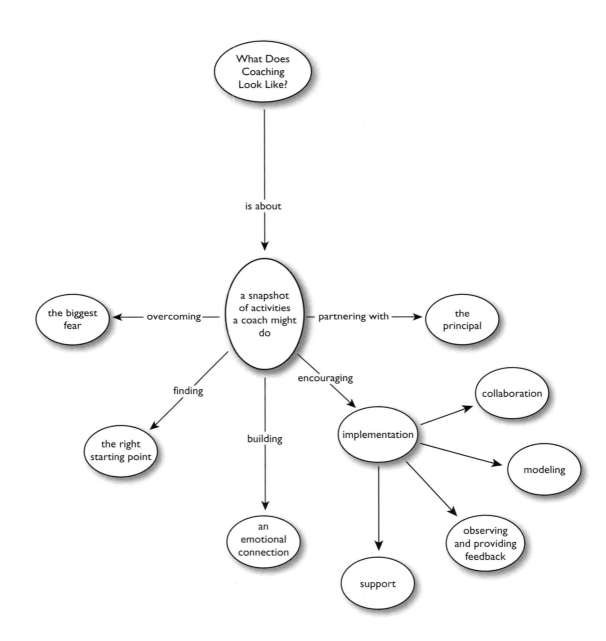

Chapter 2

What Does Coaching Look Like?

I am first a teacher. My job hasn't changed, but my audience has. Now I teach teachers to use strategies and routines. My job is still to impact kids, but now I do it by helping teachers be as focused and effective as they can be.

—Devona Dunekack,
instructional coach, Pathways to Success

CHAPTER OVERVIEW

Instructional coaching is certainly one of the most unpredictable professions in education; each day brings surprises, new challenges, and successes. However, an IC's life does have many common elements. This chapter provides a snapshot of many of those common activities, including (a) overcoming a coach's biggest fear; (b) finding a starting point; (c) building an emotional connection; (d) encouraging implementation through collaboration, modeling, observation, and support; and (e) partnering with the principal. This chapter is an overview, and all of these activities are described in more detail in subsequent chapters.

WHAT DOES COACHING LOOK LIKE?

After working as an IC for more than two years, Devona Dunekack fully understood that her job kept her moving. One day, she decided to find out just exactly how far her feet took her. Devona strapped on a pedometer and discovered that within her small middle school, she was walking more than five miles a day. "I learned," said Devona, "that anyone who wants to lose weight, just needs to do my job. I was walking everywhere."

Devona Dunekack

Devona has been an educator for 24 years. She was a middle school teacher for 16 years, and then spent 4 years working as curriculum coordinator. She has been an IC in the Pathways to Success program for five years and has been at Eisenhower Middle School for the past four. Devona is certified as a Strategic Instruction Model Content Enhancement Professional Developer and as a Learning Strategies Professional Developer. She is also a Trainer of Trainers for the Safe and Civil Schools CHAMPs approach to classroom management.

Devona's experiences are typical, if there is such a thing as a typical day for an IC. ICs find themselves completing many complex and varied tasks: meeting with teachers, modeling in their classrooms, observing, gathering classroom data, building relationships, preparing materials, facilitating learning teams, as well as doing the inescapable chores of every educational professional—attending meetings and doing paperwork. Each day brings unique surprises, challenges, and rewards that test the flexibility of even the most resilient coach. Devona considers this variety to be one of the joys of the job. "It is different every day. My whole day's plans might go out the window because a teacher's lesson plans change. Someone might snag me in the hall and open up a new opportunity for me. I love that part. I always go in wondering what will happen. I'm always challenged and surprised. And just like teaching, some days I expect trouble, and things work out beautifully; other days I expect smooth sailing, and I end up feeling flatter than a fritter."

Devona's work, as she says, is "different every day," yet what she has done over the days, months, and years at Eisenhower Middle School provides a useful example of the work done by many ICs. In this chapter I'll use Devona's experiences as illustrations for an overview of the strategies and tactics employed by ICs. All of the ideas summarized in this snapshot of the life of a coach will be elaborated in much greater detail in the subsequent seven chapters.

OVERCOMING THE BIGGEST FEAR AT THE START

For Devona and many ICs, the biggest fear when starting out is that teachers will not want to work with them. Not much will be accomplished if no one wants to work with the coach. I learned about the challenges of getting teachers on board more than eight years ago while leading a high school research project that required me to lead several curriculum changes, including integrating learning strategies into language arts classes, content enhancements into general education classes, and inclusive forms of instruction into technology classes. When I started explaining the project's work scope to people in the school, I learned quickly that most believed the technology classes would be my biggest challenge. One special education teacher's comments captured the opinion I heard again and again: "There's no stinkin' way you're going to get the shop teachers to work with you on this."

During my first meeting with the technology faculty, I began to wonder if maybe everyone had been right. We met on a hot day in May (the four men who taught technology classes, the department chair, and I) in a small, stuffy boardroom after school. As I explained the dimensions of the project, the group's antipathy to my suggestions filled the room like thick smoke. No one would look in my direction, and all four teachers seemed to focus their eyes on an invisible dot in the middle of the table. Everyone, except the department chair, had the kind of angry, resistant facial expressions that I assume most people save for auditors from the IRS. The room was hot when we first sat down, but the temperature seemed to go up by five degrees every five minutes as we proceeded.

To say the meeting was going poorly would be an understatement, so I decided to cut it short and asked if everyone would let me visit with them one-to-one so that I could learn more about what they taught. Once I knew more about their courses, I would explain, as honestly as I could, what the project might offer them, and then they could make a decision about participating. The department chair, who was probably quite excited about getting a lot of free professional development, encouraged everyone to agree, and we made plans to meet again.

When I met the teachers in their shops and classrooms, everything about our interactions improved. Meeting one-on-one, the teachers were very willing to talk with me. I was determined to listen to them, and they had a lot to tell me. In our conversations, the teachers explained that traditional professional development never seemed to be relevant to their classes. They also talked about their deep frustration with how they thought they were perceived in the school. They were professional, committed educators, but they felt the rest of the staff didn't see them that way. One drafting teacher said, "I actually had an English teacher ask me if I'd ever been to college; I just walked away and wrote her off."

After these one-to-one meetings, we all met again and, as I promised, I gave them an honest report on what I'd heard. This time, everyone was interested and involved in the conversation. At one point, one of the most resistant teachers turned to me and said, "You know, you might be the first person who has ever understood where we're coming from." That day all four teachers signed on. At the end of the two years of the project, we had worked together dozens of times to rewrite many of the units for three core technology classes, a far more ambitious accomplishment than I had hoped for when we started out. Because we met one-on-one, we found a way to work together. Without the one-on-one meetings, we would never have had the chance to find any common ground.

My experiences with the technology teachers play out daily in the professional experiences of ICs like Devona Dunekack. Many ICs find that the best way to involve teachers is to start by meeting with them one-on-one. As

Charles Bishop Jr. (2001) has commented, "the path to organizational change is through individual change" (p. 4) " . . . change happens one person at a time" (p. 1). Frequently, ICs get large groups of people on board by starting out one person at a time.

There are many ways that coaches enroll teachers, and most are described in detail in Chapter 5. Coaches might enroll teachers through large-group, small-group, or one-to-one presentations or conversations. What matters is that (a) coaches start by listening and respecting the teachers with whom they are interacting, and (b) they communicate that—more than anything else—they are another teacher willing to help.

Devona learned how to enroll teachers the hard way by entering a school where the staff was not enthusiastic about having a coach. In the year prior to her arrival at Eisenhower, fewer that 10 teachers had collaborated for a sustained period of time with their coach. However, Devona was determined to bring the school on board. Always respectful and persistent, she made it a point to spend time meeting with each teacher. She interviewed teachers in their classrooms and went out of her way to get to know teachers informally in the staff lounge, the halls, and around the school. She learned about the lives of her colleagues, built bridges, and started friendships one by one.

After Devona got to know the teachers in her school and they got to know her, they became interested in learning the best practices that Devona was able to share with them. Devona wrote a weekly newsletter in which she described the successes that school staff were having, and each week another teacher or two chose to work with her. Eventually, almost every teacher was collaborating with Devona. Not surprisingly, after being a struggling school for years, Eisenhower began to show the greatest gains on student achievement measures in the district.

FINDING THE RIGHT STARTING POINT

One challenge Devona faces every time she collaborates with a teacher is determining where to start. If ICs are unfocused in their efforts with teachers, they can waste teachers' and their own time, and ultimately, they miss a chance to improve children's learning experiences. ICs can increase their chances of having a big impact by focusing on high-leverage practices that truly respond to teachers' most pressing concerns.

Both of these concepts, focus and leverage, are important. Consider leverage: when a lever is placed on a fulcrum at the right spot, we need to exert only a tiny amount of effort to move something that is incredibly heavy. Similarly, Devona looks for scientifically proven practices that, like a lever, will have a profound impact on the quality of instruction. By focusing her efforts, Devona ensures that she brings maximum intensity to the challenge of improving instruction. One way to obtain that focus is to consider what I refer to as the Big Four issues: behavior, content knowledge, direct instruction, and formative assessment.

THE BIG FOUR

Chapter 7 provides a comprehensive explanation of the Big Four, but a brief summary is provided below.

Behavior. Teachers need to create a safe, productive learning community for all students. Coaches can help by guiding teachers to articulate and teach expectations, effectively correct behavior, increase the effectiveness of praise statements, and increase students' opportunities to respond (Sprick, Knight, Reinke, & McKale, 2007). Also, teachers can learn how to establish the essential elements of a learning community through interventions such as Talking Together (Vernon, Deshler, & Schumaker, 2000), a program researched at the Kansas University Center for Research on Learning.

Content knowledge. Teachers need to have a deep understanding of the content they are teaching. For that reason, coaches must know how to access state standards for courses and how to help teachers translate those standards into lesson plans. Coaches can use planning and teaching practices such as Keith Lenz's *Course* (Lenz, Schumaker, Deshler, & Bulgren, 1998) and *Unit Organizers* (Lenz, Bulgren, Schumaker, Deshler, & Boudah, 1994), Wiggins and McTighe's *Understanding by Design* (2nd ed., 2005), or Heidi Hayes Jacobs's *Getting Results With Curriculum Mapping* (2004) to help teachers unpack standards; plan courses, units, and lessons; and prioritize what content to teach.

Direct instruction. Over the past 25 years, researchers at the Kansas University Center for Research on Learning have identified and validated instructional practices that teachers can use to help students learn effectively. Our research suggests that instruction is improved when teachers (a) provide an advance organizer; (b) model the thinking involved in whatever processes are being learned; (c) ask a variety of high-level questions; and (d) ensure that students are experiencing engaging, meaningful activities. Many other authors, including Madeline Hunter (1994), Charlotte Danielson (1996), Marzano, Pickering, and Pollock (2001), and Joyce, Weil, and Calhoun (2001), have identified powerful instructional practices that coaches might also share with teachers so that they are better prepared to ensure that students master the content they are encountering in school.

Formative assessment. Teachers also need to know whether their students are learning the content and reasoning being taught and whether each student's skills or disposition is being affected by instruction. Teachers can make it easier for students to become motivated by (a) clearly identifying students' learning targets, (b) enabling students to see and monitor their progress, and (c) providing constructive feedback so students know what they still have to do to hit their learning targets. Richard Stiggins's and associate's *Classroom Assessment for Student Learning* (2004) provides excellent suggestions for how coaches can help their teachers form learning teams to become assessment literate.

BUILDING AN EMOTIONAL CONNECTION

Having a broad repertoire of best practices to share with teachers is only part of what a coach needs. Indeed, knowing a lot about teaching is only one part of coaching. A subtler but equally important goal for ICs is to establish emotional connections with collaborating teachers. John Gottman and Joan DeClaire (2001), who have studied thousands of hours of videotape of people interacting, conclude that "emotional communication . . . is the basic principle that regulates how relationships work" (p. xi). Their research, discussed in more detail in Chapter 4, suggests that relationship building is a subtle, unconscious dance between two partners, hinging on each person's ability to send and accept bids for emotional connection. Effective ICs skillfully act and communicate in hundreds of ways to establish that connection.

Devona and other ICs nourish their emotional connection with collaborating teachers by adopting a partnership philosophy (described in Chapter 3) and by using partnership communication skills (described in Chapter 4) to show genuine respect for the collaborating teacher. Devona comments, "As a partner, I want to help teachers feel good about what they do. Some are actually embarrassed to say they're teachers. I want them to feel competent and proud. I want them to know that the job they have is a job I love—the most important job in the universe."

What Is the Partnership Mind-set?

ICs adopt a "partnership" approach with teachers. Partnership,[1] at its core, is a deep belief that we are no more important than those with whom we work, and that we should do everything we can to respect that equality. This approach is built around the core principles of equality, choice, voice, dialogue, reflection, praxis, and reciprocity.

Equality

Partnership involves relationships between equals. Thus, in a partnership each person's thoughts and beliefs are held to be valuable. When this principle is applied to instructional coaching, it means that collaborating teachers are recognized as equal partners and, consequently, no one's view is more important or valuable than anyone else's.

Choice

In a partnership, one individual does not make decisions for another. Because partners are equal, they make their own choices and make decisions collaboratively. When this principle is applied to instructional coaching, it means that teacher choice is implicit in every communicative act and that, to the greatest extent possible, teachers have a great deal of choice in what and how they learn.

Voice

All individuals in a partnership must have opportunities to express their points of view. Indeed, a primary benefit of a partnership is that each individual has access to more than the perspective of the leader. When this principle is applied to instructional coaching, it means that teachers know they are free to express their opinions about content being learned. Furthermore, since different teachers have different opinions, ICs should encourage conversation that gives voice to a variety of opinions.

Dialogue

Partners engage in conversation that encourages others to speak their minds, and they try their best to listen authentically and to fully understand what others say. When two or more people act in such a way, they begin to think together, or engage in what many have described as dialogue. When this principle is applied to instructional coaching, it means that ICs listen more than they tell. ICs avoid manipulation, engage teachers in conversation about content, and think and learn with them.

Reflection

If we are creating a learning partnership, if our partners are equal with us, if they are free to speak their minds and free to make real, meaningful choices, it follows that one of the most important choices they will make is how to make sense of whatever we are proposing they learn. Partners don't dictate to each other what to believe; they respect their partners' professionalism and provide them with enough information so that they can make their own decisions. When this principle is applied to instructional coaching, it means that ICs encourage collaborating teachers to consider ideas before adopting them. Indeed, ICs recognize that reflective thinkers, by definition, have to be free to choose or reject ideas or else they simply are not thinking at all.

Praxis

Partnership should enable individuals to have more meaningful experiences. In partnership relationships, meaning arises when people reflect on ideas and then put those ideas into practice. A requirement for partnership is that each individual is free to reconstruct and use content the way he or she considers it most useful. When this principle is applied to instructional coaching, it means that ICs and collaborating teachers focus their attention on how to use ideas in the classroom.

Reciprocity

In a partnership, everyone benefits from the success, learning, or experience of others—all members are rewarded by what one individual contributes. When this principle is applied to instructional coaching, it has two major implications. First, one of the coach's goals should be learning along with the collaborating teachers. Thus, the coach learns about teachers' classroom, the strengths and weaknesses of the new practices when seen as an application for that environment, and so on. Second, ICs who live by the principle of reciprocity believe that teachers' knowledge and expertise are as important as their own. They have faith in teachers' abilities to invent useful new applications of the content they are exploring.

ENCOURAGING IMPLEMENTATION

The fun starts once an IC pursues the goal of helping teachers implement research-validated interventions with fidelity. This complicates the relationship between the coach and collaborating teacher. On the one hand, the coach wants to validate, reassure, and support the collaborating teacher. On the other hand, the coach has to keep encouraging that teacher to refine his or her practices until they embody the validated, critical teaching practices.

Our research suggests that teachers who implement new interventions will see much greater improvements in student achievement when their teaching practices are close to those specified in the research.[2] Consequently, coaches are most effective when they act as critical friends, simultaneously providing support and empowering teachers to see areas where they can improve.

People may underestimate the rich interpersonal complexities that are called into play when a coach talks to a teacher about teaching. As Parker Palmer (1998) has observed, "Unlike many professions, teaching is always done at the dangerous intersection of personal and public life . . . teaching is a daily exercise in vulnerability . . . No matter how technical my subject may be, the things I teach are things I care about—and what I care about helps define my selfhood" (p.17). Teachers are passionate about their subjects and their students and, unless they have distanced themselves from their students to reduce their personal vulnerability, teachers care deeply about the art and craft of their profession. ICs are in the school to improve instruction, but they need to ensure that their conversation is supportive, cautious, and respectful.

The Job I Love

There are always challenges. Some teachers were pretty standoffish the first year. They'd duck their heads whenever I walked by. It took some time to crack the hard ones. My approach was to let them know that I was a partner. I was there as a friend, a support, someone to help them if they wanted my help.

If you're going to be a coach, you can't be afraid to approach people. You have to become a part of their lives. When I started, I visited everyone so I could shake their hand and look them in the eyes. I wanted them to know that I was here for them, someone who might be a second set of hands in their classroom. Eventually, I guess I wore them down because pretty much everyone was on board.

When you've worked with someone for a while, it becomes a kind of friendship. I always start off telling them all the great things, and then just ask, "Have you ever thought about . . . ?" I try not to sound critical. They respond better to positives, and even a negative comment can be put positively.

It's exciting when you can get a teacher to a place where our ideas just mesh. I just take their ideas and restate them—make it so I'm clarifying—help them take their ideas and put them in a more learner-friendly way. I'm kind of like a backboard in tennis: they bounce their ideas off of me, and I send them back to them.

It's invigoration for teachers too. Together we enjoy what we're doing and it's contagious; they realize I'm not a part of a negative culture. It's really cool to just be relaxed and let the creative juices flow and come up with a plan together.

More than anything, I want to help them feel good about what they do. Some are actually embarrassed to say they are a teacher, but they have the most important job in the universe. I want them to know that the job they have is the job I love, and that's true.

ICs work from the assumption that knowledge is learned efficiently when it is learned on the job. ICs share ideas with teachers during one-to-one meetings, mostly held during teachers' planning time, or by modeling instructional methods in the classroom. Whenever ideas are shared by ICs, they are shared to be implemented. IC Lynn Barnes comments: "I want teachers to see that I have concrete stuff that can empower students' learning." IC Shelly Bolejack agrees: "The strategies do work, they do make a difference, and my job is to listen to issues, explain how the strategies work, model them in the classroom, and help the teachers see that these ideas work."

There are scores of actions a coach can do to accelerate teacher learning; five activities are particularly effective: collaborating, modeling, observing, providing feedback, and providing support.

COLLABORATION

Collaboration is the lifeblood of instructional coaching. Through collaboration, the coach makes it possible for teachers to engage in reflective dialogue about teaching. This is very important. We live in a time when meaningful conversation is becoming more and more scarce. Millions of people today have their only intimate conversations with complete strangers on the Internet. These are fast times, says John Gleick (1999), when "information . . . whistl[es] by our ears at light speed, too fast to be absorbed" (p. 87). There is so much to do, so much information to digest, and so little time for what counts, like conversation. It is no surprise that one of the most popular metaphors for our time is surfing: We channel surf while watching TV, pick up snippets of information from magazines, surf through our e-mails, surf the Internet, and surf relationships; we catch bits of conversation on the fly before moving on to the next urgent task.

Coaches make it possible for teachers to take time to have real conversations about teaching. IC Susan Claflin sees this as a critical part of what she does. "Some teachers are starved for attention, for someone to listen to them, to understand their point of view and respond to them. In a big system, a teacher can feel a little lost, and not a unique individual. We respond to each one of them as a human being."

Collaboration is also critical because it is in collaboration that the partnership relationship comes alive. Collaboration, at its best, is a give-and-take dialogue, where ideas ping-pong back and forth between parties so freely that it's hard to determine who thought what. Collaboration, then, is not one person telling another what to do; collaboration is people working together as partners, reflecting and cocreating together. As Peter Block (2002) comments, this collaborative problem solving is very important: "It is difficult to live another's answer, regardless of the amount of goodwill with which it is offered" (p. 6). Collaboration enables the coach and collaborating teacher to arrive at the same answer, together.

Devona values collaboration so highly that she uses the terms *instructional coach* and *instructional collaborator* interchangeably. She collaborates from the moment she starts working with individual teachers to identify what interventions they'll work on together. In some cases, the intervention she and the teacher identify together is one that leads to extensive collaborative planning. One intervention Devona frequently shares with teachers is the Unit Organizer Routine (Lenz, Bulgren, et al., 1994), a routine teachers can use to identify, plan, and teach essential information.

When she helps teachers use the Unit Organizer Routine, Devona finds herself in conversations that get to the heart of what it means to be an effective teacher. "It's exciting when you get a teacher to a place where ideas just mesh together. It's exciting, invigorating, and it's contagious." Devona might collaborate with a teacher to identify the essential questions that embody the objectives of the unit, to create a graphic organizer that maps the essential content to be taught, and to identify the content structures that will be important in the unit. Such conversations about these core components of instruction also help Devona create deeper and healthier relationships with her collaborating teachers.

MODELING: YOU WATCH ME

When coaches model, described at length in Chapter 6, they go into teachers' classrooms and show them examples of how to employ the particular best practice that they are learning about. Devona explains that "people need to see it. They need to see it done right at first. They might tweak it, but they need to see it done right." By going into the classroom and showing teachers how to implement an intervention, ICs help teachers obtain a deeper understanding of the intervention in the context where it matters most: their classroom. Teaching is such a rich and artful activity than no manual comes close to capturing all that is involved in the healthy, joyous, effective interactions between teachers and students.

The artful part of teaching, to borrow Michel Polanyi's words (1958), involves a "tacit dimension." Great teachers, like other great performers, employ habits, routines, practices, and ways of communicating that they themselves are completely unaware of. Like an athlete who can't explain how he was able to make a great play, many great teachers are not able to tell you how they taught a great class (Knight, 2002). Modeling, as Devona fully understands, helps teachers grasp the subtle or "tacit" elements in implementing a way of teaching. "Modeling is more than demonstrating a technique. I show them a different way of relating to students, a different style of classroom management. They might have a teacher's manual, but they need to see it, to see how you can take a scripted manual and put your personality into it—and still get across what needs to happen." Devona adds, "they also get to see me teach; they know I can step in and do it because they've seen me teach."

OBSERVING AND PROVIDING FEEDBACK

Observing and providing feedback are other important ways in which ICs enable teachers to teach interventions with a high degree of fidelity to the research-validated practices. On the surface, this sounds simple: coaches watch teachers and tell them what they need to do to improve. However, the practice is more complex than it appears. Observation involves the vagaries of perception, and no two people will see the same class the same way. As a host of writers have explained in the past decade, we all see the world through the window of our own personal mental model (Kuhn, 1970).

I learned about the complexity of perception in a simple enough way, sitting on the couch listening to a baseball game on a Sunday afternoon. The game occurred late in September, and the Toronto Blue Jays were on the verge, I hoped, of clinching the division title. Toronto was ahead 1–0 in the ninth inning. Toronto's pitcher was Tom Henke, who had a spectacular fastball, and the batter was Kirk Gibson, who had a spectacular ability to hit important home runs. Since the game was critical, I was completely engaged in it, literally leaning forward to catch every word.

My son David, who was almost three at the time, was listening to the game with me. As the intense narrative of the game played out, David walked over to the stereo speaker from which the announcer's voice was booming. As the tension built, he looked at me, and he looked at the speaker, and then he turned to me and commented on the only sound that mattered to him at the time, saying "hot dog." David didn't notice the announcer's commentary on the game, the balls and strikes and the eventual Kirk Gibson home run; David only cared about what he heard, someone selling hot dogs in the stands, calling out that they had hot dogs for sale.

What struck me at that moment was that although I was totally engaged by the game, even though I was listening as carefully as I possibly could, David heard sounds that totally escaped my perception. What David heard, from his 2½-year-old perspective, was completely outside my hearing—even though I was listening as hard as possible. David's listening was completely different than mine. What else am I not hearing every day, I wondered? What else is out there that others see, hear, and perceive that is totally beyond my ability to perceive? No doubt a lot.

What I learned about perception while observing my son taking in a baseball game on the radio has helped me understand what I need to do when I observe teachers. I need to be certain that I am watching for the right things; otherwise, I may miss something very important. On the Pathways to Success project, ICs recognize the limited nature of perception, and we try to be careful not to miss too much when we watch teachers.

ICs have several tools at their disposal to ensure that they focus their eyes and ears on the right things. First, the IC and collaborating teacher need to clarify what critical teaching behaviors are being observed. To make this process work better, coaches can identify the teaching behaviors that are fundamental to any teaching practice being learned. Once they have identified those behaviors, they can create checklists of those that research has identified as important. Devona comments, "checklists help me show teachers what I'm looking for when they use, say, the Unit Organizer. If you show them the target you're aiming at, they'll hit it."

Many coaches focus their own and their collaborating teacher's attention by co-constructing a checklist (an example is included in Chapter 6) with teachers. The co-constructed checklist contains all of the behaviors that the coach considers important so long as the collaborating teacher agrees that they are important. Also, the co-constructed form includes behaviors that the teachers believe are important.

No checklist can capture every important action that a teacher does, so coaches must also be purposeful about watching for other behaviors. Coaches need to focus their attention on all that the teachers do well. Observers can slip into the habit of seeing the weakness more than the strengths, but coaches will be less effective if they fall into that pattern. Devona observes that "you can always find something positive."

After observing teachers, coaches need to discuss the notes or data they recorded while observing. When reviewing data, many coaches again find the partnership perspective to be helpful. Thus, rather than telling teachers what they have done "right or wrong," ICs guide teachers to make their own sense of the observation data. If coaches tell teachers what they did right, they run the risk of offering a commentary that their collaborating teacher might brush off as untrue (Kegan & Lahey, 2002). If they tell teachers what they did wrong, coaches run the risk of attacking a teacher's personal identity, and thus making it difficult for him or her to hear suggestions. The coach's and teacher's collaborative exploration of data, described in Chapter 6, enables supportive but honest dialogue about instruction.

SUPPORT

For most of our professional lives, we have heard about people "resisting change." Although this cliché does capture some truth, it fails to account for the fact that people change every day. In the past few days, for example, you may have used a computer, surfed the Internet, downloaded music, read or sent e-mail, used a cell phone, withdrawn cash from an ATM, watched a DVD, listened to a CD or iPod, and used your credit card at the gas station to pump your own gas. If you're old enough, you can probably remember a time when all of these activities, which today consume so much of our time, didn't exist. Next time you think people resist change, look around and notice how many of us are doing something that was impossible 10 years ago. We change, and I'm sure we'll keep changing.

Csikszentmihalyi's description of how ideas evolve shows that changes that people embrace generally have two qualities: they are more powerful than older technologies and they're easier to use. According to Csikszentmihalyi (1994), "ideas, values, technologies that do the job with the least demand on psychic energy will survive" (p.123). In other words, an appliance that does more work with less effort is preferred. People today use Macintosh or Windows computer operating systems because they are easier to use and because they do more than the now primitive DOS operating systems. If something is easier, if it does more, people will embrace it.

ICs believe that the same notion holds true with educational interventions. First, as explained in detail in Chapter 8, ICs must share teaching practices that are proven to work and that address real challenges facing teachers. Jan Bulgren's Concept Mastery Routine (Bulgren, Deshler, & Schumaker, 1993), for example, is a simple and powerful way for teachers to ensure that all students share a complete understanding of the meaning of a concept. Similarly, Randy Sprick's CHAMPs approach to classroom management (Sprick, Garrison, & Howard, 1998) is an easy-to-use way for teachers to identify and communicate their classroom expectations and to reinforce safe and civil behavior in the classroom. The fact that these interventions help teachers to help students increases the likelihood that they may be adopted by many teachers in a school.

Just because a teaching practice or program works is no guarantee that it will be adopted. A very powerful program that is difficult to use is likely going to be dropped very quickly. Interventions catch on and spread when they are powerful and easy to implement. This is where ICs become very important. The IC's job, in large part, is to make it as easy as possible for teachers to implement a new practice. For Devona, this support can involve a wide range of tasks: "I do whatever I can to provide support. I make copies. I get them transparencies if they need them. I model in their classrooms. I give them feedback. Sometimes support is just showing that things are happening even when the teachers are too close to the class to see it."

PARTNERING WITH THE PRINCIPAL

Three variables, in my experience, are the most important predictors of the success of a coaching program. One is that coaches have received appropriate professional development in what and how to coach. A second is that coaches have the discipline, skills, and personality required to be effective coaches. The third is that coaches are working in schools with principals who are effective instructional leaders.

A well-prepared and talented coach can accomplish a great deal, but every coach's impact will be magnified when she or he works in partnership with an effective instructional leader. What's more, the coach and principal have to have a shared understanding and vision of what instructional coaching can accomplish. Creating that shared vision was one of Devona's goals. She met weekly with her principal to discuss how school reform was progressing in the school. She developed brief summaries that made it easier for her principal to learn the many teaching practices that she had to offer, and she acted quickly on her principal's concerns regarding teachers who needed support.

Once a critical mass of teachers in a school or on a team have become committed to the change initiative introduced by the IC, the coach and principal can then turn attention to the task of building networks for change across the school. Real, profound change will not happen in a school until groups of teachers come together to orchestrate schoolwide implementation and support of interventions. This work may be the most challenging that a coach can face.

When it comes to developing networks for change in schools, the IC must be continually watching for an opportune moment to develop learning networks. At times, this may mean that the IC takes on, at least initially, a leadership role in the smooth working of school-based teams or professional learning communities. To accelerate organizational learning, coaches can help teams establish learner-friendly team norms and can introduce protocols

for setting priorities, surfacing issues, solving problems, or planning implementation. Coaches can also lead the teams until they have developed the
capacity to be independent, professional learning communities.

GOING DEEPER

The National Staff Development Council's *Standards for Staff Development*,
Revised (2001), suggests 12 standards for professional development: learning
communities, leadership, resources, data driven, evaluation, research based,
design, learning, collaboration, equity, quality teaching, and family involvement. The International Reading Association's *Standards for Middle and
High School Literacy Coaches* (2006), the result of a collaborative partnership among the National Council of Teachers of English, the National Science
Teachers Association, and the National Council for Social Studies, identifies
and articulates leadership standards for collaboration, job-embedded skills,
and evaluation of literacy needs along with content-area standards.

TO SUM UP

- Coaching is about building relationships with teachers as much as it
  is about instruction. The heart of relationships is emotional connection.
- To get around barriers to change, coaches often start by working one-
  to-one with teachers.
- ICs adopt a partnership philosophy, which at its core means that they
  have an authentic respect for teachers' professionalism.
- The partnership philosophy is realized in collaborative work between
  the coach and the collaborating teacher. Together, coach and teacher
  discover answers to the challenges present in the classroom.
- ICs model in the classroom so that teachers can see what correct
  implementation of an intervention looks like.
- ICs model in the classroom so that teachers can see what research-
  based interventions look like when they reflect a teacher's personality.
- To be truly effective, coaches must work in partnership with their
  principals.

NOTES

1. A study conducted by researchers at the Kansas University Center
for Research on Learning compared a partnership and a traditional approach to
professional development. At the end of the study, the partnership approach yielded
significantly higher results on measures of teachers' engagement, enjoyment, comprehension, and readiness to implement interventions during professional development (Knight, 1998).

2. In a Pathways to Success study of the relationship between teacher fidelity and student outcomes ($N = 1,868$), we found that teachers who taught the Sentence Writing Strategy (Schumaker, 1985) with a fairly high degree of fidelity saw their students' ability to write complete sentences improve by 14%. Teachers who taught with less fidelity saw an improvement of 4% in the number of complete sentences. This study is discussed in more detail in Chapter 6.

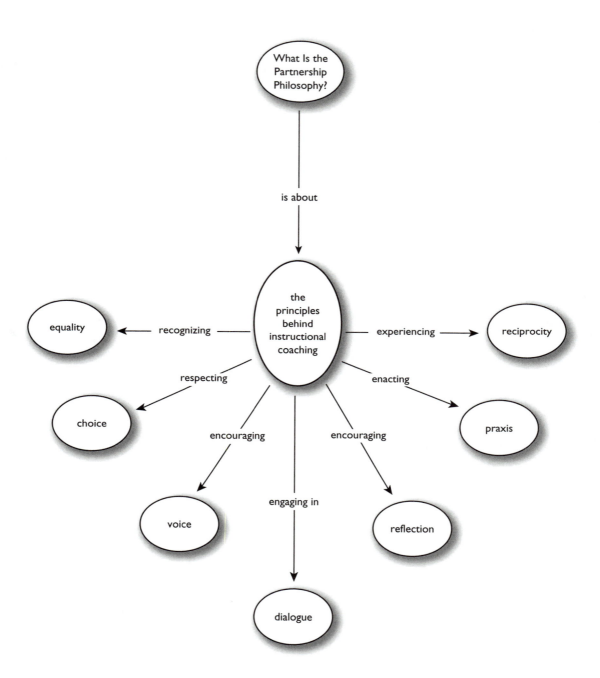

Chapter 3

What Is the Partnership Philosophy?

Partnership, ultimately, is about treating somebody like a human being.

—Ric Palma, instructional coach, Topeka High School

CHAPTER OVERVIEW

Instructional coaches who do not reflect on their philosophy may find it very difficult to be successful. For that reason, an important first step for coaches is for them to reflect on their principles, the theory behind their actions. In this chapter, I introduce the Partnership Approach as one possible theoretical framework for instructional coaching. The Partnership Approach is based on the principles of equality, choice, voice, dialogue, reflection, praxis, and reciprocity. Each of these principles is described below.

WHAT IS THE PARTNERSHIP PHILOSOPHY?

Theory has gotten a bad rap. When I ask teachers what they like and don't like about professional development, one of the first criticisms they make is that professional development is often too "theoretical." For many, the word *theory* has become synonymous with the word *impractical*. While sharing ideas in schools, I've learned that if a teacher says "that's great in theory," my idea has just received the kiss of death.

In part, I agree with the criticisms. An idea that has no practical application shouldn't be at the top a teacher's to-do list. If teachers are expected to spend their limited free time on learning new ideas or teaching practices, they are being sensible and realistic when they ask to learn something that will help them in their classrooms.

Why then would I include an entire chapter on the theory behind instructional coaching? My answer is quite simple: as Kurt Lewin (1951), one of the pioneers of social psychology, said in a now famous statement, "There is nothing as practical, as a good theory" (p.169). The value of a good theory is that it provides a way for people to organize, prioritize, and choose how they will act and what they will do in any situation, and for that reason a theory can be very practical. A little joke I loved to tell when I was a child nicely illustrates just how important a theory can be. The joke goes as follows:

Emily and Cameron are driving down the road together in a car. Emily is driving, and when she comes up to a red light, she guns the car and races right through the intersection. Not surprisingly, Cameron is shocked. He turns to Emily and asks, "What the heck are you doing?" Unfazed, Emily glances at Cameron and says, "Don't worry about it; my brother does it all the time." A few minutes later, Emily roars right through another red light, and before Ben says anything, she turns to him and says again, "Don't worry about it; my brother does this all the time." By this time Cameron is very nervous, but they drive for some time before they see another traffic light. Finally, Cameron sees an intersection in the distance, and he is relieved to see the signal light is green. However, his relief quickly disappears when Emily slams on the brakes and brings the car to a full stop at the green light. Stunned, Cameron asks the only sensible question: "What in the world are you doing stopping at a green light?" Without missing a beat, Emily quickly answers back, "Hey, you never know when my brother might be driving along."

In this joke, Emily is able to drive the car—she can start and stop, and turn the steering wheel; she clearly has a well-worked out theory about how to drive. However, I think we would all agree that Emily will find herself in real trouble unless she changes her theory of driving. Real life is no different. The principles we base our actions on have very practical implications. For example, an IC can have a PhD in instruction and know dozens upon dozens of useful teaching techniques, but if that coach bases her or his coaching activities on principles that are counterproductive, the coach may fail to bring about meaningful changes in schools. Simply put, if a coach comes from the wrong place, the coach will have a hard time leading change.

Whether fully conscious of it or not, we all live our personal and work lives according to theories, at the most profound and most mundane levels. When we drive down the road, we drive according to our own theory about what other drivers will do as they approach an intersection. When we leave a tip for a server who we don't know and will never meet again, we do it because we have a certain ethical theory. So, whether we are honest, dishonest, selfish, or selfless, we act according to various theories of life. What's more, if you think that this talk about theory is a bunch of hooey, that people don't live their lives according to any theories, that people just live free and in the moment at all times without any kind of theory, that's a theory, too.

So what is a theory? My wife Jenny's fourth-grade teacher taught her that "a theory is not the truth; it is something that cannot be proved." When the teachers I interview complain about interventions that are "too theoretical," I think their definition is something like Jenny's teacher's: theory is an abstract idea that is a long way from reality. I use the word *theory* in a different sense. One definition of *theory* in *The Oxford English Dictionary* is "a systematic conception or statement of the principles of something." William Isaacs (1999) has described the important role that theory of this sort can play in our lives:

> When we undertake any task, like run a meeting, negotiate an agreement, discipline a child—even meditate—we operate from a set of taken-for-granted rules or ideas of how to be effective. Understanding these tacit rules is what I mean by *theory*. The word *theory* comes from the same roots as the word *theater*, which means simply "to see." A theory is a way of seeing . . . Without a theory, however— some way to assess what is happening—we shall be forever doomed to operate blindly, subject to chance. (p. 73)

Theory is the gravity that holds together any systematic approach, such as instructional coaching, for example.

I identified the principles behind this approach to instructional coaching by studying the fields of education, business, psychology, philosophy of science, and cultural anthropology. By reading such authors as Paulo Freire, Riane Eisler, Michael Fullan, Peter Block, Peter Senge, Richard Bernstein, and William Isaacs, I discovered an alternative model for how people can work together; indeed, several similar principles resurfaced in many of these authors' works. Ultimately, I narrowed those principles to the following seven: equality, choice, voice, dialogue, reflection, praxis, and reciprocity.

I first studied the partnership approach in 1997 by comparing a bottom-up approach to professional learning, Partnership Learning, to a more traditional approach to professional learning (Knight, 1998). The traditional approach was primarily a lecture provided by an expert, who focused on ensuring that teachers learned the correct way to teach scientifically proven teaching practices. The partnership approach was based on the principles described in this chapter. The results were compelling. Teachers reported that in the partnership sessions, they learned more, were engaged more, and enjoyed themselves more than in the traditional sessions. Additionally, they were four times more inclined to implement teaching practices they learned during partnership sessions than those learned during traditional sessions (Knight, 1998).

This chapter describes the partnership principles and provides practical examples of what those principles look like when they are acted on by ICs.

Ric Palma, an IC at Topeka High School, knows a lot about the principles behind the instructional coaching approach. As part of his professional learning to be an IC, Ric learned, explored, and discussed the principles. Like other coaches on the Pathways to Success team, Ric refers to these principles as partnership principles because partnership seems to be the most appropriate metaphor for describing the kind of relationship he strives to establish with teachers.

Ric's knowledge of the partnership principles gives him a foundation to work from when he collaborates with teachers. As Ric observes, "the teachers here know that I'm one of them; they don't look at me as someone who is coming from a different angle and surely not from above them. I'm a peer with them." Like Ric, ICs see themselves as equal, respect others' choices, and encourage others to voice opinions. Whether they are observing a class, modeling an instructional practice, building an emotional connection with a teacher, or providing constructive suggestions, coaches use the partnership principles as a point of reference for their behaviors and actions. Sue Woodruff, a leader of professional developers from Grand Rapids, Michigan, states that "the [partnership] principles really help me think through what should happen when I work with teachers. On those occasions when I don't feel I've been successful, I go back to the principles and I usually discover that I failed because I violated one of the principles."

Ric Palma

Ric Palma is in his third year as an IC on the Pathways to Success project at Topeka High School. Prior to being a coach, Ric taught language arts at Topeka High School for 12 years. Although he is now a Kansas University employee, Ric continues in his role as the Topeka High School announcer and is known affectionately as *The Voice of the Trojans*.

The seven principles are intended to provide a conceptual language for ICs to describe how they go about working with teachers. I hope coaches will find, as Ric Palma says, that the principles "put into words why we feel good about what we do because we know that when we were teachers this is how we would have wanted to be treated." The partnership principles are described below.

Equality: Instructional Coaches and Teachers Are Equal Partners

The central idea behind instructional coaching is the central idea behind most democracies and republics: the belief that all people are created equal. We say we believe in equality, our votes count equally, and we share equal rights and responsibilities. Nevertheless, if we peek in on a traditional professional development session, we might not see equality in action. On many occasions, traditional professional development looks more like the antithesis of equality.

What might happen on a traditional staff development day? Teachers might go to a training session that they did not choose. At the session, a trainer at the front of the group might do most of the talking. The entire session might be based on an assumption that the teachers would implement whatever they were told to implement, and yet the teachers might spend most of the session quietly (and sometimes not so quietly) resisting the trainer's efforts. When a teacher disagrees with the trainer or points out some reason why an innovation might be difficult to implement, chances are the teacher wouldn't be listened to, and might even be considered a troublemaker. Unfortunately, the ensuing clash of wills between trainer and teacher can end up poisoning the entire event.

Instructional coaching changes all of that by embracing the principle of equality. "They see me," Ric Palma says, "as somebody who is coming in as one of them, instead of somebody who is coming in to *impart* all this . . . knowledge." A simple example illustrates the way the partnership approach helps. Imagine that you felt compelled to offer parenting advice to your sister. My guess is that if you found yourself in such a situation, you would approach your sister cautiously. Rather than showing up at her house with a collection of PowerPoint slides and handouts to show just how she needs to improve, you would tread lightly. You would ask what her ideas were and listen with all your heart. You would make suggestions, and then let her decide if your suggestions had any merit. Since parenting is so personal, you would phrase every statement cautiously and infuse your conversation with respect and compassion.

Teaching is almost as personal as parenting, yet too often professional developers do not tread lightly. If teachers are truly equal, then their ideas must count. Equality does not mean that coaches and teachers have equal knowledge on every topic, but it does mean that the collaborating teacher's opinions are as important as the coach's, and both points of view are worth hearing. An IC who acts on this principle communicates in every interaction that collaborating teachers are no less important than coaches. Teachers who work with ICs should walk away from all interactions feeling like they are valued and that their opinions matter.

When Ric Palma collaborates with teachers, he ensures that they know they're equal partners. Ric shares ideas provisionally, making certain that collaborating teachers realize their expertise is important. Says Ric, "the first thing I always ask teachers is whether they think the strategy or device we're talking about would work with kids in their classroom. I want them to see that I'm looking at the materials the same way they would. I want them to know right off the bat that our conversation is about them." Ric also demonstrates equality by being careful to respect his collaborating teachers' points of view: "I let them know that their opinions are important, and I draw on their knowledge and experience."

Choice: Teachers Should Have Choice Regarding What and How They Learn

If ICs believe that people are equal, it follows that they also believe the people with whom they work should have a say in what they do and do not do. Imagine what would happen to most partnerships if one partner decided how to spend the money, how to run the business, whom to hire, and so on. Imagine how you'd feel if you were supposed to be in a partnership, and yet your partner didn't consult with you before acting, never asked your opinion, never allowed you to say yes or no. Chances are you wouldn't feel like a partner at all.

True partners choose to work together; that is a defining characteristic of a partnership. Partners enter more or less as equals. Partners are people who have a say, who guide the direction of whatever endeavor they share, who have the right to say yes and no and make choices, as long as they are partners. Peter Block (1993), in his book *Stewardship*, points out that if there is no choice, there really is no partnership:

> Partners each have a right to say no. Saying no is the fundamental way we have of differentiating ourselves. To take away my right to say no is to claim sovereignty over me . . . If we cannot say no, then saying yes has no meaning. (pp. 30–31)

One reason why traditional professional development usually fails is because teachers frequently have little choice in what they learn. Often, teachers "do not have a right to say no," as Peter Block says. Too often, teachers are told to attend compulsory training sessions even if the sessions don't meet their needs or if they've heard the speaker previously. Teachers often are told that their school has adopted a new innovation that, whether they want to or not, they will be asked to implement. Not surprisingly, many teachers resist being forced to change. Like a partner who has not been listened to, they turn away, saying enough is enough.

Taking away teachers' "right to say no" is one way schools take away teachers' professionalism. Personal discretion is in many ways the heart of being a professional. Doctors, lawyers, or teachers are professionals because we trust them to make the right decisions, to use their knowledge skillfully and artfully. That is, what makes someone a professional is her or his ability to choose correctly. When we take away choice, we reduce people to being less than professionals.

Ric sees choice as the "most important thing." By allowing teachers to choose the extent to which they will work with him, Ric demonstrates his respect for their professionalism. "They know they don't have to use this stuff, and in most cases they aren't forced to learn it." On the one hand, Ric and the other ICs he works with have found that offering choice actually increases both teachers' desire to teach with fidelity and the likelihood that teachers will implement learning strategies and teaching routines. On the other hand, when you force teachers to learn something, like most people would, teachers often choose to dig their heels in and resist.

Choice should be limited at times for good reasons. A principal might know that schoolwide implementation of a strategy would be better for students, and therefore, she might require every one of her teachers to implement it. A researcher might know that a teaching routine was used a certain way during clinical study, and therefore, he might want teachers to teach exactly as it was done during clinical study.

The principle of choice, Ric believes, is one reason why many teachers implement what he has to share. "Teachers know when it comes to us, it's all about choice. Every one of them knows it in this district. They know that I'm here if they want me." What's more, for Ric, offering choice is also one way of providing better support for students. "I give them as many options as possible, not just my biased opinion. The more choices we can give them, the more variety and choices they can give their students. And the more their students are going to learn."

Offering choices does not mean that everything is up for grabs. Teachers have to strive to help their students meet standards, and if teachers are to be treated professionally, they must act professionally. In some cases, compulsory training is necessary, unavoidable, or legally mandated. In some cases, teachers have lost their calling, lost their love of kids or their ability to respect children, and they need to either rekindle that love and respect or move on to other work that does not involve shaping the hearts and minds of children. Nonetheless, even when teachers have no choice about participating in training, a professional developer can offer teachers choices about how they might adapt instruction, how they want the learning experience to be structured, how frequently they want breaks, what kind of support they would prefer, and whom they want to work with during a session. ICs who offer meaningful choices take steps toward making real partnerships come alive.

Voice: Professional Learning Should Empower and Respect the Voices of Teachers

If partners are equal, if they are free to choose what they do and do not do, they should be free to say what they think, and their opinions should count. For that reason, ICs value the opinions of everyone with whom they collaborate—even collaborating teachers who strongly disagree with them. In fact, coaches often learn the most when they carefully listen to the viewpoints of people who may appear to be disagreeing or resisting ideas being shared. When coaches listen to and value teachers' voices, they do a lot more than learn. Coaches who temporarily set aside their own opinions for the sole purpose of really hearing what their colleagues have to say are powerfully demonstrating that they truly value their colleagues' perspective. In a very real sense, when a coach empathetically listens to another person's ideas, thoughts, and concerns, the coach communicates that the other person's life is important and meaningful. This may be the most important service that a coach can provide.

ICs who act on this principle sometimes find that they have to help teachers find their voice. The urgency of the everyday professional life of a teacher is overwhelming, to say the least, and many teachers are weighed down with planning, meeting paperwork demands, responding to and involving parents, preparing students for standardized tests, contributing to team meetings, coaching athletic teams, and attending courses at night. For many teachers, those competing urgent demands make it difficult to find time to reflect on priorities and give voice to what really matters. An IC who takes the time to listen to teachers and collaborates with them can create a situation where an overwhelmed teacher is able to take time to reflect and exchange ideas, and perhaps even give expression to what really counts: her voice.

Sarah Lawrence-Lightfoot, in her book *Respect* (2000), tells a story from her childhood that captures what can happen when we attend to the voices of others. Dr. Lawrence-Lightfoot describes how she felt and what she learned when a family friend sketched a picture of her as a young girl. At its heart, Dr. Lightfoot's story also depicts why ICs should truly listen to the voices of their collaborating teachers:

> The summer of my eighth birthday, my family was visited by a seventy-year-old black woman, a professor of sociology, an old and dear friend. A woman of warmth and dignity, she always seemed to have secret treasures hidden under her smooth exterior. On this visit, she brought charcoals and a sketch pad. Midafternoon, with the sun high in the sky, she asked me to sit for her . . .

> What I remember most clearly was the wonderful, glowing sensation I got from being attended to so fully. There were no distractions. I was the only one in her gaze. My image filled her eyes, and the sound of the chalk stroking the paper was palpable. The audible senses translated into tactile ones. After the warmth of this human encounter, the artistic product was almost forgettable. I do not recall whether I liked the portrait or not . . . This fast-working artist whipped the page out of her sketch pad after less than an hour and gave it to me with one admonition: "Always remember you're beautiful," she said firmly. To which I responded—beaming with pleasure and momentary embarrassment—"Now I know I'm somebody!"

> In the process of recording the image, the artist had made me feel "seen" in a way that I had never felt seen before, fully attended to, wrapped up in an empathic gaze. (p. 211)

Seeing people in a way they have never been seen before involves an almost reverential commitment to listening with care, empathizing, and creating an environment where others feel comfortable talking honestly about what matters most. Part of voice is simply taking the time to truly hear what people have to say.

Voice also involves helping others find the words to express what really matters in their lives. Helping people find their voice, collaborating with friends and colleagues in activities that enable them to bring shape to their deepest passions—that is profound and important work. Stephen Covey, who has spent his career describing what it takes to live a fulfilled life, explains: "there is a deep, innate, almost inexpressible yearning with each of us to find our voice in life" (2004, p. 5). Covey describes how significant an activity it is to collaborate with others to help them find their voice:

> The power to *discover* our voice lies in the potential that was bequeathed to us at birth. Latent and undeveloped, the seeds of greatness were planted. We were given magnificent birth gifts—talents, capacities, privileges, intelligences, opportunities—that would remain largely unopened except through our own decision and effort. Because of these gifts, the potential within an individual is tremendous, even infinite. (p. 40)

More than a decade ago, I conducted a study on the role of voice in professional growth with a small group of teachers, ranging in age from their early 20s to their 50s, who taught English in middle and high school. The teachers donated their personal time to articulate their voices in personal vision statements. They then helped me gather data on whether or not having a vision changed anything about their professional lives.

This little study ended up being much more interesting and complicated than I had anticipated. Indeed, having a personal vision led one teacher to significantly change the way she planned her lessons. After writing her personal vision in which she committed to teaching all students, this teacher began to plan her lessons by visualizing a high-, average-, low-, and other-achieving student in her class. Similarly, a first-year teacher told me that writing a vision helped her get through her first year: "I am really glad I wrote a vision because I think I would be a lot more negative right now if I hadn't done that. My vision reminded me of why I am doing this, and what I am trying to accomplish. It's kind of forced me to hold on to all that idealism that I may have lost a little bit of this year."

The most interesting finding was that writing a personal vision affected everyone differently. One outstanding teacher of the year said that writing a vision had very little impact on her because she knew exactly what she intended to do in every classroom. Writing her vision took her less than an hour, and the document read like a poem to teaching. Another teacher told me that she couldn't write a vision because she was too deeply disappointed by the wide gap between her real professional goals and what occurred in her classroom. Yet another teacher said that after she wrote a vision statement that emphasized the importance of having a balanced life, she decided that she would stay home more and have children; indeed, before the end of the project she was pregnant with her first child.

In most cases, writing a vision helped teachers give voice to ideas and beliefs that had been dormant inside their souls somewhere. Articulating a vision helped many of these teachers find their voices, and that discovery helped them be more of the kind of person they wanted to be. Finding a voice was, in a real sense, finding out who they were.

Ric Palma encourages teachers to use their voices by listening carefully when he collaborates. "Listening is what gives them a voice. You have to listen to them, so that they know that when they speak, they're going to be heard, and they're going to be taken seriously." By listening with care to the voices of teachers, ICs can make teachers feel "seen" and "fully attended to." Validation is a gift that can be given to anyone, but it is a gift that many overwhelmed or pressured teachers receive with a tremendous amount of gratitude.

Dialogue: Professional Learning Should Enable Authentic Dialogue

If people come together as equals, if they feel free to voice their opinions, if they are listened to, and if they act on the exhilarating belief that they are free to agree, disagree, and reflect on ideas as they choose, something marvelous can happen. When conversation between a coach and a teacher comes alive, ideas can bounce around like balls in a pinball machine, and people can start to communicate so well that it becomes difficult to see where one person's thoughts end and another's begin. An exciting community of thought can arise, and two individuals or a group can start to think as one, a partnership between differently talented, unique individuals sharing the joy of muddling over a problem. This kind of communication can be called *dialogue*.

At the heart of instructional coaching is a deep belief that a true partnership should involve dialogue. Dialogue brings people together as equals so they can share ideas, create new knowledge, and learn. Specifically, a coach and a teacher engaged in dialogue attempt to open up discussion and share what is on each other's minds. During dialogue, people inquire into each other's positions at least as much as they advocate their own point of view, and they use specific strategies to surface their own and others' assumptions.

Dialogue is not the same as simple discussion, where individuals advocate their points of view in competitive conversation with little, if any, reflection on the assumptions that underlie their points of view. The problem with such a competitive form of communication, as David Bohm has noted, is that by defending an assumption, we "push out what is new." Bohm (2000) explains the unique qualities of true dialogue as follows:

> In a dialogue, there is no attempt to gain points, or to make your particular view prevail . . . It's a situation called win/win, whereas the other is win/lose—if I win, you lose. But a dialogue is something more of a common participation, in which we are not playing a game against each other but with each other. In a dialogue everybody wins. (p. 7)

Dialogue often arises naturally when coaches and teachers talk about practices they are learning, adapting, or implementing in their classrooms. Buckminster Fuller made this point in a well-known quotation, "If you want to teach people a new way of thinking, don't bother trying to teach them. Instead, give them a tool, the use of which will lead to new ways of thinking" (quoted in Senge, 1994, p. 28). Thus, an IC who is collaborating with a teacher for implementation of a Content Enhancement Routine might explain that one of the principles of Content Enhancement is that the needs of all students, both individually and as a group, are to be addressed. Together, the coach and the teacher could explore whether the teacher truly felt this was possible, whether or not the teacher held this assumption. In the best cases, the conversation would lead to dialogue—a meaningful conversation between a teacher and a coach about the assumptions that most profoundly affect both teachers' class-room behaviors.

ICs use many other communication strategies to make it possible for authentic dialogue to occur. They engage participants in honest, respectful, empowering conversation about content, and they think and learn with participants during the conversation. By seeing others as equals, by listening empathically, and by encouraging everyone to speak their minds, ICs can encourage dialogue.

For Ric Palma, dialogue is motivating both for teachers and for him. "Dialogue makes things happen. It makes changes occur, and ultimately dia-logue is kind of like natural selection when it comes to education. The more ideas you have, the more opportunities for survival and growth. When you have teachers that have been teaching the same way for 35 years, and they come [away from a dialogue] saying, I want to try all this stuff, it makes you feel great about your job."

Reflection: Reflection Is an Integral Part of Professional Learning

If ICs create learning partnerships through dialogue, if their collaborat-ing teachers are equal, if teachers are free and encouraged to speak their own minds and to make real, meaningful choices, it follows that one of the most important choices teachers will make is how to make sense of whatever it is that they are learning with their IC. ICs don't tell teachers what they should believe; respecting their partners' professionalism, they provide them with enough information to make their own decisions.

Offering teachers the freedom to consider ideas before they adopt them is central to the principle of reflection. Indeed, reflective thinkers, by definition, have to be free to choose or reject ideas, or else they simply are not thinkers at all. As Brubaker, Case, and Reagan (1994) explained, "the reflective teacher is first and foremost a decision-maker, who must make his or her decisions con-sciously and rationally" (p. 24). Reflection is only possible when people have the freedom to accept or reject what they are learning as they see fit.

More than 25 years ago, Donald A. Schön (1987) wrote about the need for reflection in all sorts of professions. According to Schön, reflection is necessary for learning since often the most important parts of skillful or artistic activities, like teaching, are hidden from our conscious understanding. People are skilled or artistic practitioners because they have a repertoire of competencies and skills that they may not even be able to identify. Polanyi (1983) described this as tacit knowledge. For that reason, Schön observes, becoming skilled at anything is as much about "getting the feel" of an activity as it is about learning specific skills. Reflection enables people to become more aware of their tacit knowledge, to understand the assumptions that are implicit in their actions, and to get the feel for whatever it is they are learning.

Schön (1987) distinguishes between "reflection in action" and "reflection on action." Reflection in action occurs while people are in the midst of an activity. During reflection in action, "our thinking serves to reshape what we are doing while we are doing it" (p. 26). Reflection on action occurs after an activity. This form of reflection involves "thinking back on what we have done in order to discover how our knowing-in-action may have contributed to an unexpected outcome" (p. 26).

Killion and Todnem (1991) extend Schön's description of reflection by observing that in addition to looking back and reflecting on practice, or thinking on the spot and reflecting in practice, reflective practitioners often think about how an idea can be used in the future, what they call *reflection for practice*. This is the kind of reflection most likely to be found when a coach and teacher sit together. During instructional coaching, teachers should be empowered to consider how an idea might be shaped, adapted, or reconstructed so that it fits with their way of teaching and also meets the most pressing needs of their students.

Ric Palma describes reflection as "two-pronged," that is, he sees reflection as important for his own professional growth as much as for his collaborating teachers' professional growth. For his own part, Ric observes that "reflection is always about self-improvement. I take notes on how I'm doing, and look back on them every week. I used to look back every day. I'm constantly thinking about how I do presentations, how I deal with opinions that are different from mine. I'm not encouraging reflection if I expect everyone to think the same as me."

Ric's "second prong" of reflection is empowering teachers to reflect as they learn new practices. "I think it's important that we give teachers the ability to reflect, not just tell them that they need to reflect. We need to give them tools and lead by example on how reflection can be a part of the collaboration. Reflection can and should be an important part of teaching, really with any profession, but especially teaching. I think the best teachers are the ones that are the best learners."

Reflection ultimately provides opportunities for teachers to think about what Parker Palmer (1998) calls "the inner landscape of the teaching self." As Palmer has observed, reflection can enable teachers to ask profound questions about what, how, why, and who teaches. His comments are revealing: "Teaching, like any truly human activity, emerges from one's inwardness, for better or worse . . . teaching holds a mirror to the soul. If I am willing to look in that mirror and not run from what I see, I have a chance to gain self-knowledge" (p. 2).

Praxis: Teachers Should Apply Their Learning to Their Real-Life Practice as They Are Learning

What do we desire as ICs? Most likely, we want the people with whom we work to learn new ways to help students, to think about what they do—to change for the better. To encourage such reflective action, we give teachers many chances to mull over how they might plan to use the new ideas being discussed. In some ways, when coaches and teachers work together, they are like children having fun with modeling clay, as together they reshape each new idea until they can see how it might look in their classroom. When ICs are acting on the principle of praxis, teachers have opportunities to think about how to shape new ideas to their real-life practices.

Praxis is the act of applying new ideas to our own lives. Moacir Gadotti (1996) defines it as "the unity that should exist between what one does (practice) and what one thinks about what one does (theory)" (p. 166). When teachers learn about Course Organizers (Lenz, Deshler, & Kissam, 2004) and spend a great deal of time thinking about and developing Course Questions that focus and reshape their courses, they are engaged in praxis of a sort. When they learn about telling stories and then create their own new stories to weave into their lessons, they are engaged in praxis. And when they learn about a new teaching practice or theory, think about it deeply, and decide not to use it in their classes, they are engaged in praxis. In short, when we learn, reflect, and act, we are engaged in praxis.

The concept of praxis has many implications. Most important perhaps is the assumption that if we are to apply new knowledge to our lives, we need to have a pretty clear understanding of our current reality. Paulo Freire (1970) has suggested that praxis is a profound and important activity because it leads to really analyzing our lives and the world in which we learn. For Freire, praxis is revolutionary: "it is reflection and action upon the world in order to transform it" (p. 36).

In many ways, it is easier to describe what praxis is not, rather than what it is. Praxis is *not* memorizing a new routine so that we can teach it in our classes exactly as we memorized it. Praxis is *not* running a workshop so that the picture in our mind ends up exactly the same in the minds of all the participants. Rather, true praxis is established when teachers have a chance to explore, prod, stretch, and recreate whatever they are studying—for example, really consider how they teach, really learn a new approach, and then reconsider their teaching practices, and reshape the new approach, if necessary, until it can work in their classroom.

A simple example illustrates what praxis is and why it is important. Imagine two different ways of learning how to use PowerPoint. In the first, you sit in a workshop for three hours and listen to an expert lecture on PowerPoint. In the second, an expert sits beside you as you prepare a presentation that you plan to give in the near future. When would you learn most? My guess is that most of us would learn most if we had a chance to apply our new knowledge to a real-life issue, as in the second situation above. When you do that, you're experiencing praxis as I have come to understand it.

Because reflection is central to this approach to learning, praxis enacted between people is impossible without a partnership relationship. As Richard J. Bernstein (1983) has observed, "praxis requires choice, deliberation, and decisions about what is to be done in concrete situations" (p. 160). In other words, if teachers are going to make plans to use what we're explaining, they need to feel free to make their own sense of the materials. They have to be true partners, equal, free to say yes and no, free to reflect, and, we hope, excited by possibilities offered by the new ideas they are learning.

Ric Palma sees praxis as enabled by every teacher's ability to tailor learning to his or her unique classrooms. "I think for praxis to work, they realize with us that what we're selling, what we're espousing, isn't just another way to do things. Our devices when we give them to them are blank, and then they fill them in to fit their classroom. What we give them is effective and based on research, but it's something that can be changed to better fit each teacher's classroom."

Praxis has another and perhaps more profound meaning. When people are reflecting, applying knowledge to their lives, honestly talking about how they will use what they are learning, they are fully engaged in the experience. Ric comments, "They aren't sitting there twiddling their thumbs thinking, 'Maybe I should be taking notes.' They aren't wasting time. They are doing something important for their students and for themselves."

Reciprocity: Instructional Coaches Should Expect to Get as Much as They Give

In a partnership, all participants benefit from the success, learning, or experience of others (Freire, 1970; Senge, 1990; Vella, 1995). All members are rewarded by what each individual contributes. When this principle is applied to coaching, it has some fairly obvious implications. ICs who operate from the partnership principles enter relationships with teachers believing that the knowledge and expertise of teachers is as important as the knowledge and expertise of the coach. By encouraging teachers' voices, through dialogue, and by observing teachers' reflection, ICs demonstrate that they have faith in teachers' abilities to invent useful new applications of the content they are exploring. Coaches expect to learn from teachers and they do. Richard Beckhard, discussing executive coaching, succinctly describes the reciprocal nature of effective coaching:

Coaching is one of the deepest, mutually satisfying experiences a person can have. The coach helps the person being coached to learn and grow and realize their dreams. At the same time, the person being coached brings out the noblest sentiments and brings out the deepest gratification for the coach. Coaching is the quintessential win–win experience. (Goldsmith, Lyons, & Freas, 2000, p. xiii)

ICs learn about collaborating teachers' classrooms and schools, the strengths and the multiple perspectives on the content being presented when seen through the eyes of participants. The reward ICs reap for adopting the partnership principles is that they are continually learning from their collaborating teachers.

Ric Palma sees reciprocity in the rewards coaches and teachers experience together. "Teachers' knowledge and their experiences are important. Reciprocity means an equal give-and-take. Mutual respect builds, and we know that we're helping each other. And that's important. The ICs on my team, we're all passionate, and I think that allows for the reciprocity to happen, because, on a basic level, when our teachers are happy and effective so are we. We know we had a part in that, and we think, oh man, this is going to be great."

How They Define Themselves as Good People

One of the things I used to love about teaching was that one kid who used to stick around class just to tell you something. It didn't necessarily have to do with why he wanted to stick around; it was his weird way of saying that he knew you cared about him, that he appreciated the fact that you cared. What he wanted to talk about might be something silly, like showing you a picture of his car, or telling you that he has a pet frog. Telling you some weird thing is students' little way of reaching out to you to let you know that you made a difference. You can have the same experience with a kid who comes back four years after graduating, saying, "You had the most impact on me, and I'm doing well now." They kind of want to brag, but they want to brag and let you know that you helped them.

When I became an instructional coach, I was worried that I would miss that kind of impact the most because I can't have the same kind of direct effect on kids now. But I've learned that I can have a positive effect on many more kids. And, instead of a kid coming into my classroom or my office and talking to me, I can now have a teacher come into my office to say, "Hey! This is great. I love this stuff."

I can see it in their eyes, that they're remembering why they loved teaching, that they feel and see why teaching is such a neat profession. They feel validated as teachers, as professionals, and more important, they feel validated as people. For most teachers, to teach well and to reach people, to reach those kids is how they define themselves as good people. I kind of had to trade off where that positive feedback comes from, but I think I now can have more of a profound effect on the kids in the long run.

Other Principles

This list of principles is by no means exhaustive or definitive. I presented these at a conference sponsored by Riane Eisler, who has written more about the concept of partnership than anyone. When I asked for Riane's thoughts, she suggested adding the principle of caring. For Riane, a partnership is a caring relationship, and when she talks about partnership relationships in schools, she stresses the importance of compassionate action and concern for others. I agree that caring is an authentic manifestation of a true partnership.

Others could argue, and I would agree, that quality is also an extremely important principle. What good does it serve students if an IC and teacher work together in a healthy relationship but their friendly conversation has no impact on the quality of the teacher's teaching? Quality is important. One study (Knight, 2004) showed that teachers who taught a comprehensive, metacognitive approach to sentence writing, *The Sentence Writing Strategy* (Schumaker & Sheldon, 1985), in ways that were similar to those described in the research-validated instructor's manual saw the number of complete sentence in their students' writing ($N = 1,302$ students) increase by 13% (from 74% to 87% complete sentences). We refer to this as "hi-fi teaching." Teachers who taught in ways that varied significantly from research-validated practices, what we refer to as "low-fi teaching," saw the number of complete sentences in their students' writing ($N = 562$ students) increase by about 4% (from 76% to 80%). Clearly, quality counts.

There are other principles you might choose to adopt. What matters is that ICs, and those setting up coaching programs, reflect deeply on and articulate their principles. Many coaches succeed or fail because of the principles on which they base their actions. Coaches need to think deeply about the assumptions that define the way they choose to work with teachers.

At the heart of the teacher-coach collaborative relationship, as I define it, there is a deep respect for the professionalism of teaching. We base our work with teachers on the principles of equality, choice, voice, dialogue, reflection, praxis, and reciprocity. Our hope is that we will be considered to be just like any other teacher in the school. If we are viewed in such a way, and teachers come to see us as colleagues they can trust, there is a good chance that together we can make a difference in the way teachers teach and students learn in schools.

GOING DEEPER

Paulo Freire's *Pedagogy of the Oppressed* (1970), which describes methods for literacy education for adults in Brazilian villages, is a challenging but highly rewarding description of the power of dialogue, praxis, and the mutual humanization that can result from people learning together as partners.

Peter Block's *Stewardship* (1993) explores the significance of the partnership metaphor as a way of understanding human interaction in organizations.

Block suggests that leaders will be more effective if they adopt a stewardship approach, as opposed to a top-down autocratic approach.

Riane Eisler's *Chalice and the Blade: Our History, Our Future* (1988) provides anthropological data to support her contention that world cultures have always been based on either a "dominator" or a "partnership" form of social organization. For Eisler, partnership is superior to patriarchy, and she details what it will take for western civilization to shift from its current patriarchal mind-set to a more humane partnership mind-set. Eisler's *Tomorrow's Children: A Blueprint for Partnership Education for the 21st Century* (2000), offers a critique of the prevalence of the "dominator" model in today's schools and provides a comprehensive explanation of what schools would look like if they were based on the partnership model.

Stephen Covey's *The Eighth Habit: From Effectiveness to Greatness* (2004) is, among many other things, an articulate defense of, and sophisticated "how to manual" for, finding our voice and helping others find their voice in their personal and professional lives.

Dialogue is discussed in several books mentioned in this chapter. More information on dialogue is included in the Going Deeper section of Chapter 6.

TO SUM UP

Human action is based on a theory, or principles, and to fully understand what we stand for, we should think deeply about what principles we embrace for our work and personal lives. ICs who know a lot of valuable information but base their actions on inappropriate principles may inadvertently provoke others to resist their ideas because of those principles.

In this book, I propose seven principles (equality, choice, voice, dialogue, reflection, praxis, and reciprocity) as the theoretical foundation for instructional coaching.

- *Equality* is believing the people we collaborate with are no less important than us or anyone else, and that consequently their ideas, thoughts, and opinions are no less important than our own.
- *Choice* is believing that choices lie at the heart of professional practice, and that when we take away others' choices, we treat them as if they are not professionals. We have found that when we offer others choices, we actually increase the likelihood that they will embrace what we have to offer. Taking away choice is a bona fide recipe for resistance.
- *Voice* is believing that a part of learning is helping people find the words they need to say what matters to them. Another important part of voice is making it possible for others to openly communicate what they think.
- *Dialogue* is believing in the importance of conversations that enable people to think together.

- *Reflection* is believing that learning can be enhanced when we have numerous opportunities to consider how what we're learning might impact what we have done in the past, what we are doing now, and what we will be doing in the future.
- *Praxis* is believing that learning is most meaningful when we reflect and recreate knowledge so that we can use it in our personal or professional lives.
- *Reciprocity* is believing that every learning experience we create provides as much of a chance for us to learn as it does for our learning partners.

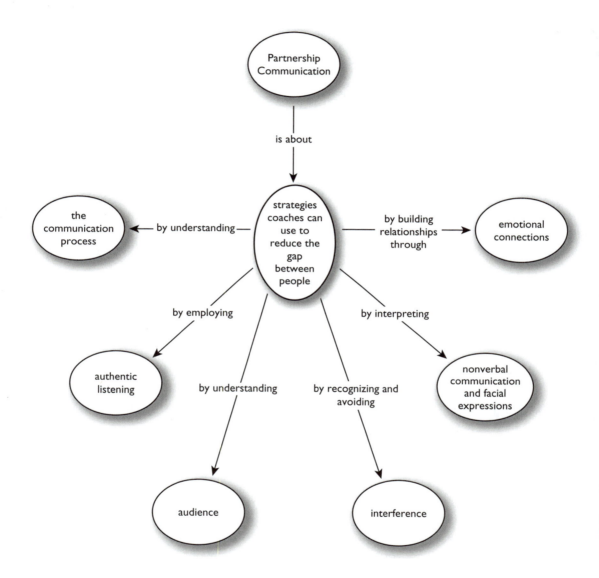

Chapter 4

Partnership Communication

Creating Learning Conversations

I love communicating with people. I love making people feel good about themselves and what they teach. This is the perfect job to make people feel good about themselves, to feel good about their profession, and to help kids learn.

—Lynn Barnes, instructional coach,
Jardine Middle School

CHAPTER OVERVIEW

The success or failure of a coaching program hinges on the coach's ability to communicate clearly, build relationships, and support fellow teachers. A coach who struggles to get along with others will likely struggle to be successful. This chapter introduces six aspects of effective communication: (a) understanding the communication process, (b) employing authentic listening, (c) understanding our audiences, (d) recognizing stories, (e) interpreting nonverbal communication and facial expressions, and (f) building relationships through emotional connection. Coaches who learn and apply these aspects of communication to their professional and personal life should be better prepared to connect with people in meaningful, healthy relationships.

CREATING LEARNING CONVERSATIONS

We face a crisis of communication. Although we may talk with dozens of people every day, we can go through entire weeks or longer never having a single, meaningful conversation. Margaret Wheatley, author of *Turning to One Another: Simple Conversations to Restore Hope to the Future* (2002), describes our situation as follows:

> We have never wanted to be alone. But today, we are alone.
> We are more fragmented and isolated from one another than

ever before. Archbishop Desmond Tutu describes it as "a radical brokenness in all of existence. (p. 4)

On those occasions when we work up the courage to share a few honest words, we often find that things fall apart. We try to make a simple point, to express a well-thought-through opinion, and find ourselves silenced, or ignored, or inadvertently offending someone whom we meant no harm, or offended by someone who meant us no harm. In a time when many people long for more intimacy, we struggle to find a common language to make meaningful conversation possible. For many, the only place where intimate conversations exist is on the Internet, with strangers.

Communicating an important message can be one of the most authentic, rewarding experiences in life. When we communicate, we learn; share thoughts, experiences, and emotions; and become colleagues, friends, and soul mates. Words and language, messages sent and received, can build a tie between people that is deep, strong, and even lifelong. Effective communication can enable the kind of faithful relationship that we build our lives around. Unfortunately, words can also destroy relationships. A simple, innocent comment can do damage that may take years to repair, or damage that may never be repaired. Getting our messages through is a messy business.

Our common struggle to communicate is doubly important for ICs. The ability to communicate effectively stands at the heart of what ICs do, not just inside the walls of a school, but inside every important relationship in which they live. An IC who is a highly effective communicator is well on the way to a successful career. An IC who struggles to communicate effectively, however, faces a world of challenges. We may not be far off the mark if we say that ICs cannot be effective in their profession unless they understand how to be effective communicators.

Lynn Barnes, an IC at Jardine Middle School, believes that communication and relationship building lie at the heart of being an effective coach. "You have to build a relationship before you can do anything. You have to truly care about the individuals and students you are working with. At all times, you have to be compassionate, empathetic, patient and understanding. There's no place for sarcasm with kids or adults."

Lynn Barnes

Lynn Barnes, an IC at Jardine Middle School, has a total of 35 years of teaching experience. Of the 35 years, she has been an IC for 6 years and taught language arts for 15 years. Lynn won Topeka's Middle School Teacher of the Year Award and is certified as a Strategic Instruction Model Content Enhancement Professional Developer, a Strategic Instruction Model Learning Strategies Professional Developer, and a Professional Developer for Randy Sprick's Safe and Civil Schools program.

THE COMMUNICATION PROCESS

Understanding the communication process can help us see why communication frequently falters and fails. As the figure below illustrates, communication of any sort is more complicated than meets the eye (or ear, I suppose, depending on the way the message is shared) and the process of communication involves several components.

Figure 4.1   The Communication Process

- Speaker
- Message
- Listener
- Interference
- Perceived Message
- Feedback

Components of the Communication Process

Communication usually begins with an intended message, that is, an idea, thought, opinion, or statement that someone wishes to communicate to another person or persons. The person who expresses the idea, thought, opinion, or statement we call the *speaker*, and the person(s) receiving the message we call the audience. As simple as this sounds, a funny thing happens to the message on the way from the speaker to the audience, however. Interference messes with the message. Like static on the radio, interference is anything that stands in the way of us sending or receiving our message.

Consequently, the audience receives a modified version of the intended message—we call this the perceived message. Unfortunately, the perceived message can be quite a bit different from the intended message, but the audience doesn't know that and believes the perceived message is real. Since interference hinders the transparent communication of ideas, a speaker has to evaluate the reaction of his or her audience to ascertain whether or not the intended message has made it through the interference. This reaction, which we call feedback, can be spoken loudly and obviously (laughter, shouts, smiles) or transmitted so subtly as to be almost imperceptible (a momentary look away).

The moment the audience arches an eyebrow, smiles, or breaks into tears, the audience becomes a speaker sending a new message. Indeed, even if the audience didn't intend to send a message, nothing still communicates something, and any reaction can be understood to convey countless additional perceived messages. Such is the way communication proceeds, with speakers and audiences sending out messages all with the goal of getting the message through interference.

Interference can occur in a multitude of ways. Interference can literally be some real noise that makes it difficult for an audience to perceive a message. If Pandora Radio is playing loudly when your daughter is talking about her applications to college, and you find it difficult to hear her over the music on the computer speakers, obviously the sound is causing interference. If you're leading a two-hour workshop exploring a complicated teaching practice and the school secretary has a riotous time sending out messages over the PA, the sound of the PA would be interference.

Interference is manifested more subtly as well. If your friend applies for an important position in an executive firm and shows up for the interview wearing a Sex Pistols T-shirt, her clothing might interfere with her audience's ability to perceive her intended message that she really is qualified for the job (though there may be one or two settings where that T-shirt might communicate that she is the perfect person for the job).

Interference frequently is invisible, existing in our audience's preconceptions, competing priorities, experiences, prior knowledge, or lack of prior knowledge. Our thoughts, perceptions, beliefs, values, emotions, and prior knowledge can keep us from being effective audiences for others' important messages.

The art of effective communication is finding ways to get around interference so that the message we want to communicate more or less becomes the message that is perceived by our audience.

Partnership Principles and Communication

ICs who ground their actions in the partnership approach (see Chapter 3) find it easier to send and receive messages effectively. If they believe that they are partners with others and that everyone has something to teach them, they are more inclined to be respectful and open to the people with whom they interact. Respect, equality, and openness are good starting points for learning conversations. Lynn Barnes believes that the respect inherent in the partnership approach makes it much easier for her to connect with teachers: "Teachers know that if they tell me something, I won't get upset. I accept their opinions, and as a partnership, we just value each other's opinion, and we are more accepting of each other. They're willing to share ideas; they're willing to meet with me, and they share their kids with me. They don't share their kids if they don't believe and trust you."

EMPLOYING AUTHENTIC LISTENING

If you pick up just about any book on communication, leadership, relationships, or self-help, there is a good chance you will find several pages or chapters dedicated to the art of listening. Many authors have emphasized the importance of this skill. For example, Robert K. Greenleaf, who first described the concept of servant leadership (1998), states that "the inability to listen may be the most costly of the human relations skills to be without" (p. 71). Douglas Stone, Bruce Patton, and Sheila Heen (1999) observe that "listening well is one of the most powerful skills you can bring to a difficult conversation. It helps you understand the other person. And, importantly, it helps them understand you" (p.163). Margaret Wheatley (2002) even goes as far as stating, "I believe we can change the world if we start listening to one another again" (p. 3).

We need to listen better. We know it, and yet we do not do it. We zone out of conversations, we argue with others before we fully hear what they have to tell us, and we turn the focus back to us when we should be focused on those with whom we are talking. We want to listen, but we just do not seem to be getting much better at it. Or we are blithely unaware of how poorly we listen. And the people around us don't seem to be very good listeners either. If only they'd listen, things could be so much easier.

How Misconceptions Keep Us From Listening

Of course, the problem usually isn't the other person. The problem is that we frequently misjudge our ability to listen. To paraphrase R. D. Laing, if we don't know we're not listening, we think we're listening. If the other person isn't listening well, maybe our best solution is to listen to them. Over time, I have learned that when I listen with great care, the person I'm speaking with almost always becomes a much better listener.

So why is it so difficult to listen? William Isaacs explains that "if we try to listen we find it extraordinarily difficult, because we are always projecting our opinions and ideas, our prejudices, our background, our inclinations, our impulses; when they dominate, we hardly listen at all to what is being said" (1999, p. 84). Our memories, especially, interfere with our ability to listen. For example, an IC who remembers he was criticized by a teacher in a team meeting a month ago may find that memory interfering with his ability to listen objectively in the here and now. Even if the teacher makes a positive statement, the IC's memory might make it difficult to hear the positive comments.

We also struggle to listen simply because we may not want to hear what others are saying. We are usually drawn to those messages that confirm our hopes or affirm our assumptions about ourselves. Even after years of communication training, for example, many find it easier to listen to praise than criticism. David Bohm (2000) explains that if someone examines the way they listen,

> If one is alert and attentive, he can see, for example, that whenever certain questions arise, there are fleeting questions of fear, which push him away from consideration of these questions and of pleasure, which attract his thoughts and cause them to be occupied with other questions . . . can each of us be aware of the subtle fear and

pleasure sensations that block his ability to listen freely? Without this awareness, the injunction to listen to the whole of what is said will have little meaning. (p. 4)

Attentiveness

In a now famous quotation, Woody Allen reportedly once said, "eighty percent of life is just showing up." I think that much the same can be said about listening. More than anything else, the defining characteristic of effective listening is being attentive. An IC who truly wants to listen better has to make the effort. Listening is an act of will as much as it is a skill or an art, and no matter how many coaching books ICs read, they won't be effective listeners unless they decide to roll up their sleeves and stay focused on the person with whom they're speaking. Susan Scott (2002) explains the importance of attentiveness as follows:

Think for the moment about the kind of attention you bring to your conversations. While someone is talking, where are your thoughts? When you are face-to-face, do you look at the individual in front of you or do your eyes roam in a sort of perpetual surveillance? While you're talking with someone on the telephone, do you scan your email? And can you tell when someone is scanning his? (p. 95)

IC Lynn Barnes works very deliberately to pay attention to collaborating teachers when she listens.

Sometimes when they come with their stories, and there are 15 other things I have to do, I have to tell myself, "put your pencil down, give them eye contact, put yourself in their shoes." I've had the experience happen to me when I was talking to someone and they were typing an email or doing something else, and it was like they could care less about me being with them. I need to value each moment that a teacher wants to be with me. I make sure when someone comes to my office, I make sure that I'm really listening, all there. I'm not thinking about what pressing engagement I have to do. I can't have that distraction. I'm needed. I try to think of them first.

Self-Awareness

Aside from attending to "the kind of attention" brought to listening, coaches should also consider whether or not they are listening in a biased manner. Are they only hearing information that confirms their assumptions? Are their memories biasing them as they listen? William Isaacs (1999) explains, "You can begin to listen by listening first to yourself and to your own reactions. Ask yourself, 'What do I feel here? Or how does this feel?' . . . To learn to be present, we must learn to notice what we are feeling now" (p. 92).

In order to be better listeners, ICs need to learn to distinguish between experiencing and evaluating during conversation. We need to ask, are we listening through the filter of our personal biases? Do we judge as we hear? Or, when we experience a conversation, do we focus our attention on simply hearing exactly what the other person is saying? ICs who listen effectively do not paint the words of others with their biases; they simply focus on understanding fully what the other person says.

Honesty and Authenticity

No matter how many listening techniques ICs learn, they will not be effective listeners unless they honestly want to hear what others have to say. As Stone et al. (1999) have observed,

> Scores of workshops and books on "active listening" teach you what you should do to be a good listener . . . The problem is this: you are taught what to do and how to sit, but the heart of good listening is authenticity. People "read" not only your words and posture, but what's going on inside of you. If your "stance" isn't genuine, the words won't matter . . . If your intentions are false, no amount of careful wording or good posture will help. If your intentions are good, even clumsy language won't hinder you . . . Listening is only powerful and effective if it is authentic. Authenticity means that you are listening because you are curious and you care, not just because you are supposed to. The issue, then, is this: Are you curious? Do you care? (p. 168)

Empathy and Respect

Stephen Covey (1989) has been very articulate in describing the importance of empathy in the act of listening. "Empathic listening gets inside another person's frame of reference. You look out through it, you see the world the way they see the world . . . The essence of empathic listening is not that you agree with someone; it's that you fully, deeply, understand that person, emotionally as well as intellectually" (p. 240). Without empathy, little true listening takes place. However, with empathy, deep communication, nourishing humanizing communication is possible.

What must we do to be empathetic? I believe that we begin to be empathetic when we begin with humility. The goal of empathy, what Covey refers to as *empathic listening*, is to silence ourselves and attend to others. We need to teach ourselves to put our personal concerns aside, and to concern ourselves with whomever we are speaking to. This may mean that we learn to duck, metaphorically speaking, when we are criticized or attacked, or that we put our opinions or agendas aside temporarily to hear others. To really listen to others, we have to learn to keep our personal needs for attention, self-defense, prestige, or power from interfering with our ability to hear what is being said.

An empathic response is also a powerful way to demonstrate respect. William Isaacs (1999) reminds us, "Respect is not a passive act. To respect someone is to look for the spring that feeds the pool of their experience . . . it involves a sense of honoring or deferring to someone. Where once we saw one aspect of a person, we look again and realize how much of them we have missed. This second look can let us take in more fully the fact that before me is a living, breathing being" (p. 111). To respect is to commit fully to the belief that each other person carries within him or her a humanity that must be recognized, validated, and listened to.

Isaacs (1999) suggests that one way we can increase respect is to remind ourselves, "This, too, is in me," when we hear something that provokes in us an un-listening reaction. Isaacs explains that "we may be tempted to say that a given behavior is all 'theirs'—I do not have anything like that in me! Maybe so. But the courage to accept it as not only 'out there,' but also 'in here,' enables us to engage in the world in a very different way" (p. 124). Isaacs goes on to say that we can build respect by demonstrating "the willingness to forgive that which we see in another and come to the point where we can accept it as being in us" (p. 124).

The kind of respect Isaacs describes is central to the partnership approach. We believe that the others with whom we interact are equal to us, that our voice is no more important than theirs, and that they have something to teach us. Even more fundamentally, we believe that it is a moral necessity to see the value in those with whom we interact. We don't tell them what to do or make their decisions; we respect them as fellow human beings traveling a road very similar to our own.

Listening Strategies

Developing inner silence
Listening for what contradicts our assumptions
Clarifying
Communicating our understanding
Practicing every day
Practicing with terrible listeners

Some Listening Strategies

Developing inner silence. We can improve our ability to listen by training ourselves to silence thoughts we have that lead us to judge rather than simply experience the comments of others.

Listening for what contradicts our assumptions. Since we are frequently attracted to messages that reinforce our biases and predispositions, we can improve our listening if we direct our brain to listen for messages that contradict our assumptions.

Clarifying. An obvious but frequently overlooked listening strategy is to check with our colleagues to ensure that we understand what they are saying. Clarifying might take the form of a paraphrase ("let me tell you what I'm hearing you say, and you tell me if I've got it right") or might simply involve asking our colleague to slow the pace of conversation or to repeat an idea that we missed the first time it was spoken.

Communicating our understanding. Being a good listener does not mean that we sit silent and frozen like a rock. Good listeners ask questions, clarify, and communicate that they understand what is being said. We can communicate our understanding verbally or nonverbally. The important thing is that we communicate that we understand, and thus encourage the speaker to keep talking.

Practicing every day. Listening, Stephen Covey (1989) reminds us, "is something you can practice right now" (p. 258). I find it most effective to plan specific times or situations when I will work on my listening skills. Like other healthy habits, we become better listeners the more we practice.

Practicing with terrible listeners. Stone et al. (1999) assert that "the reason why the other person is not listening to you is not because they are stubborn, but because they don't feel heard" (pp. 166–167). To prove their point, the authors suggest a simple test: "Find the most stubborn person you know, the person who never seems to take in anything you say, the person who repeats himself or herself in every conversation you ever have—and listen to them. Especially, listen for feelings, like frustration, or pride or fear, and acknowledge those feelings. See whether that person doesn't become a better listener after all" (p. 167).

UNDERSTANDING OUR AUDIENCE

Becoming an effective listener is a great start for one of the most important communication strategies—learning how to present information so that it can be understood easily by an audience (in this case collaborating teachers). A coach's best intentions, a coach's communication goals, or a coach's obvious intended message doesn't matter a whit if the collaborating teacher doesn't hear it. The message that matters is the one in the teacher's mind, not the one in the coach's mind. For that reason, coaches who are effective communicators structure every message so that it can be accurately perceived by their audience. If coaches start by understanding their audience, they then can frame their message so that it will be heard.

What Questions Can Instructional Coaches Ask to Focus on Their Collaborating Teachers?

What are my collaborating teacher's most pressing concerns?
What does my collaborating teacher know about this topic?
What are my collaborating teacher's learning preferences?
What are my collaborating teacher's values?

ICs communicate better with their teachers if they first ask a few questions. An IC might start working with a teacher by asking these questions in an actual learning conversation, or an IC might consider these questions on her own as she prepares for a future conversation with teachers.

1. *What are my collaborating teacher's most pressing concerns?* The importance of this question might seem obvious, but far too many of us have shown up with ideas to share with a teacher without really ever knowing what is on that teacher's mind. As Lynn Barnes explains, "I have to meet their needs, when they need it." Put another way, ignorance of what is most important to a collaborating teacher can interfere with a coach's ability to have an impact. If a teacher is really concerned about classroom management, and I fail to address that when I meet with her, I may or may not be able to create a sustained relationship focused on professional learning. However, if I can respond to a teacher's pressing concern that he needs to learn classroom management techniques quickly, and as a coach I hear that concern and provide the teacher with tools that help him keep his kids on task and learning, I can make a difference.

2. *What does my collaborating teacher know about this topic?* Chances are, all of us have been in learning situations where teachers misjudged what we knew about a topic before they started teaching us. On the one hand, if an IC assumes I know a lot about a topic and dives in full-throttle without checking to make sure I have sufficient background knowledge, the IC runs the risk of leaving me behind in the dust of her rapid-fire explanations. On the other hand, if an IC tediously explains a topic I already know well, the IC can be even more frustrating because she is wasting my precious time or, more problematic, appears to be patronizing me by teaching me something I know very well.

Effective ICs, then, must do their best to understand as fully as possible how much their audience knows about a topic. Coaches can start by making some assumptions based on their prior knowledge of a given teacher and others who hold similar positions in the school. However, as quickly as possible, the IC needs to check with the teacher to see if her assumptions are correct, asking a few quick questions to determine how much the teacher knows. Then, throughout future collaborative conversations with teachers, the coach should continually check to make sure that the explanations are sufficiently complete without being overly comprehensive.

Lynn Barnes says that the secret of assessing teachers' prior knowledge is to "ask questions. You find out what they know about this, if they've had training, if they really know it or not . . . you ask questions and you start formulating in your own mind an idea of how much they know."

3. *What are my collaborating teacher's learning preferences?* Asking this easily overlooked question can yield some very useful information. If we can get a better understanding of how our collaborating teachers prefer to learn, that can help us communicate more efficiently. Jane Kise's *Differentiated Coaching: A Framework for Helping Teachers Change* (2006) appears to be the definitive work on learning preferences and coaching. Kise compares several ways of explaining learning types but employs the Myers-Briggs Type Indicator tool (MBTI) to explain why coaches should understand learning types and how they can use that information when coaching teachers.

The MBTI is a self-reporting instrument that people can complete to better understand their learning preferences. The MBTI sorts our learning styles into four pairs of preferences: (a) judging and perceiving, (b) extraversion and introversion, (c) sensing and intuition, and (d) thinking and feeling. Kise's definitions of each preference pair are included in the tables below:

Judging and Perceiving: How We Approach Life	
Judging	"A preference for planning their work and working their plan. They are not more judgmental but rather prefer to come to judgment (closure) on things" (p. 86)
Perceiving	"A preference for staying open to the moment. They are not more perceptive but rather prefer to continue to perceive (gather) more information" (p. 86)

Extraversion and Introversion: How We Get Energy	
Extraversion	"Gaining energy through action and interaction, the outside world" (p. 89)
Introversion	"Gaining energy through reflection and solitude, the inner world" (p. 89)

Sensing and Intuition: How We Gather Information	
Sensing	"*First* paying attention to *what is*, to information you can gather through your five senses—the facts" (p. 93)
Intuition	"*First* paying attention to what *could be*, to hunches, connections or imagination—a sixth sense" (p. 93)

Thinking and Feeling: How We Make Decisions	
Thinking	"Making decisions through objective, logical principles" (p. 96)
Feeling	"Making decisions by considering the impact of each alternative on the people involved" (p. 96)

Since ICs can personalize learning experiences for each collaborating teacher, they seem uniquely capable of responding to teachers' learning preferences. An IC who recognizes that a collaborating teacher has a "judging" learning preference, for example, might take care to spend much more time collaboratively planning with that teacher. Similarly, an IC with an extroversion learning preference should be careful to adapt her communication when working with a teacher who gets energy from solitude. Extroverts who try to energize introverts can sometimes push them away if they do not recognize the introverts' learning style.

ICs can benefit by deepening their understanding of learning preferences by reading works such as Kise's *Differentiated Coaching*. However, even without extensive knowledge of learning types, coaches should be attentive to the unique learning preferences of those with whom they collaborate. IC Lynn Barnes observes that learning styles are important to consider when planning group presentations. "I think it's good to realize that we all have different learning styles, like students. In our trainings we have to incorporate multiple learning styles so that we meet the needs of all those styles in our trainings."

4. *What are my collaborating teacher's values and how do my own values affect my relationship with this teacher? What is most important to this teacher?* An IC who understands a teacher's values, that is, knows what a teacher considers to be important or valuable, has a significant advantage when it comes to communication. For that reason, coaches should do their best to understand each teacher's values so that they can communicate in the most efficient manner.

Consider, for example, the value teachers ascribe to standardized test scores. Some teachers are very concerned about the results their students and school achieve on standardized test scores, so when working with those teachers, ICs would be prudent to explain how particular interventions might help students do better on standardized tests. Other teachers view standardized tests negatively, believing they promote a narrow understanding of what education is and can be. When working with a teacher who ascribes a negative value to standardized tests, an IC would be prudent to explain how interventions address other aspects of education that the teacher values.

ICs also have to consider other values a teacher holds that might enhance or interfere with communication. Teachers' time, for example, is something that Lynn Barnes is very careful to respect. "Their time is valuable, and when you show them you understand that, that's important to the relationship." At the same time, Lynn also avoids topics that might put her at odds with collaborating teachers. "You know, the older I get, the wiser I get. I try to really be conscious of what I say, really conscious about the way I say it. I'm never flip with people. I could care less about persuading them to vote Democrat in the next election or persuading them to be a Protestant rather than a Catholic. I'm not at the job to talk politics. I'm there because I truly care about helping them in their profession and meeting the needs of those kids."

RECOGNIZING AND OVERCOMING INTERFERENCE

Effective communication, more than anything else, is all about getting the message through various forms of interference. If we are at a Yo La Tengo concert, for example, and the band is playing very loud, we may have to resort to sign language, touch, or notes to get our message through the interference of the music. Similarly, when we work with teachers, we have to employ strategies that help us get through the interference that keeps them from hearing what we have to say.

One common form of interference has been identified by Stone et al. in *Difficult Conversations: How to Discuss What Matters Most* (1999). The authors explain that when a conversation has implications for someone's identity, when it becomes what they refer to as an *identity conversation*, a person often finds it difficult to hear the intended message being communicated:

> The identity conversation looks inward: it's all about who we are and how we see ourselves. How does what happened affect my self-esteem, my self-image, my sense of who I am in the world? What impact will it have on my future? What self-doubts do I harbor? In short . . . the identity conversation is about what I am saying to myself *about me*. (p. 14)

Communication is difficult in schools when change leaders are insensitive to the identity implications of what they are proposing. Teachers don't resist new ideas as much as they resist the suggestion that they are not competent and they need to be helped or improved. When coaches clearly communicate their genuine belief that their collaborating teachers are competent and skilled, that is, when they take the partnership approach, there is a chance that those teachers will hear what their coaches have to say. However, when coaches communicate even ever so slightly that they are in the school to fix the "bad teachers," then teachers hearing that message will resist to protect their identity no matter how great the information is that a coach has to share. Simply put, to make sure people hear you, be careful not to start the conversation by attacking their identity.

A second form of interference exists inside ourselves. Our stories about events can also interfere with our ability to communicate. Over the past few decades, authors such as Michel Polanyi (1983), Thomas Kuhn (1970), and Peter Senge (1990) have shown that our ability to understand the world is limited or incomplete. What all these authors communicate, whether they discuss "the tacit dimension" of perception, or "paradigms," or "mental models," is that what we see, hear, and perceive is dramatically shaped by our prior knowledge (both conscious and unconscious).

An experience I had at a party for my son Geoff's hockey team helped me gain insight into just how incomplete our perceptions can be. Geoff and his young teammates were celebrating the end of a fun season. A kindly grandmother of one of the players had videotaped the final game. After all the food had been eaten, kids and parents herded into the basement recreation room to watch the video of the game. While at first everyone was excited to see the game, within a few minutes, the kids began to get restless. The proud grandmother had filmed every move of her grandson, whether or not he was involved in any action on the ice. During those moments when her grandson was in the midst of the play, everyone in the room was excited to watch. However, during those minutes (and to the children they seemed like very long periods of time) when her grandson was not in the action, the videotape of the boy standing on the blue line, back from the action, was, to say the least, disappointing to all the other players on the team. In short, the boys got to see a tape of the game, but because the tape focused on only one boy, the tape missed most of the game.

Our perceptions of the world are very similar to this grandmother's videotape. We only get a partial view of the action, and our personal interests tend to focus us on some things more than others. Patterson, Grenny, McMillan, and Switzler (2002) illustrate this phenomenon by discussing the impact of stories, stating that stories "are our interpretations of the facts. They help explain what we see and hear. They're theories we use to explain *why, how, and what*" (p. 99).

ICs must be careful not to let their personal stories interfere with their ability to understand what is really happening. On occasion, the stories we tell ourselves about reality shape our perceptions much more than the bare facts right in front of our faces.

When my colleague Mary Brieck came into our research center as our administrative manager a few years ago, every researcher at the Center breathed a sigh of relief. With someone carefully managing our office, we hoped, we would be able to spend more time working on what we felt mattered and less time on bureaucratic minutiae. At first, mind you, I was concerned that Mary was not helping at all. In her first few weeks on the job, Mary instituted several procedures that seemed to be anything but helpful. First, she instituted a policy that compelled all of us to sign out the center's state car if we wished to drive it—up until that point the car had had a nickname that I liked quite a lot, "Jim's car," and I had simply used it whenever I wished. Now I had to sign it out, and sometimes others signed it out ahead of me. Then Mary introduced a policy that she had to approve all grant-related purchases before the orders could be processed. I found myself writing time-consuming e-mails to Mary explaining why I needed a digital camera or why I needed to attend a particular conference. Worse than that, sometimes she wrote back to say I couldn't make the purchase.

As time went on, Mary's impact on my work life grew, and I wasn't happy about it. What was the point of all these new rules, I thought, except for making Mary feel like she was in control? Each week, I found myself increasingly frustrated, going home at night to complain to Jenny about how the new office administrator was a "control freak" who seemed determined to be a thorn in my side.

I got more and more frustrated with her policies and actions. Finally, my feelings and thoughts came to stand in the way of my ability to work with Mary, and I decided to confront her about her behavior. I knew what her problem was, and I was going to fix it, I reasoned. Fortunately, when I sat down and talked with her, I started by asking her to explain why she was doing what she was doing. I quickly discovered that my story was the problem, not Mary's actions. Mary tactfully explained that she was told when she was hired that her chief task was to create systems to organize the way we functioned and to increase our accountability. "My job here, and the way I will be evaluated," Mary said, "is whether or not I can create systems that make sure we don't do anything that will get us in trouble with our funding agencies."

Understanding how Mary perceived her actions made a world of difference to how I perceived what Mary did. Once I knew that she was only interested in ensuring that we were efficient and legal, our relationship changed. I realized that Mary wasn't someone intent on making my life difficult—she was intent on making sure I stayed out of jail. From that day on, when Mary e-mailed me to ask why I needed to make a particular purchase, I no longer saw her as a control freak, but as someone intent upon ensuring that we use our funds correctly and thereby ensuring we continue to get funding for our research. She wasn't against me; she was very clearly pulling for me, working on my side.

If ICs are not careful, they can make the same mistake I made with Mary and allow their personal stories to interfere with an accurate perception of reality. For example, a coach might come to believe that teachers are stubbornly resisting change when in reality they are simply taking time to balance competing demands on their time. If a coach writes off teachers as being resistant, hostile, or negative, they may dismiss teachers who might actually be open to change. By failing to inspect their own stories, coaches can do teachers and their students a real disservice.

Lynn Barnes told me a story that illustrates how she keeps herself from letting stories interfere with her ability to reach out to teachers. When Lynn first met "Alison" at her school, Alison brushed Lynn off, telling her, "I know all about graphic organizers, so you won't have to deal with me." Although tempted to take Alison at her word, Lynn said, "I continued to do what I do—greeting her in the hall, giving her positive notes, inquiring about her life, finding positive things about her as a person. It ended that she was all for our strategies. She didn't need me right away, but she was able to see the benefits of our strategies in her classroom. We should never dismiss teachers; there is always some way we can help them."

Patterson et al. (2002) identify what they refer to as "vicious stories" we tell ourselves that interfere with our ability to communicate. One such story is the story in which we paint another person as a villain. Thus, an IC might develop a story that an administrator who questions every intervention a coach offers is a bad person who is determined, for selfish or evil reasons, to destroy everything good that the coach is doing.

I spend a great deal of time in schools across the nation, and everywhere I go I hear educational leaders described as if they are villains (even one loving, dedicated coach I know, who seems to have a kind word for everyone, once referred to her administrator as a witch when the administrator failed to support her). The reality is that few people wake up in the morning determined to do evil to adults or children in schools. However, when coaches fall prey to the villain story, it is very difficult for them to reach out to those they consider villains. If I'm sure you're my enemy, I will find it difficult to listen to, empathize with, respect, or connect with you.

A second type of vicious story is the helpless story. Here, we create a story in which we convince ourselves that we are helpless in the face of some challenge. "How can I ever teach these students," a teacher might ask, "when they're not motivated, when their parents don't care, when the class size is far too big?" By telling ourselves that our situation is helpless, we create a situation where the only appropriate reaction seems to be to give up.

It is easy to understand why an IC might give in to helpless stories because at times the challenges of school improvement can seem overwhelming. I have indeed met many coaches who are seduced, momentarily at least, by the story that they cannot make a difference. But a primary message of this book, and a major conclusion to be drawn from our research, is that ICs are not helpless. Indeed, our data show quite clearly that ICs can have a profound impact on the way teachers teach and students learn. In fact, the ICs who are most helpless are those who choose to give in to the vicious story of their own helplessness.

The art of communication involves finding ways to get around inter-ference that stands in the way of the transparent sharing of ideas. In some instances, the interference comes from within ourselves. Our stories about people can stand in the way of us understanding them. Thus, an IC who wants to connect with others needs to be aware of the ways in which his or her own preconceptions might block communication.

Just Talking Together

I had a meeting a while back that I thought was going to be awful. I got an e-mail from the principal, who wrote, "I'm not happy with how things are going. We need to talk." Sometimes it seemed as if the principal just didn't want me to help her with her kids, you know, and at first I didn't like that e-mail a bit. But I knew I couldn't ignore it. As it turned out, the next day was a day when teachers were out of the building, so I sug-gested we get together.

That night I thought a lot about how to handle the meeting. I decided that my main goal would be to listen. I wanted her to know that I got what she was saying. I wanted to see the world through her eyes and feel her feelings. When I went in she had a lot of criticisms, and I just listened. I didn't agree, but I didn't argue. I just said, "I can see why you feel worried. I can see why you might be concerned." I asked about her work, and the frustrations she was facing. She was overwhelmed and I was amazed that she could handle so many things at once. I told her that, too, and it seemed to help.

Something happened during the conversation. Somehow we shifted from her criticisms to talking about all kinds of things, her son, her new teachers, the new vice principal, our philosophies of life. It became a fun conversation, and I started to like her a lot more. In the midst of the conversation, I explained why I was doing what I was doing. My goal wasn't to trick her. We were just talking, and like never before, she understood me. Everything worked out that day. Sometimes you get lucky.

THE SUBTLE LANGUAGE OF COMMUNICATION: FACIAL EXPRESSIONS AND EMOTIONAL CONNECTIONS

When we think about communication, we might think about things that are fairly easy to see or hear, such as speech, e-mails, memos, letters, or touch. I would contend, however, that most communication is more subtle. When we communicate with others, much of what takes place in the interaction happens beneath the surface. We watch for nonverbal cues, we read body language, we look for eye contact, and we pay attention to how we feel as we talk with others. Furthermore, we often respond positively or negatively to a speaker for reasons that we can't really explain. We like someone, like the way they communicate, like their message. We often find it easier to hear the same message from one person than it is to hear it from another.

Facial Expressions and Nonverbal Communication

Most of us have read about, learned about, or studied nonverbal communication. The basics are well known. The way we carry ourselves, the way we move and gesture, often communicates louder than words ever could. Nonverbal communication can reveal whether we feel affection for, are interested in, want to control, or trust those with whom we communicate.

Strategies for effective nonverbal communication include such tactics as (a) facing people when you speak with them, (b) making eye contact, (c) avoiding distracting gestures, (d) nodding your head in an encouraging way, (e) finding an appropriate place for communication, (f) paying attention to how close we sit with others, (g) choosing an appropriate tone of voice for the message we want to communicate, and (h) touching or not touching others appropriately depending on the situation. These are important, if well-known, skills every IC should master. In particular, it is important to ensure that what we communicate nonverbally reinforces the messages we intend to communicate verbally.

The most important part of nonverbal communication is facial expression. Paul Ekman and his colleagues have studied people's emotional responses worldwide (in primitive and modern cultures). They conclude that facial expressions represent a universal language that can be interpreted in the same way we interpret other forms of language. Ekman's Facial Action Coding System, developed in 1978, "is now being used by hundreds of scientists around the world to measure facial movements" (2003, p. 14).

Ekman (2003) explains that facial expressions often communicate in "micro expressions," "very fast facial movements lasting less than one-fifth of a second" (p. 15). Ekman suggests that our "micro expressions" can trigger emotions in others, or others' "micro expressions" can trigger emotions in us. Simply put, the communication of emotion happens in a flash, and we must be very conscious to recognize what others' facial expressions communicate to us. As Ekman observed, "As an emotion begins, it takes us over in . . . milliseconds, directing what we do and say and think" (pp. 19–20).

According to Ekman "seven emotions each have a distinct, universal, facial expression: sadness, anger, surprise, fear, disgust, contempt, and happiness" (p. 58). In *Emotions Revealed* (2003), Ekman describes the facial expressions for each of these emotions in detail, including illustrations that, in some cases, are difficult to look at given how evocative they are. ICs would be wise to study Ekman's work to gain a deeper understanding of the subtle way in which facial expressions can communicate messages that support or undercut what is being spoken. By watching facial expressions carefully, ICs can learn a lot about their collaborating teachers and can improve their ability to communicate clearly.

Over the years, Lynn Barnes has learned a lot about reading body language. When she meets with teachers, she says, she "pays attention to the obvious things, eye contact, their body stance, whether they're nodding." Lynn also looks at her collaborating teachers' nonverbals to determine whether the teacher is ready and willing to learn. "We need to take consideration that maybe they have something else pressing, they might be agitated, they might need to call a parent, and maybe we should meet at another time. A lot goes into it." Lynn goes on to say, "it's just about being aware and acting upon it."

BUILDING AN EMOTIONAL CONNECTION

Facial expressions and nonverbal communication are an important part of another part of the subtle side of communication—emotional connections. To be effective, ICs, we have found, must become masters at building emotional connections with their teachers. When I interviewed teachers who had collaborated with Lynn Barnes, they were quick to heap praises on their IC. Although the teachers said they appreciated the valuable tools and teaching practices Lynn had to share, more frequently they noted that they liked working with Lynn because they flat out liked her as a person. Hannah Waldy, for example, told me, "I think you picked the right person to do this job because she is smart, intelligent, with-it, and also has a very kind heart." Jim Edmiston said, "Lynn's got a very outgoing personality. She's an awesome listener, and I think what helps us most is she has an uncanny knack to sense when something is not going the way we expected and offer some suggestions." Linda Lake told me that Lynn is "such a comfortable person to be around." Others commented on Lynn's warmth, kindness, attentiveness, compassion, sense of humor, and positive nature. Jim Edmiston summed up the opinions of all of the teachers: "You could get somebody else to do that job, but it's the person in that job that makes the difference, and Lynn's that person."

These comments, as complimentary as they are to Lynn, might trouble the rest of us. Does an IC have to be born with a super personality? Can ICs learn to connect with teachers the way Lynn does? Fortunately, research conducted by John Gottman suggests that we do not have to be born perfect to be an IC. Much of what Lynn accomplishes can be learned. Gottman, who has spent his professional life studying people in relationships, describes the specific practices that shape relationships as follows:

> We have discovered the elementary constituents of closeness between people, and we have learned the basic principle that regulates how relationships work and also determines a great deal about how conflict between people can be regulated. That basic idea has to do with the way people, in mundane moments in everyday life, make attempts at emotional communication, and how others around them respond, or fail to respond, to these attempts. (Gottman, 2001, Preface)

Gottman describes "the elementary constituent of closeness between people" as an emotional bid: "A bid can be a question, a gesture, a look, a touch—any single expression that says, 'I want to feel connected to you.' A response to a bid is just that—a positive or negative answer to somebody's request for emotional connection" (2001, p. 4). People extend bids for emotional connection to others all the time, he contends, and in healthy relationships, both members extend and respond positively to these bids. Emotional bids can be obvious gestures, such as inviting someone out to dinner, or incredibly subtle, such as a second of sustained eye contact. Bids can be verbal or nonverbal, funny or serious, physical or intellectual. Bids for emotional connection can be questions, statements, or comments about thoughts, feelings, observations, opinions, or invitations.

When someone makes an emotional bid, Gottman argues, we can respond in one of three ways: (a) turning toward, (b) turning away from, or (c) turning against.

When we turn toward someone who offers us an emotional bid, we respond positively toward that invitation. If someone shakes our hand, we might pat them on the back. If we are invited out to dinner, we say yes, or acknowledge the thoughtfulness of the invitation. If someone smiles, we smile back.

Though she might not refer to them as emotional bids, Lynn Barnes does many acts that enhance her emotional connection with teachers in her school. "I find out their interests, personal things at home. I try to connect with them on things that are near and dear to their heart." Lynn tries to make a personal connection with each teacher every day. "My daily goal is to try to find something to do to validate each person. Recognition is what babies cry for and grown men die for. We need it for the good things we do."

When we turn away from a bid, we fail to respond to the bid for emotional connection. For example, an overwhelmed administrator might be too preoccupied by the countless work-related demands on her time and turn away by failing to notice or acknowledge a colleague's complimentary comments. Gottman observes that turning away "is rarely malicious or mean-spirited. More often we're simply unaware of or insensitive to others' bids for our attention" (2001, p. 5).

The impact of turning away can be devastating. Gottman reports that "When somebody turns away from a bid, the bidder loses confidence and self-esteem. In our observational studies, we see how people almost seem to 'crumple' when their partners turn away. The bidders don't get puffed up with anger; they don't get indignant; they just seem to fold in on themselves. On video we can see their shoulders sag slightly as if they've been deflated. They feel defeated. They give up" (2001, p. 47). Lynn Barnes is very aware of teachers who turn away from her during the school year. "If I go home and there is a person who has turned away, not wanting to make that emotional connection, I try to figure out a way to do something positive for them. You have to give them personal recognition."

When people turn against bids, they react in argumentative or hostile ways. If someone makes a bid by offering to cook dinner, for example, a person turning against might respond by saying, "Are you kidding? I've tasted your cooking." For me, the perfect example of a couple that turns against is George Costanza's parents on *Seinfeld*. Each conversation between George's parents proceeds like a verbal boxing match in which both partners throw disdainful comments at each other. When we watch these conversations on TV, we laugh, but when we experience them in our own lives, they can be far from funny—the results can be profoundly destructive. Lynn Barnes admits that teachers who turn against her can be difficult to handle. "I'm really working hard on not taking things personally," she says, "but it can take its toll. I have to respect their decision. I read a quotation a while back and I thought, I had to memorize it: 'respect those you want to silence.' I'm working on that. You've just got to respect them and go on."

ICs can increase their effectiveness if they are fully aware of how bids for emotional connection function, almost like an invisible undercurrent in any relationship bringing people together or keeping them apart. An IC who carelessly adopts a sarcastic tone may inadvertently turn against his or her colleagues' bids for connection.

ICs also need to train themselves to be very sensitive to the ways in which teachers extend emotional bids for connection, which Gottman refers to as mindfulness. ICs should be attentive to collaborating teachers' thoughts, emotions, and concerns, so they can recognize emotional bids for connection and respond in ways that enrich their emotional connection with others. If they miss their colleagues' emotional bids, they will likely have a more difficult time making a difference in their teaching practices. As Gottman has observed, "if you don't pay attention, you don't connect" (2001, p. 66).

Gottman's research should also be a caution to ICs to be careful not to misinterpret a colleague's behavior. On occasion, a loud, aggressive, or hostile manner can be a teacher's way of reaching out. If an IC is too quick to assume she will never build an emotional connection with a colleague, she runs the risk of writing off someone who might benefit from becoming more connected with the coach. Time and again I have found that my first impressions of people can be disproven if I work to build some kind of respectful common ground with them. Gottman observes:

> If you can see past a person's anger, sadness, or fear to recognize the hidden need, you open up new possibilities for relation. You're able to see your coworker's sullen silence as a bid for inclusion in decisions that affect his job, for example. Or you can recognize that your sister's agitation says she's feeling alienated from the family. You can even see the bid in your three-year-old's temper tantrum: He not only wants the toy you can't buy for him, he wants your comfort in a frustrating situation, as well. (2001, p. 36)

HOW IT ALL FITS TOGETHER, SORT OF

The ideas, strategies, tactics, and concepts discussed in this chapter reinforce and overlap with each other frequently. For example, if we have carefully built an emotional connection with teachers, then we should find it easier to discuss topics that might come close to unearthing an identity conversation with teachers. If we become aware of our own "vicious stories" about others when they start to take root, we may find it much easier to build an emotional connection with people whom we might have otherwise have avoided.

If we are aware of our own body language and become more adept at reading others' body language, we can become better listeners. Our listening skills can help us construct our message in a way that our audience can understand, and by listening we can also build connections, get around our own and others' stories, and make connections with others that make a difference. What's more, if we learn to share positive comments with others, we stand the chance of improving the kind of conversations that take place in our schools. We then can start to transform our schools into settings where respectful, supportive interchange takes the place of stories about villainy, helplessness, and victimization.

Underlying all of this is the importance of the partnership orientation. When we authentically see our collaborating teachers as equal partners, when we engage in dialogue and encourage reflection, when we focus on praxis, when we respect teachers' choices, when we listen to and encourage teachers' choices, when we expect to learn from others as much as they can teach us, we remove many of the barriers that interfere with communication. People resist our supportive efforts when they feel they are being tricked, manipulated, or bullied. When we treat others as partners, more often than not, they open themselves up to us as collaborators, as partners, and frequently, as friends.

ICs who adopt a partnership approach and who become fluent in many of the partnership communication skills described here will find themselves in healthier, more rewarding relationships, both inside and outside their schools. This ultimately is the great reward of the partnership approach. If it is true that we live in a time of communication crisis, perhaps ICs have, so to speak, something to say about that. By nourishing meaningful conversations in their day-to-day work, ICs may move all of us closer to a world where more intimacy between people becomes a reality. Coaches can shorten the gap between people one conversation at a time.

GOING DEEPER

John Gottman's *The Relationship Cure* (2001) is an accessible summary of his research suggesting that emotional bids are at the heart of personal relationships. Gottman and Silver's *Seven Principles for Making Marriage Work* (1999) relates the insights gained from his research to the specifics of marital relationships. Malcolm Gladwell's *Blink* (2005) offers another perspective on Gottman's work, along with many insights regarding the interrelationship of perception and interpretation.

Stephen Covey's *The 7 Habits of Highly Effective People* (1989) remains the best, most useful handbook on listening, in particular the chapter "Seek First to Understand, Then Be Understood," in which Covey introduces the concept of empathic listening.

Patterson and colleagues' *Crucial Conversations* (2002), Stone and colleagues' *Difficult Conversations* (1999), and Scott's *Fierce Conversations* (2002) introduce several communication strategies that enhance our ability to get around interference and deal directly with the most important issues. Stone and colleagues provide an especially helpful description of different types of difficult conversations that can very quickly disrupt our efforts at communication.

Paul Ekman's *Emotions Revealed* (2003) offers a thorough, well-researched discussion of facial expressions, what they mean, what they reveal about us, and what they can tell us about those with whom we are communicating.

Tony Jeary, who has written *Life Is a Series of Presentations* (2004), is a kind of modern-day Dale Carnegie, offering many practical tips on how to successfully deliver the many presentations we give each day—whether they are to an audience of thousands or to our 3-year-old son. The original Dale Carnegie's *How to Win Friends and Influence People* (1936) may seem a little dated, but it remains, in my opinion, a tremendously valuable work for anyone working with people—and that is pretty much anyone.

TO SUM UP

- The communication process involves a speaker, with a message, who tries to penetrate interference to communicate with an audience, who receives a perceived message, and whose reactions to the message function as feedback for the speaker.
- Effective communicators start by trying to understand their audience, and they shape their messages so that it is easier for their audience to perceive them.
- An authentic desire to listen to others may be our most important communication skill.
- How well a person connects or fails to connect emotionally with others profoundly affects the quality of relationships that person experiences. John Gottman refers to the essential constituent of emotional connection as a bid; people turn toward, turn away from, or turn against bids.
- Our personal stories, and the stories held by those with whom we communicate, can block our ability to build emotional connections and to communicate effectively.
- If we take a partnership approach, we frequently find it much easier to communicate transparently with others.
- ICs make the world safer for more meaningful communication, one conversation at a time.

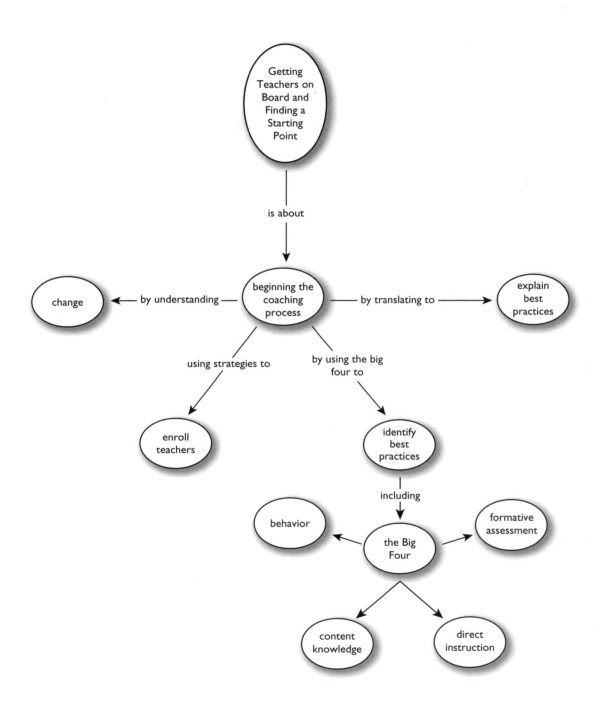

Chapter 5

Getting Teachers on Board and Finding a Starting Point

It will fail if we go in as experts. If we do not honor who teachers are as people, what they need. That's why I think instructional coaching is unique. We have to go in and listen, and tailor our conversations individually, and offer particular tools that we have expertise in. We have to value where they're coming from, what they're doing, what their goals and desires are as well.

—Sue Woodruff, a nationally
recognized leader of instructional coaches

CHAPTER OVERVIEW

There are several strategies ICs can employ to bring teachers on board and to identify the point of departure for coaching. This chapter introduces three components of coaching: (a) enroll, strategies for getting teachers on board; (b) identify, methods for finding the most appropriate teaching practices to share during instructional coaching; and (c) explain, tactics for insuring that teachers fully understand the materials we are sharing with them. The chapter also introduces the Big Four, a framework ICs can use to sort out the various scientifically proven teaching practices available to share with teachers.

GETTING TEACHERS ON BOARD

When instructional coaching was introduced at Kim Wilson's inner-city middle school, Kim, a language arts teacher, wasn't impressed. She stated bluntly that she did not want any of whatever her IC, Alison Shanahan, was offering. Kim refused to meet her coach, telling her straight-out, "I don't need anyone to help me teach my class, and I'd appreciate it if you'd refrain from wasting my time." When Alison tried to set up an interview with Kim to better understand Kim's concerns, Kim pointedly replied, "I'd prefer not to have anyone spying on me if you don't mind."

Kim was hostile, and suspicious, and, some might say, rude in her dealings with her coach. Lucky for Kim and her students, Kim's IC was an outstanding relationship builder. Alison respected Kim's request, didn't mention coaching for many months, in fact, and concentrated instead on building a trusting relationship with Kim. Alison was friendly, positive, supportive, and caring in all of her interactions with Kim, even though for a long time Kim did not respond in kind. Eventually, however, Alison and Kim began to have brief conversations in the staff lounge, the hallway, or before or after school. During these little interactions, Alison learned about Kim and showed a genuine interest and concern for her, asking questions about Kim's family and life outside of school. This wasn't a technique or trick. Alison truly was interested; she really did care.

Over time, Kim warmed to Alison. Alison began to ask Kim for advice on different aspects of teaching writing (Alison learned quickly that Kim had a lot of expertise to share), and during those conversations Kim eventually began telling Alison about the challenges she was facing. Alison came to understand that Kim was very proud of the writing scores her students achieved, and equally frustrated when she couldn't get through to her students. At first, when Kim expressed her frustrations, Alison simply listened empathetically. Then, when she thought it was appropriate, every so often she would mention some of the effective practices that she was introducing with other teachers and the results those teachers were achieving.

Through these informal conversations, Alison learned that Kim was especially frustrated by her students' struggles to organize their writing. Alison decided that Kim's pride in her students' skills and her frustration with her students' organizing challenges might be a way to open the door to a collaborative relationship with Kim. When Alison was sure she had Kim's trust, she asked her if she was willing to try a little experiment and let Alison teach the Framing Routine (Ellis, 1998) with a class of Kim's students. Since the Framing Routine employed a graphic organizer students could use to organize their ideas, Alison suggested that after the class, they look at the data and see whether or not the strategy helped the students organize their thoughts. "This will be quick and easy," Alison said. "I promise it won't hurt. If it works, we will have found another way to improve your kids' scores. If it doesn't work, we'll know what not to do." Keen to increase student achievement, trusting Alison, and aware that she was in the risk-free position of only having to watch, Kim said yes.

After Alison's lesson, a simple informal assessment showed that the strategy had helped students. Kim grew more interested and, after talking with Alison, decided that her students might benefit from learning an essay writing strategy, the Theme Writing Strategy (Schumaker, 2002b).

At first, perhaps because she was uncomfortable being observed, Kim didn't want to teach the strategy herself and asked Alison to do it. Alison would likely have refused Kim's suggestion if she felt that Kim was simply trying to get out of teaching. However, Alison had a hunch that if Kim watched her teach parts of the strategy a few times, she might get on board. Alison guided Kim to watch for and gather data on certain teaching practices she used during the model lessons, and sure enough, after watching a few lessons, Kim began to feel confident that she too could teach the strategy.

Alison then arranged to meet during Kim's planning time. Alison explained in direct, simple language exactly what to do to implement the strategy. She also shared an instructor's manual with Kim, and even highlighted some sections she considered especially important. When Kim first taught the strategy, Alison was there more as a support than an observer. Although she had some helpful tips after the first class, Alison mostly offered genuine, specific positive comments about Kim's performance. Kim lit up like a Christmas tree when Alison gave her specific, positive feedback on her teaching methods.

In all of her subsequent actions with Kim, Alison was careful to support Kim first, always offering suggestions in a way that was supportive, not critical. Alison gathered data on the critical teaching practices both she and Kim agreed should be observed (the same practices Kim had watched for when Alison provided her model lessons), and then, like partners, they reviewed the data together. Alison never judged or evaluated Kim; Alison simply collaborated like a friend, a support, a second pair of hands, to help Kim help her students be better writers.

Alison and Kim's hard work paid off. After learning the writing strategy, Kim's students' scores improved dramatically. Kim was hooked. She began to tell others about how effective the strategy had been, and teachers around the school realized that if Kim liked it, there must be something to it. Indeed, at the start of the next school year, Kim spoke out at a district language arts meeting in favor of the strategy. "I'm going to be doing this strategy in my class, no matter what, and I plan on trying some other new strategies this year. I actually think that's what we all should be doing," she said, "because this helps our kids." It took a long time, it took false starts, overcoming rejection, patience, and support, but Alison's efforts were rewarded. The students in her school and district truly were better learners thanks to Alison's efforts.

Alison and Kim are fictional names, but they are real people whom I have observed. Their story is one that I have witnessed time and again across the nation. Confronted with a resistant teacher, effective ICs react as relationship builders first, and then employ the tools of coaching to align themselves with teachers. Sue Woodruff, who coached Muskegon High to national recognition for school reform, found the partnership approach to be essential for successfully enrolling teachers at the start of the coaching process. Sue reports, "I made a lot of mistakes; I don't want you to think any of this was easy. I mean it was scary because you are kind of putting yourself on the line. But I knew it was the right thing, and people understood that my intention all along wasn't to push it on them. I wasn't trying to beat them over the head with a hammer and say you have to do this. I was essentially their guide through it, and they found they enjoyed it."

Sue Woodruff

Sue Woodruff is a nationally recognized leader of school improvement efforts based in Grand Rapids, Michigan. A leader of leaders for the Strategic Instruction Model and the Content Literacy Continuum, Sue spends her time identifying excellent ICs and mentoring them for their district. Sue was an IC at Muskegon High for 15 years. Muskegon High received national recognition when it won the Pete and Carrie Rozelle National Award from the National Center for Learning Disabilities for addressing the educational and social-emotional needs of all children, including those with learning disabilities.

In this chapter, we'll explore the techniques Sue has employed at Muskegon High and across the nation to win over collaborating teachers (the enroll, identify, and, explain components of instructional coaching). In Chapter 6, we'll look at the coaching components ICs can use to teach and support teachers' high-quality implementation of scientifically proven teaching practices (model, observe, explore, support, and reflect).

The partnership approach that Sue employed to promote professional learning is significantly different from more traditional one-shot approaches to professional development. Since employing instructional coaching techniques, Sue reports that she can't see herself going back to conducting traditional professional development. "It's not a pleasant experience for me anymore to go in if I haven't had personal interactions with the teachers. I don't even do it any more. It's just very difficult."

The traditional approach, in which teachers spend a day or a half day listening to an expert and then return to their classrooms, is based on the assumption that change happens in single events. Increasingly, researchers studying personal change (Hall & Hord, 2005; Prochaska, Norcross, & DiClemente, 1994) suggest that change, as Hall and Hord have said for some time, "is a process, not an event" (2005, p. 4). Indeed, one reason why traditional, one-shot professional staff development has such a poor success rate (Joyce & Showers, 2003) is that it appears to be based on an imperfect understanding of the complexity of change. For that reason, I'd like to review one well-researched change model before turning directly to our discussion of the specific components of instructional coaching.

STAGES OF CHANGE: PROCHASKA, NORCROSS, AND DiCLEMENTE

Prochaska, Norcross, and DiClemente are researchers who have conducted "more than fifty different studies on thousands of individuals to discover how people overcome problems of smoking and alcohol abuse, emotional distress, weight control" (1994, p. 14), and so forth. The researchers conclude that "successful self-changing individuals follow a powerful and, perhaps most important, controllable and predictable course. Along this course are various stages, each calling for particular and different approaches to change" (p. 15). The researchers identify six stages within the process of personal change, which are described below.

Prochaska et al.'s Stages of Change (1994)

Precontemplation
Contemplation
Preparation
Action
Maintenance
Termination

Precontemplation

People in the precontemplation phase of personal change ignore data that suggests they should change. Precontemplators, according to Prochaska and his colleagues, are often also "demoralized. They don't want to think, talk, or read about their problem because they feel the situation is hopeless" (1994, p. 41). "When their problem comes up in the conversation, they shift the subject; when newspaper articles reveal new information about it, they turn the page" (p. 41).

Contemplation

During the contemplation stage, people begin to consider why they might need to change; in particular, they begin to weigh the losses and gains of adopting a personal change. If they identify enough gains, people reach a personal tipping point and decide that they must change. However, Prochaska and his colleagues warn that "Many people remain stuck in the contemplation stage for a very long time . . . That is often the nature of contemplation: You know your destination, and even how to get there, but you are not quite ready to go yet" (1994, p. 42).

Preparation

Once people decide that they really want to change, they must make plans for whatever change they are planning. A person planning to develop a habit of exercising, for example, might locate a gym to attend and fill out a daily calendar, making a personal appointment that they will keep to work out every day. Prochaska and his colleagues note that "most people in the preparation stage are planning to take action within the very next month, and are making the final adjustments before they begin to change their behavior" (1994, p. 43).

Action

In the action phase, people initiate the change in behavior for which they have been preparing: smokers quit smoking, drinkers quit drinking, people planning to get in shape start exercising. During the action stage, people, as the Nike slogan says, "just do it."

Unfortunately, people frequently jump to the conclusion that action is all that matters in personal change. Every one of us has known someone who has proudly announced that he has given up smoking, fatty foods, or drinking for life, only to return to the old unhealthy habits in a matter of days or weeks. Prochaska and his colleagues remind us that "the action stage is not the only time you can make progress toward overcoming your problem. Although modifying your behavior is the most visible form of change, it is far from the only one; you can also change your level of awareness, your emotions, your self-image, your thinking, and so on. And many of those changes take place in the stages that precede action" (1994, pp. 44–45).

Maintenance

After action comes what may be the most important stage of change: maintenance. Maintenance is the stage when people live out their ongoing personal struggle to stop self-destructive behaviors, to adopt healthier habits, to improve. "During maintenance," Proschaska and his colleagues note, "you must work to consolidate the gains you attained during the action and other stages, and struggle to prevent lapses and relapse. Change never ends with action" (1994, p. 45).

Termination

When people achieve the termination stage of change, they are no longer struggling to make change happen. For example, a drinker who has reached the termination stage can sit in a bar with friends who are drinking and not be tempted to drink. Termination, as the word suggests, is the end of the change process, "your former addiction or problem will no longer present any temptation or threat; your behavior will never return, and you will have complete confidence that you can cope without fear of relapse. In the termination stage, all of this holds true without any continuing effort of your part. You will have exited the cycle of change and won your struggle" (1994, p. 46).

The Spiral Model of Change

People who successfully complete a personal change, the researchers suggest, move through all of the stages from precontemplation to termination, but they do not necessarily move through them in a linear, step-by-step sequence. They move back and forth, sometimes moving in and out of the same stage several times, or getting stuck at one stage for a considerable period of time. Thus, a person trying to make a change might be in the maintenance phase for a while, and then after some time slip back to the contemplation phase before returning to action and maintenance once again. In truth, people who are successful at personal change usually move back and forth between the various stages before they arrive at termination.

Successful change, according to Prochaska and his colleagues, moves forward in a pattern more like a spiral than a straight line. "Several . . . setbacks may make you feel as though you are going around in circles rather than solving your problem. And, to some extent, that is the case, but the good news is that the circles are spiraling upward. A successful self-change is like climbing the Leaning Tower of Pisa: First, you walk up, but as you approach the lower part of each floor, you begin to head down. A few steps later you resume your ascent" (1994, p. 48).

THE STAGES OF CHANGE AND PROFESSIONAL LEARNING IN SCHOOLS

Educational researchers have begun to explore how Prochaska's stages of change may apply to coaching and professional learning in schools (Reinke, 2005). Even a casual observer of organizational learning likely sees that the model is richly applicable to the way teachers might learn new ideas.

Teachers in the *precontemplative stage* might blame the students, the principal, the parents' lack of support, the large class size, and in fact, anything other than themselves for the problems in the classroom. At the start of our story above, Kim was clearly in the precontemplative stage.

Teachers who are precontemplative are not facing a life sentence, imprisoned by their inability to see evidence suggesting they should change. Like others who experience personal change, teachers can move to the *contemplative stage*. At this point, they start to think about and consider the causes, resources, and possible methods they could use to improve their classroom management skills, for example, rather than affix blame for behavior somewhere outside themselves. "I have got to do something to get these kids under control, but I just don't know what to do" is the kind of phrase that might be spoken by someone at this stage.

In our story, Alison masterfully leads Kim out of precontemplation (in which Kim had isolated herself from opportunities for learning and growth) and into contemplation (where she opened herself up to learning). Alison helped Kim move from one stage to the next by asking her questions about her goals, about the challenges she faced trying to achieve those goals, and by proposing, in a nonthreatening way, several practices that might help Kim get around those challenges, specifically helping her students improve their ability to be organized.

Teachers in the *preparation stage* take time to plan what they have to do to implement the change they are planning to implement. ICs can greatly help. ICs can assist with curriculum mapping or co-construct teaching plans. ICs can make sure teachers are ready, willing, and able to implement. In our story, Alison helped Kim into the preparation phase on several occasions. She prepared Kim for the first model lessons of the Framing Routine, she prepared Kim for the model lessons of the Theme Writing Strategy, and she prepared Kim to do her own teaching of the Theme Writing Strategy.

Teachers in the *action stage* are trying out some new teaching practice. Alison did everything she could to make it easier for Kim to teach the Theme Writing Strategy. She showed her what it would look like in her classroom. She shared an instructional manual. She highlighted and clearly explained important information. She even prepared materials so that Kim did not have to worry about anything except teaching. "The IC's job," as IC Tricia McKale has commented, "is to remove every barrier to implementation that a teacher might face."

Of course, the IC's job does not end with action. Too frequently, ICs make the false assumption that once a teacher is implementing a new teaching practice, the work is done. Nothing could be further from the truth. My experience observing ICs in many settings has shown that if an IC overlooks the *maintenance* aspects of supporting a teacher, there is a good chance that the teacher will eventually put her teacher's manual back on the shelf and forget about what she learned with the coach. To enable meaningful improvements that stick, ICs must provide support long after the action phase. In our story, Alison dropped in on Kim frequently to observe, collaborate, and generally provide support to Kim as she worked through the Theme Writing Strategy.

A teacher in the *termination stage* has totally integrated a new teaching practice into the way she teaches—she no longer needs support from an IC on the practice she's mastered. Frequently, teachers, like others experiencing change, stay in the maintenance phase for a long time, and they benefit from ongoing support from their IC. However, ICs have a limited amount of time, so they must be careful not to tie themselves up too much by maintaining only teachers. An IC should provide as much support as necessary, but no more. What the right amount of support is must be determined on a case-by-case basis by the IC.

Kim in our introductory story may still need more support before she reaches the termination phase of change—but she is well on her way. She has learned a new way of teaching that helps her students, and she is committed to making that new way of teaching a part of how she reaches her students. Since Kim had a coach who understood how complex it is to support someone making a personal change, Kim learned, implemented, and kept implementing something that improved the quality of learning experienced by her students.

Sourpuss

I love watching people change over time. The ones who don't accept ideas right away are the most interesting to watch. I like to see if I have any effect at all, and then to figure out why or why not. I think of this guy who, when we first met, we called Sourpuss.

Sourpuss was really obnoxious, and initially he totally rejected our teaching practices. He was really, really negative and wasn't afraid to share his negativity. I'm telling you, the man was a piece of work. He was negative; he was all grumpy. I don't know . . . I honestly didn't think he would ever come around.

But the man is coming around. I think it's because of the partnership principles. We haven't forced him to do anything; we've listened. He's been able to have his voice, which he's shared on many occasions. I think he's really benefiting from the collaboration and being a part of this initiative. And I know he's benefiting personally. The man's smiling now.

It's almost like watching a kid who is learning to read when you see somebody change from being really difficult, really confrontational, to really becoming a part of the group. He is changing as a professional, to the point where he's actually very pleasant and . . . he's different. I'm sure it's wearing off on his colleagues and his students, too. So watching that impact, or watching the change, is gratifying because he's becoming a better person.

THE COMPONENTS OF COACHING: ENROLL, IDENTIFY, AND EXPLAIN

In working through the stages of change with Kim, Alison employed the components of coaching we have identified at the Kansas University Center for Research on Learning. Instructional coaching, as we define it, has very clear components that enable an IC to respond to the challenges of change. The first three components of this process (enroll, identify, and explain) are described in this chapter. The additional five components of the instructional coaching process (model, observe, explore, support, and reflect) are introduced in Chapter 6.

Enrollment: Getting Teachers on Board

One of the first questions many novice ICs ask is, "How do I get people to work with me?" As we have seen, teachers can be suspicious of change initiatives or school reform plans. This is especially the case in schools or districts where programs have come and gone in rapid succession. If teachers watch a number of imperfectly implemented programs embraced and abandoned in rapid succession, they are understandably suspicious when new ICs arrive. As systems thinkers have shown for decades (Senge, 1990), every time a district or school adopts a quick-fix solution, the chances of a real-fix solution taking hold go down.

So how does an IC get people on board? We propose five methods: (a) one-to-one interviews, (b) small-group presentations, (c) large-group presentations, (d) informal conversations, and (e) administrator referral. Each of these approaches will be described below, but because one-to-one interviews have proven to be especially powerful, more time will be spent describing that process.

One-to-One Interviews

Sue Woodruff has come to see interviews as a very effective way to enroll teachers. Interviews help her build rapport with teachers and learn invaluable knowledge about those with whom she's working. "Interviews," Sue says, "provide teachers a chance to see you not as a professional developer, some expert coming in, but as someone like them. It's that principle of equality, that you're together, its one-to-one, it's not I'm better than you, or I'm going to come tell you something. It's we're going to have a conversation."

Why should you consider using interviews? One-to-one interviews help ICs achieve at least three goals. First, they are a way to gather specific information about teacher and administrative challenges, student needs, and cultural norms specific to a school. Coaches can use this information to tailor coaching sessions and other professional learning to the unique needs of teachers and administrators.

Sue Woodruff reports that the information gathered from interviews "helps to open my eyes to reality. If you don't have a handle on the issues that are going on—what makes life difficult in that school, or what teachers find really rewarding, you might make some big mistakes when working with a school. What I learn during interviews really helps to put into focus where I need to begin my professional development."

Sue learns a lot about the politics and dynamics of the school from interviews as well. "It helps to have a conversation about the school. I get to see the alliances; who are the leaders, and who are the vocal people. Very quickly I get to see who are the naysayers as well."

Interviews also enable ICs to educate participants about the philosophy, methods, and opportunities offered by instructional coaching. As we've noted before, professional learning in schools is tricky. Effective coaches have to motivate teachers to move forward and change, while at the same time communicating that they authentically respect, value, and believe in their collaborating teacher. If a teacher feels his or her identity is being threatened by coaching, the teacher will not engage in the coaching experience. For that reason, an IC who does not deeply respect the profession of teaching usually struggles to get teachers on board.

During interviews, ICs can explain their partnership approach to coaching, listen to teachers' concerns, and explain that as coaches they are there to help, not to evaluate. IC LaVonne Holmgren, who has also used interviews to enroll teachers, has found that "a lot of the interview is just answering questions and explaining what is going to happen—and that is essential." Sue Woodruff says that the interview also allows her to communicate that "I have had experiences in schools with real kids and real teachers." Sue explains, "I want them to see that I've been in the trenches like they are. I want them to see that the real reason I do this is because I believe in it. I have a passion for it. I'm not doing it as a job."

Interviews also provide an opportunity to develop one-to-one relationships with teachers. Sue explains that "in most cases no one has ever come in and asked these questions. It's validating them as a person because you want to hear what they have to say. You communicate that what they've got to tell you is interesting and important. It's all about empathic listening." According to LaVonne Holmgren, "after the interviews, people feel like you genuinely care about them—that's the beginning of the relationship."

How should one-to-one interviews be conducted? Interviews are effective when they last at least 30 minutes and more effective when they are 45 minutes to one hour long (generally, one planning period per interview). While a longer interview allows more time to learn about each person's particular burning issues and provides more time to build a relationship, a great deal of information can be gathered from 15-minute interviews.

Whenever possible, interviews should be conducted one-to-one. The experience of ICs around the country has shown that a 10-minute one-to-one interview is a more effective way to build relationships than a two-hour focus group session with a school team. This is partly because in a group people tend to comment in ways that are consistent with the cultural norms of their group (Schein, 1992). People talking one-to-one speak much more candidly. Since effective instructional coaching may involve overcoming negative or even toxic cultural norms, creating a setting where teachers can step outside their culture and speak frankly is important.

Scheduling Interviews

One of the easiest ways to schedule interviews is to conduct them during teachers' planning time. Usually, an administrative assistant in the school or a department chair can set up a schedule. Sometimes the IC is responsible for setting up the interviews. Whoever draws up the schedule must ensure that the people who will be interviewed know when and where their interview will be and that the purpose of the interview is simply for the IC to learn more about their unique teaching situation so that the IC can provide coaching that is most effective for each teacher and student in the school.

Many ICs schedule interviews informally over the first few weeks of the school year. They may send out a memo or newsletter informing teachers of their goal to meet just to learn from everyone. Then, ICs can meet each teacher in the hallway, staff lounge, or classroom and schedule meetings. An important first step for coaches is to get a copy of the school's staffing schedule, so that they will know when teachers might be free for a brief conversation and eventually for an interview.

During the Interviews

During the interview, ICs should take detailed notes and record teachers' actual words and phrases as much as possible. Tape-recording interviews is a good idea because it allows you to revisit what was said. Some professional developers play their tapes in their car tape deck to stay in touch with the issues the teachers are facing, including the tone and feelings expressed by the teachers. Most teachers accept the tape recorder as a necessary tool so long as the IC is clear that the interview is confidential. If you think your teachers will object to you using a tape recorder, forgo its use.

In most cases, your goals during an interview will be the same regardless of the amount of time available. We have found that it is most valuable to seek answers to at least five general questions:

1. What are the rewards you experience as a teacher?

2. What are your professional goals?

3. What obstacles interfere with you achieving your professional goals?

4. What are your students' strengths and weaknesses?

5. What kinds of professional learning are most/least effective for you?

When you have more time to conduct interviews, you can broaden or focus the scope of your questions depending on the nature of the professional development session you are planning to lead. A fairly extensive list of interview questions from which you might draw in structuring your interview is included below.

Interview Questions You Might Consider Using

Questions About Teachers' Current Realities

- Describe a typical day on the job.
- What do you really like about your job?
- What kinds of pressures are you facing?
- What challenges are you facing?
- What kinds of changes are you experiencing?

Questions About Students' Current Realities

- Tell me about your students.
- What are the major needs of your students?
- What would most help your students?
- What outcomes are you striving for with your students?
- How many students are you teaching each day?
- Please estimate the number of students with various disabilities that you teach.
- What could have a significant influence on the happiness and success of your students?

Questions About the School's Current Reality

- How would you describe the relationship between special education teachers and general education teachers in your school?
- How would you describe the relationship between senior high school teachers and junior high school teachers in this district?

Questions About Changes Being Experienced

- How has your job changed over the past five years?
- How has your philosophy changed over the past five years?

Questions About Instructional Practices

- Are you teaching (name of intervention) at this point?
- If yes, which (intervention) are you teaching?
- What modifications, if any, have you made in your teaching of (intervention)?

Questions About a Desired Future

- What changes in your school do you think could have the greatest influence on your students' success?

- Describe the ideal school.
- What would you like to change about your job?

  Questions About Professional Development

- Talk about the kinds of professional development you've attended in the past few years.
- What have you liked about professional development?
- What have you not liked about professional development?
- How can the coming session be structured to best meet your needs?
- How do you learn best?

HOW TO BUILD RELATIONSHIPS DURING INTERVIEWS

Using interviews as a way to build an emotional connection with collaborating teachers can make it easier for you to communicate your message. As IC Shelly Kampschroeder observes, "There's a certain amount of natural defensiveness on the part of any audience. We can get around much of that defensiveness when we show that we care enough to listen to their concerns."

By positioning themselves as listeners during the interviews, ICs have a chance to make many bids for emotional connection with participants (Gottman, 2001). ICs can share stories, laugh and empathize, offer positive comments, discuss personal issues, and listen with great care during an interview. Sue Woodruff notes that being a good listener is an essential part of what she does during interviews. "To move someone out of the precontemplative stage, to thinking about it, to actually doing something, you really have to learn to listen." If done well, preworkshop interviews provide ICs with many opportunities to listen with empathy, offer encouragement, and reveal themselves as real, caring people.

Asking Teachers to Commit: Contracting

As important as the interview process is for providing you with information about teachers, students, and your school, the most important outcome of the interview process is to obtain commitment from teachers to the coaching process. Many coaches in business and education refer to this as contracting. ICs must find time during the interview to tactfully explain how instructional coaching works and what benefits it might offer for the teacher being interviewed. This is tricky. If teachers feel manipulated during the interview, they may reject the offer of assistance.

When explaining what they do or have to offer, ICs must avoid acting like high-pressure salespersons. Sue says, "If we go in trying to tell them what to do, it's not going to work; it's going to fail." Rather, an IC should search for appropriate times in the middle of the interview to explain aspects of instructional coaching in response to comments of the teacher being interviewed. The goal is to ensure that the teacher knows enough about coaching so that she can make an intelligent choice about whether or not she will work with the coach. For that reason, ICs should see the interview as their first chance to demonstrate the respectful, partnering relationship that is at the heart of instructional coaching. At the end of the one-to-one interview, ICs should know whether or not a teacher is ready to collaborate with them and, In most cases, the interview is an IC's best strategy for enrolling teachers.

Small-Group Meetings

In some cases, one-to-one interviews are not practical or necessary. For example, if an IC is certain that a group of teachers are interested in collaborating, the need for interviews isn't as great. Also, in a few cases, there may not be time for interviews—though in most settings it should not be too difficult to organize them. Nonetheless, an alternative to one-to-one interviews is small-group meetings. Usually an IC meets with the teachers during a team meeting, a grade-level meeting, or whatever small-group meeting is available.

During the meeting, an IC's goals are quite simple: (a) to explain the opportunities that exist for teachers' professional growth, (b) to clarify the partnership perspective that underlies the coaching relationship, (c) to explain other "nuts and bolts" issues related to instructional coaching, and, most important, (d) to sign up teachers who want to work with their coach.

The presentation during small-group meetings should be short, clear, and respectful. In many cases, this initial conversation is the IC's first opportunity to communicate an authentic respect and admiration for the important activity of teaching. If ICs honestly communicate their genuine respect for teachers, that may go a long way toward opening doors. On the other hand, if ICs appear to communicate a lack of respect for teachers, that may put them into a hole that will be very difficult to climb out of. Word of mouth in a school travels very quickly if an IC has useful tools and if the IC demonstrates an authentic respect for teachers. Word of mouth will travel even quicker if an IC does not appear to appreciate the challenges, rewards, and complex professional work of educators.

We suggest that ICs plan for about 20 minutes during small-group meetings. Following the informal presentation, ICs should answer any questions teachers raise. ICs can also provide a one-page summary of the teaching practices teachers can learn as a result of instructional coaching to help with classroom management, curriculum planning, teaching to mastery, or formative assessment.

At the close of the small-group presentation, after teachers have heard about the IC's partnership philosophy, the way the IC works, the teaching practices that the IC can share, ICs should hand out a short form (see example below) asking teachers to note whether or not they are interested in collaborating with their IC at this time. The form provides an opportunity for teachers to communicate their interest privately. Our experience has been that teachers are much more willing to commit to a coaching relationship if they are not asked to do it publicly. A simple form, asking people to let you know if they're interested, is an easy way to enroll teachers.

Large-Group Presentation

In some cases, ICs enroll teachers through a single large-group presentation to the entire staff. Such a presentation is usually held at the start of

Figure 5.1 Are You Interested?

Instructional Coaching
Progress through Partnership

ARE YOU INTERESTED?

NAME: ____________________

DATE: ____________________

I am most interested in:

____
____
____
____
____
____
____
____

☐ Times good for me:

____
____

☐ Maybe some other time

the school year, ideally before classes begin, or at the end of the year, to enroll teachers for the following year. A large-group presentation is a good idea when an IC wants to ensure that all teachers hear the same message. Large-group presentations are also effective when an IC is confident that teachers are interested in collaborating with an IC. As a general rule, the greater the resistance an IC expects to experience with teachers, the smaller the group should be, and when there is any concern that teachers will resist collaborating with ICs, one-to-one interviews are recommended.

When conducting a large-group presentation, ICs should do what they would do in a small-group presentation. ICs should explain the partnership philosophy, the details of how they will collaborate with teachers, and the specific interventions that teachers can learn. Just as they do during the small-group presentations, ICs should have a one-page handout, as well as a feedback form teachers can complete to indicate their interest in collaborating with an IC. Coaches should resist the temptation to hand out too many pages. Simplicity guru Bill Jensen has what he describes as the "Grand Poobah Guarantee." "There is a running joke about CEOs: 'If it has a staple in it, it doesn't get read'" (2000, p. 77). ICs will find that teachers are much like CEOs. If coaches want their handout to be read, they need to do the hard thinking that allows them to synthesize their knowledge into a one-page summary document.

ICs can enhance large-group presentations by employing Partnership Learning Structures (Knight, 2000), learning activities that foster dialogue in the middle of the presentation. For example, ICs might ask teachers to work in groups to identify the top needs of students and then match possible interventions to the identified needs. ICs can also enhance presentations by asking one or several teachers to give testimonials about the effectiveness of teaching practices they learned from their IC. Even though an IC is truly a teacher among teachers, sometimes hearing another classroom teacher discuss the benefits of coaching is especially persuasive.

As with small-group presentations, large-group presentations are important since they set the stage for the future and ICs can set a positive tone for the entire year with a well-organized session. For that reason, the IC should be careful to prepare anyone else who might speak about coaching during the presentation. For example, a well-intentioned principal who wants to support the IC but tells the staff they absolutely must work with the coach may, in fact, do more damage than good.

At the end of the session, the IC asks participants to complete a form to indicate whether they are interested in collaborating with them. The form might be the same as the one proposed for the small-group session, or the IC might have participants complete a form throughout the presentation. When they employ this presentation tactic, ICs provide a brief explanation of a few teaching practices or interventions, and then they pause to provide time for the audience to write down their thoughts or comments about the practices or interventions that are described. In this way, the teachers have an opportunity to express their thoughts about what they are hearing, and ICs get a lot of helpful feedback. What is essential is that at the end of the session, each person has a chance to write down whether or not they are ready to work with the coach, and the IC will have a list of people with whom to start coaching.

One-to-One Informal Meetings

Frequently, ICs enroll teachers through casual conversations around the school. ICs who are skilled at getting teachers to commit to collaboration usually are highly skilled relationship builders. As we will see in Chapter 8, an IC shouldn't feel compelled to get every teacher on board immediately. A better tactic is to win over a few teachers with high-quality professional learning on an intervention that really makes a difference for students. In most cases, the IC should seek out a highly effective solution for a troubling problem a teacher is facing. If you respond to a real challenge a teacher is facing with a real solution, word will travel through the school, and teachers will commit to working with their coach.

Principal Referral

When an IC and a principal work together in a school, inevitably there will be occasions when the principal or other administrators identify teachers who need to work with the IC. Principal referral can be a powerful way to accelerate the impact of coaching in a school, but it must be handled with care. If the partnership principles are ignored and struggling teachers are told they must work with a coach (or else!), the IC can be seen as a punishment, not a support, and teachers may come to resent the coach's help.

We suggest a different approach for principal referral, one consistent with the partnership principles. Rather than telling teachers they must work with coaches, we suggest principals focus on the teaching practice that must change, and offer the coach as one way the teacher can bring about the needed change. Thus, a principal might say, "John, when I observed your class I noticed that 10 of your 24 students were off task during your lesson. You need to implement ways to keep those kids on task. Our instructional coach Tamika is great at time on task. You might want to talk with her about this, but if you can find another way, that's fine, too. What matters is that more kids are learning. I'll check back in a few weeks, and I expect to see a difference."

In this way, the principal can apply pressure on the teacher while at the same time leaving the IC as one option. Thus, the coach isn't a punishment forced on the teacher, but a lifeline, someone who provides a meaningful support for teachers doing this important and complex work in the classroom. When led to the coach in this way, many teachers are grateful for their coach's support and assistance. If other teachers are able to address the problem in the class in other ways, that is fine too, and it provides ICs with more time to work with teachers who want to work with their coach.

Whether ICs enroll teachers through one-to-one informal conversations, one-to-one interviews, small-group conversations, large-group presentations, or principal referral, what remains most important is that they communicate their genuine respect for the task of teaching. Sue Woodruff explains, "I want them to see that I realize how difficult teaching is now, that the profession has changed. I want them to see that I respect them as professionals."

Identify

After enrolling teachers (through interviews, in one-to-one meetings, in small groups, in large groups, or through teacher referral), the IC will have a list of potential collaborating teachers. It is important that ICs reply promptly to every teacher expressing an interest in working with them. If the coach waits too long, the teachers may run out of time to collaborate, become focused on other priorities, or lose their desire to collaborate with the coach.

ICs shouldn't worry too much if their starting list of potential collaborating teachers is short. The list could include most of the school's teachers, but frequently it consists of less than 25% of the staff. The length of the list is not that important initially. What really matters is that the coach is on his or her game from the start. The experiences of the first few teachers the IC collaborates with are very important because they will start the word-of-mouth process that should eventually lead to widespread implementation of the teaching practices provided by the coach.

The First Meeting

A lot can be accomplished during the first conversation after a teacher has enrolled in the coaching process. Both parties share the goal of identifying which of the teaching practices the coach has to offer might be most helpful to the teacher. On many occasions, the first conversation is all that is needed for the teacher and coach to identify the teaching practices to be implemented in the teacher's classroom. For example, a teacher might come to a coach because she has heard through word of mouth about a teaching practice someone else learned from the coach, and she may want to use it with her students. On other occasions, if a teacher has a specific concern, say that he wants to increase student time on task, and the IC has something powerful to help with that concern, then the two learning partners can be off to the races.

Sue Woodruff explains how this conversation might proceed: "I start off with questions. I have some typical questions that I ask, but I only use those as a guide. I try to listen and let the teachers talk. As they begin to answer questions, some other questions might come to mind, so we have a conversation. If I start to hear something in what the teacher is saying, I might ask leading questions to lead us down a path [to a starting point]."

The first conversation, what some call a *preconference*, does not always provide enough data to identify where the coach and teacher start. In some cases, the collaborating teacher might not know where to start. Many ICs prefer to observe teachers before identifying a teaching practice (Chapter 6 includes a detailed explanation of the observation component of coaching). What counts, whether as a result of observation or conversation, is that the IC and teacher together identify a particular best practice that has the greatest chance of making a difference for students and naturally teachers' lives.

The Big Four

How do a coach and teacher determine where to start? ICs working with the Kansas University Center for Research on Learning focus their thinking when identifying teacher practices by considering four specific questions, "The Big Four," to determine the point of departure for the coaching partnership. While coaches may not ask these questions out loud, they keep them in mind as they consider where to start. In Chapter 7, we'll explore several effective practices ICs can share with teachers once they have identified which aspect of the Big Four they intend to address in a teacher's classroom.

The Big Four

Behavior: Is classroom management under control?

Content: Does the teacher understand the content, have a plan, and understand which information is most important?

Instruction: Is the teacher using teaching practices that ensure all students master content?

Formative assessment: Do the teacher and students know if students are mastering content?

Behavior: Is classroom management under control? If a teacher's students are on task and learning, an IC and collaborating teachers can turn to a variety of other issues related to student learning. However, if student behavior is out of control, in our experience, the coach and collaborating teacher will struggle to make other practices work that do not address behavior. As Sue Woodruff explains, "If teachers are struggling with behavior, they're struggling with everything." For this reason, many ICs begin with classroom management with teachers.

The emotional consequences for teachers when a classroom is out of control are immense. Many budding careers have ended prematurely because a novice teacher was unable to master the fine art of classroom management. If a coach helps a teacher get control of her or his classroom, a coach can make a powerful contribution.

There are several subquestions that might help identify whether or not behavior is an issue of the first concern:

- Are students on task in class?
- Does the teacher make significantly more positive comments than negative comments (at least a three-to-one ratio)?
- Has the teacher developed clear expectations for all activities and transitions during the class?
- Has the teacher clearly communicated those expectations, and do the students understand them?
- Do students have frequent opportunities to respond during the class?

More difficult to identify, but more important to ask, perhaps, are:

- Does the teacher care about the students' welfare?
- Does the teacher respect students?
- Does the teacher communicate high expectations?
- Does the teacher believe his or her students can achieve those expectations?

Content: Does the teacher understand the content, have a plan, and understand which information is most important? If a teacher's class is well managed, a second question is whether the teacher has a deep knowledge of the content. Teachers need to know which content is most important, and they also need to know how to explain that content clearly. Sue Woodruff adds, "Today, teachers need to know and teach a lot of content in order to be in alignment with standards. This means they have to be diligent and efficient in figuring out how they're going to teach all of this content to all of these kids."

There are many subquestions that might help a teacher determine whether or not a teacher has mastery of his or her content. They include the following:

- Does the teacher have a complete, detailed plan for teaching the course?
- Has the teacher developed essential questions for all units?
- Do those questions align with the state standards?
- Can the teacher identify the 10 to 15 core questions that are answered by the course?
- Can the teacher identify the top 10 concepts in the course?
- Can the teacher clearly and simply explain the meaning of each of the top 10 concepts?

Instruction: Is the teacher using teaching practices that ensure all students master content? If teachers hold a deep understanding of their content, and if they can manage their classroom, the next big question is whether they can teach their knowledge to their students. Effective instruction involves numerous teaching practices, the need for which may surface with the following questions:

- Does the teacher properly prepare students at the start of the class?
- Does the teacher effectively model thinking and other processes for students?
- Does the teacher ask questions at an appropriate variety of levels?
- Does the teacher use cooperative learning and other activities to keep students engaged?
- Does the teacher provide constructive feedback that enables students to improve?
- Does the teacher use language, analogies, examples, and stories that make it easier for students to learn and remember content?
- Does the teacher effectively sum up lessons at the end of the class?

Formative assessment: Do the teacher and students know if students are mastering content? If a teacher's students are on task, and if the teacher has a deep knowledge of the content, knows what's most important, and can communicate that knowledge using effective instructional practices, the final question is whether the teacher and student know how well the students are learning. Several questions will help ICs explore a teacher's understanding of formative assessment.

- Does the teacher know the target the students are aiming for in the class?
- Do the students know the target they are aiming for in the class?
- Does the teacher use formative assessment effectively to gauge how well students are learning?
- Are students involved in the development and use of formative assessments?
- Can a teacher look out into the classroom and know with some degree of accuracy how well each student is doing?

Sue Woodruff reports that the Big Four has proven to be a valuable tool for assessing where to begin with teachers. "Before I learned about the Big Four, it was all jumbled up. I might have known a teacher was struggling, but I wouldn't have known where to begin. Now I can pinpoint the best place to start." Sue also likes the way that the Big Four is organized in a quasi-hierarchical manner. "I like how it is a continuum. It helps my teacher and me to focus on what to do, where to improve. If the teacher is good on behavior, knows their content, we just move up the hierarchy. Even an excellent teacher can improve."

Explain

Once the IC and teacher have identified a proven practice to be implemented, the IC has to explain the teaching practice. This is not as easy as it seems. Many teachers' instructional manuals are more than 100 pages long, filled with fairly abstract language and concepts. On occasion, the scientifically proven interventions are described in ways that show a conspicuous lack of knowledge or naivety about what happens in the classroom. Add to this the reality that the amount of time a coach and teacher might spend together can be quite short, and no doubt, their meeting will occur in a context of competing priorities. Clearly, the coach has her work cut out for her.

In many cases, the instructional manuals and research articles an IC is intent on explaining do not come in teacher-friendly formats. As Sue Woodruff observes, "There is the researcher and there is the reality, and the research is often done in control groups without the constraints of the everyday classroom." Consequently, the IC must translate research into practice.

Five tactics enhance ICs' ability to translate research into practice:

Five Tactics for Translating Research Into Practice

1. Clarify: read, write, talk
2. Synthesize
3. Break it down
4. See it through teachers' (and students') eyes
5. Simplify

Clarify

First learn the meaning of what you say, and only then speak.

—Epictetus, Greek Stoic philosopher in Rome
(cited in Jensen, 2000, p. 46)

One of the most important and most frequently overlooked practices that ICs can employ is the simple task of reading, writing, and synthesizing what they plan to tell teachers. If an IC does not have a deep knowledge of the interventions he or she shares, the chances of having a positive impact on children are severely diminished.

Read. ICs need to read, reread, take notes, and reread the manuals and research articles that describe the instructional practices that they are sharing. A simple overview of a manual is not sufficient. Coaches need to mark up their books, highlight key passages, write in the margins, and cover their manuals with sticky notes. They should have read these materials so frequently that they know the page numbers for key sections and recognize most pages in a manual the way one recognizes and old friend. If ICs have not read their articles or instructional manuals with care, they have not done their job.

Write. In the middle of and after reading, ICs should write out their understanding of the materials they have read. This activity might take the form of writing outlines of documents, creating semantic maps or webs, or paraphrasing what has been read into simple language. Dennis Sparks (2005) offers the following:

> Writing is a way of freezing our thinking, of slowing down the thoughts that pass through our consciousness at lightning speed, so we can examine our views and alter them if appropriate. Writing enables us to note inconsistencies, logical flaws, and areas that would benefit from additional clarity. I recommend writing progressively shorter and shorter drafts to crystallize and succinctly express key intentions and beliefs so they can be powerfully stated in a sentence or two. (p. 38)

Talk. Once they have read, written about, and synthesized the materials they've been studying, ICs should seek out opportunities to explain, clarify, modify, and expand their understandings by communicating with others who are knowledgeable about the same interventions. Some ICs use the Internet or have telephone conversations with other ICs who are sharing the same practices. Others even contact the authors of the research articles and manuals to ask for their insights. In the best-case scenario, ICs set up informal or formal professional learning communities so they can meet with other ICs to discuss and deepen their knowledge of teaching practices. The ICs on the Pathways to Success project in Topeka, Kansas, for example, meet once a week (they call their meeting the ICPLC [pronounced "ick plick"], which stands for Instructional Coaches Professional Learning Community) to share ideas, review research reports and other documents, and to learn from each other.

Synthesize

After clarifying the meaning of research articles and manuals, ICs need to synthesize what they have learned and describe the essential features of the teaching practices they've studied. For some, this is accomplished by writing one- to two-sentence statements that capture the essence of the interventions they are sharing with teachers. What matters is that coaches are able to identify and summarize what is most important about the teaching practices they are sharing.

ICs can develop short checklists (see Instructional Coach's Tool Kit at the end of this book) that summarize the critical teaching behaviors that are essential components of the teaching practices they're sharing. Checklists can provide focus to conversations with teachers and shape the modeling and observing practices used to enable teachers to be successful in teaching new practices. As we'll see in Chapter 6, checklists created by coaches are a starting point for much that happens when teachers are learning new practices.

Break It Down

In many cases, the materials ICs share with teachers are complicated, elaborate, or very detailed. As translators, ICs break down teaching practices into manageable components related to the specific teaching practices to be implemented. For example, the Paragraph Writing Strategy (Schumaker, 2002a) is a highly effective method for teaching students how to master many writing strategies embedded in paragraph writing. The manual is a tremendously valuable resource, scripting every part of an eight-stage instructional model and including resources for teaching paragraph writing, but it clocks in at more than 300 pages. No doubt, some teachers will find the materials overwhelming unless a coach breaks down the manual into the various parts that need to be taught day by day and week by week.

There is much a coach can do to make teacher manuals more accessible. Some literally tear apart manuals and divide them into easy-to-understand sections that they put into binders. ICs can also highlight important passages or put sticky notes beside especially important sections of a manual. When breaking down materials, ICs need to ensure that teachers know exactly what needs to be done next. As personal productivity guru David Allen (2001) has observed, "It never fails to greatly improve both the productivity and the peace of mind of the user to determine what the next physical action is that will move something forward" (p. 237).

See It Through Teachers' (and Students') Eyes

ICs who wish to make it easier for teachers to learn new teaching practices must plan their explanations by thinking carefully about what the new practice will look like in the classroom. In this way, ICs can address the practical concerns that teachers might have. For example, they might think through a number of classroom management issues, such as explaining how to manage handing out papers, movement in the classroom, or organizing grading assignments. ICs might also discuss how to incorporate formative assessments into a lesson, or explain what expectations should be taught when a certain teaching practice is introduced. Throughout the explanation, the IC should be intent on removing teachers' anxiety and making it easier for them to understand and eventually use a new teaching practice. By considering exactly what an intervention will look like in the classroom, ICs can increase the likelihood that teachers will implement new teaching practices effectively.

Sue Woodruff believes that it is very important to see the material she shares from the perspective of her collaborating teachers. She summarizes her approach as follows:

> I always ask, "How would I want somebody to talk with me?" I think it is important to explain that the manual is a guide that they should only use as needed, but I also try to explain it fully enough so that they can operationalize the strategy. I try to explain how it will

work. Really I take cues from the person. Take a reality check. Take it step by step. Sometimes teachers are perfectionists, so I need to give them that reassurance that they don't have to be perfect. I give them permission to try the things they want to try.

Simplify

ICs should not dumb down complex ideas and make them simplistic. As Bill Jensen has said in his book *Simplicity* (2000), we should not confuse *simplistic* with *simplicity*. Simplicity, Jensen explains, is "the art of making the complex clear" (p. 2). And "making the complex clear always helps people work smarter. Because it is a lot easier to figure out what's important and ignore what isn't" (p. i). The ability to make complex ideas understandable without reducing the complexity of the concept is an essential skill for ICs. Mike O'Brien, referenced in Jensen's book, describes simplicity as "unbelievable clarity. Not reduced to ducks and bunnies explanations . . . but the exciting, passionate clarity of ideas" (p. 15).

There are many things coaches can do to attain simpler explanations. Jensen (2000) again explains that storytelling is a communication strategy that "easily creates common meaning and purpose for everyone" (p. 88). ICs can use stories to help teachers see what a teaching practice might look like in the classroom. Additionally, ICs should look for analogies, anecdotes, or simple explanations and comparisons that bring the materials to life. Sue Woodruff uses stories to clarify teachers' understanding.

> I tell stories to make it more real. I put it in the first person. I give them suggestions based on personal experience. Sometimes a good story is more important than 50 graphs and charts with awesome proof that something works. Teachers usually just want to know if something is going to work, and stories help them figure that out.

GOING DEEPER

Interviews are described in more detail at www.instructionalcoach.org, a resource where ICs can also download PDF files of many of the forms described in this chapter.

Bill Jensen's *Simplicity* (2000) is a very valuable book describing powerful strategies people can use to sharpen and focus their thinking, and to enhance their ability to communicate their ideas.

Partnership Learning Structures are ways of delivering content so that conversation becomes a central part of professional learning. A short book describing the six learning structures and the research that was conducted to validate those structures may be downloaded for free from www.instructionalcoach.org.

TO SUM UP

- ICs recognize that change is a process. They are better able to meet teachers' needs when they consider all of the stages of change identified by Prochaska and his colleagues (1994): (a) precontemplation, (b) contemplation, (c) preparation, (d) action, (e) maintenance, and (f) termination.
- There are several ways in which ICs can get teachers on board. Usually, the greater the likelihood teachers will be resistant, the smaller the number of teachers the IC meets when introducing coaching. The most effective approach is usually one-to-one interviews.
- The Big Four—behavior, content knowledge, direct instruction, and formative assessment—can help teachers and ICs make decisions about where to start with coaching.
- Translating research into practice involves identifying the essence of a work created by researchers in a clinical setting and then reconstructing it so that it can be appreciated and implemented by teachers in the classroom.
- ICs can enhance their explanations of interventions if they use five tactics: (a) clarify, (b) synthesize, (c) break it down, (d) see it through the eyes of teachers and students, and (e) simplify.

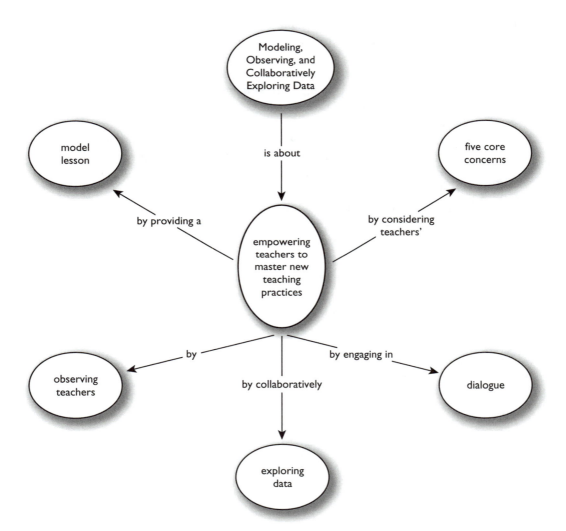

Chapter 6

Modeling, Observing, and Collaboratively Exploring Data

Modeling is where the rubber meets the road. I mean, it's really easy for us to stand back as instructional coaches and say, You should be doing this. You should interact with kids like this. You should follow the strategy like this. But until they see you do it, it's just words.

—Tricia McKale, instructional coach,
Robinson Middle School

CHAPTER OVERVIEW

Once teachers are enrolled in coaching, and the IC and the teacher have identified which teaching practice they'll implement and the coach has explained it, then the IC focuses on empowering the teacher to implement the new teaching practice in a way that is consistent with what research describes as best practice.

ICs can foster high-quality implementation of best practices through use of the components of coaching discussed in this chapter: (a) model, providing a model lesson in a teacher's classroom with that teacher's students; (b) observe, watching a teacher teach a lesson and gathering data; (c) explore, collaboratively exploring the data gathered during the observation of the teacher; (d) support, using all the components of coaching to provide support the teacher needs to implement and sustain implementation; and (e) reflect, pausing to consider what has been learned during the coaching activity. Additionally, the chapter will show how ICs can increase their chances of success by using several strategies to foster dialogical conversations and by considering five core concerns that teachers might hold.

EMPOWERING TEACHERS TO MASTER NEW TEACHING PRACTICES

My first coach was my father. When I was a child growing up in Canada, like most of my friends, my passion was hockey. As early as I can remember, I used to watch the Toronto Maple Leafs on television, and almost as soon as I could walk, my father gave me a pair of skates and a stick so I could learn how to play the game. I was lucky to live on a farm in Southern Ontario with a fairly large pond that froze up and turned into a local hockey rink in the wintertime. Children and adults from miles around used to come to Knight's Pond to play hockey on weekends and holidays.

On cold, Canadian mornings, Dad would take me down to the pond to teach me the basics. When I was first learning how to skate, my father showed me how to line up my skates so that I'd be able to turn properly. Dad would lace up his skates, show me exactly how to turn, tell me what he was doing, and then he'd ask me to do it. When I messed up, or when I did it right, he promptly gave me feedback. Time and again, the same pattern repeated itself. Dad showed me what to do; then he watched me until I got it. This was the way I learned how to play hockey—watching my father, practicing, getting his insight.

The way I learned hockey from my father is the way I've learned many, perhaps most, of the skills and behaviors picked up in my lifetime: how to drive a car, fix a flat tire, fold a shirt, or use PowerPoint. I seem to learn best when someone shows me how to do it, watches me, and then gives me feedback. Sometimes I have to see it demonstrated a few times before I master the skill, but I learn best when somebody shows me first. This is not an earthshaking insight. Educators have known for decades that modeling is an important component of learning, and numerous research studies have demonstrated the power of modeling. When teachers are helping students master reading strategies or math problem solving, they frequently model the practice for students before they ask them to perform independently. Anita Archer, a wise and marvelously enjoyable educator, describes how teachers can use the "I Do It, We Do It, You Do It," format for instruction so that their students see a model, then work as a group, and then practice independently to learn a new skill or strategy.

Modeling, observation, and feedback, then, are important, sometimes essential, for learning. We wouldn't teach someone to drive by giving them a lecture, tossing them a book, and then turning them loose on the freeway. Nonetheless, when we provide traditional staff development in schools, that is pretty much what we do. Even today (when there is a growing awareness that traditional forms of training do not improve teaching practice), a great deal of professional development occurs with little follow-up, and teachers often have few, if any, opportunities to see the new practice performed in their classrooms with their students.

When IC Tricia McKale collaborates with teachers, what she does is quite similar to what my father did on Knight's Pond. Tricia enables teachers to master new teaching practices by going into the classroom and showing the teacher exactly how a practice works with their children. Then Tricia watches her collaborating teachers try out the new way of teaching and provides feedback in a respectful and encouraging way until the teachers are confident they can implement the new practice without Tricia's help. Sometimes Tricia provides several model lessons, sometimes she observes several lessons, and sometimes she mostly talks with teachers about their progress. Through it all, Tricia is careful to build her relationship with her partnering teachers at the same time that she builds that teacher's competence in the new teaching practice.

Tricia McKale

Tricia McKale has been an IC at Robinson Middle School for the past five years. Prior to being an IC, Tricia was a language arts teacher for four years in North Ottawa County in Kansas. Tricia is a nationally certified professional developer for Randy Sprick's Safe and Civil Schools program and a certified professional developer for Learning Strategies within the Strategic Instruction Model. She is also coauthor of *Coaching Classroom Management* (Sprick, Knight, Reinke, & McKale, 2007).

MODEL: YOU WATCH ME

ICs, as we define them, spend a great deal of their time in classrooms modeling lessons, watching teachers teach, and having conversations about what the teacher saw when she watched the IC, or what the IC saw when he watched the teacher. Since some teachers find the business of observation somewhat intimidating, ICs try to keep the experience as informal as possible: "You watch me; I watch you."

The Observation Form

Before conducting a model lesson, an IC must ensure that the collaborating teachers are prepared to get the most out of the model lesson—that they know what to watch for and, in fact, are actually watching the model lesson. ICs can develop a shared understanding of the purpose of the model lesson by co-constructing with the teacher an observation form similar to the one included below, to help focus the attention of both the teacher and the IC. The observation form is a simple chart on which the IC, in partnership with the collaborating teacher, lists the critical teaching behaviors that a teacher should be watching for when watching a model lesson. For Tricia McKale, the observation form is an efficient way for her to clarify what the teacher should do while she does the model lesson:

> The thing about the form . . . it's the vehicle through which I can clearly communicate my expectations to the teacher. Because so many times you come in to model and the teacher is watching you but they don't have a 47-minute attention span, either. So it's very easy for them to start thinking, Well, I can watch you but I can also grade these papers. Or I can watch you but I can also check my e-mail. This form gives teachers specific things to look for.

As illustrated, the observation form includes a column for listing critical teaching behaviors that teachers should be watching for when observing the model lesson, a column where they can put a check mark every time they observe a critical teaching behavior, and a column where they can include comments, questions, or thoughts about what they observe during a model lesson. By co-constructing the form with teachers prior to the model lesson, ICs can check for teachers' understanding of critical teaching behaviors. Later, by having teachers fill out the form, they can focus the teachers' attention on what matters most in the model.

Tricia McKale encourages her collaborating teachers to use the form while they observe her model lesson to record any questions or thoughts they have about the model lesson: "I ask my teachers to record what they liked, what they didn't like, what they thought really worked, what they had trouble understanding. So it really opens up our communication and helps pinpoint strengths and trouble spots."

Why Don't We Just Give Them a Ready-Made Checklist?

In Chapter 5, I discussed the value of creating a checklist of critical teaching behaviors—as a tool to help coaches clarify and synthesize their understanding of teaching practices. Initially, I thought we would just give these checklists to teachers so that they would know what was most important. However, I found that giving a ready-made checklist to teachers was not as effective as co-constructing an observation form. Although the IC ensures that the co-constructed form includes most of the critical teaching behaviors on the original checklist, by involving the teacher in creating the form, a coach gets better buy-in to the form, and can be more certain that the collaborating teacher understands all of the items listed on it. Also, teachers frequently suggest teaching behaviors for the form that the coach might not have considered but that are important. Thus, by involving teachers in the process as partners, we actually get a better product.

Figure 6.1   Instructional Coaching Observation Form

Instructional Coaching
Progress through Partnership

OBSERVATION FORM

Teacher: _____   School: _____

Unit/Content: _____   Module: _____

Date: _____

TEACHING PRACTICE	OBS.	COMMENTS

> Tricia believes that the observation form also helps her do a better job as a coach. "Before using the form," Tricia says, "I used to go through the book to prep for modeling and just write kind of a lesson-at-a-glance, and that was what I would give the teacher. But it wasn't always action oriented; it was more informational. The observation form goes more into how it's going to happen." Tricia explains that the form also helps ensure that she provides a quality model. "I think it makes me more accountable because I know I can't cut corners. It's there in black and white, so it keeps me more true to the model as well."

Giving a Model Lesson

Before providing model lessons, ICs must ensure that they have a deep understanding of the lesson they are modeling. As explained in Chapter 5, one of the most valuable activities ICs can perform is to study thoroughly the teaching practices they will be sharing. ICs need to read, reread, and read again the instructors' manuals or research articles that describe the teaching practices they will be sharing. As we have seen, the observation form is a tool the teacher and coach can use to synthesize their mutual understanding and focus the teacher's attention on the most important teaching behaviors. The form is also a guide for ICs, to help them remember to emphasize the most important teaching behaviors during the model lesson.

Prior to the lesson, the IC and the teacher also need to clarify their roles with respect to behavior management in the classroom. In some cases, teachers want to retain their role as manager of classroom behavior. In other situations, teachers are very comfortable with the IC taking primary responsibility for managing behavior during the model lesson. Both the teacher and IC must know how behavior will be managed. As every experienced teacher knows, students seem to have a sixth sense that makes them very sensitive to any vacuum in leadership with respect to classroom management, and if no one is in control, they will be off task in minutes, possibly seconds.

Tricia McKale reports that most teachers are very happy to have the IC manage behavior. When she provides a model lesson, therefore, she is very explicit about her expectations for student behavior, and she takes advantage of the fact that she knows many of the students when communicating her expectations: "I've been building relationships with the kids outside of the classroom. When I go in, I state my expectations really explicitly."

After providing model lessons for the past five years, Tricia has learned a great deal along the way about what ICs should and should not do when conducting a model lesson. She offers six suggestions coaches might keep in mind when conducting model lessons.

Tricia's Suggestions for Model Lessons

- Talk with the students when they first enter the class so they are comfortable with the transition to you teaching a model lesson.
- Review content thoroughly so that students are clear that they have enough background knowledge to grasp the model lesson.
- Explain the expectation for the lesson explicitly and check to ensure students understand.
- Have a lot of interaction with the kids during the model lesson.
- Ensure the students know that you are a partner with their teacher.
- Expect to learn from your collaborating teacher.

First, Tricia says, before actually giving the model lesson, ICs should get into the classroom prior to the start of the class so that they can talk informally with students to make them comfortable with her being in the classroom. Tricia explains, "When I model an intervention, the first thing I do as the class is coming in is I just talk with the kids. Not about the lesson, not about here's what you need to be doing in class today, but just talking, just to get them relaxed, because for a lot of our kids, another teacher in the classroom is almost too much, and you've got to ease them into that transition."

Second, Tricia begins with a review to make sure that all students feel prepared to learn more about the content to be covered. Tricia explains, "I go over enough stuff so they feel like, oh yeah, I do know this stuff. OK, bring it on; I'm ready for the next thing." Tricia reports that when she co-constructs the observation form with teachers, she also asks about the students' background knowledge and skills. "If they're maybe lower than where they need to be for this particular lesson, we'll include more review of information. If they're higher, there may be parts of the review that we can shorten down."

Third, to ensure that students are ready for the model, Tricia clearly explains what her expectations are for the class. "I tell them," Tricia says, "here's exactly what we're going to be doing today, here's what I need you to do, and here's what you're going to see me doing. I'm very specific. I want them to know where the 47 minutes are going, and want them to see that there's also a clear ending. I think they appreciate that."

Fourth, while going through the model lesson, Tricia keeps the students actively involved. She asks numerous questions, and keeps students engaged. Tricia explains, "I have a lot of interaction with kids when I model—even when I'm doing self-talk. I'm really clear about this, saying 'OK guys, I'm going to self-talk right now and I want you to think about how this might be different from how you would do it.' And we have conversations around that. Then at the close of the lesson, I make sure the kids summarize what we've done."

Fifth, Tricia is careful to ensure that the students see that she is a partner with their classroom teacher. She includes statements in her lesson that demonstrate that she is working with their teacher, not doing something in place of their teacher. Tricia comments, "I might say, 'Ms. Dag and I are going to be walking around the class and assessing what you guys have done.' I really just do that to make sure the kids understand that I'm not a replacement for the teacher, and to make sure the teacher understands that we're partners in this process."

Finally, Tricia fully expects to learn from her collaborating teacher, which is her way of living out the partnership principle of reciprocity. As soon after the model lesson as possible, Tricia and the collaborating teacher meet to discuss the lesson. Here, the teacher shares with Tricia what she recorded on her observation form. "Hopefully," Tricia explains, "they will have some questions or notes written down—things they liked, things they didn't like, things that were unclear. Maybe they wanted some explanations for why I did certain things, or maybe they want to do something differently. Using the form really opens up the lines of communication and helps pinpoint strengths and trouble spots."

What Do Teachers Think About Model Lessons?

At the Center for Research on Learning, we have completed two studies to capture teachers' perceptions of the value of model lessons: (a) a 10-item survey that was completed by all 107 teachers who observed model lessons in Topeka, Kansas, in the academic year 2003–2004, and (b) a qualitative study that involved interviews with 13 teachers who observed IC Lynn Barnes provide model lessons when she was an IC at Chase Middle School. The results of both studies strongly support Tricia McKale's assertion included at the start of this chapter: "modeling is where the rubber meets the road."

Survey Results

In the fall of 2003–2004, we surveyed every teacher in Topeka who had seen an IC provide a model lesson the previous year. The survey consisted of 10 items addressing five questions. Two questions assessed whether or not model lessons helped teachers teach with fidelity to research-based practices ("Watching my IC model in the classroom helps me know the correct ways to implement interventions" and "When I watch my IC, I get a better idea of what I should and should not do when I implement Pathways interventions"). The combined mean score was 6.40, with 1 standing for "strongly disagree" and 7 standing for "strongly agree."

On questions assessing whether teachers perceived that model lessons increased their confidence about implementing interventions ("I am more certain about my teaching practices after I watch my IC in my classroom" and "I am more confident about teaching a Pathways to Success intervention after I watch my IC use it with my students in my classroom"), the combined mean score was 6.22.

Other survey results also suggested that teachers perceived model lessons as beneficial. On items assessing whether teachers believed model lessons made it easier for them to implement new teaching practices ("I am more certain about my teaching practices after I watch my IC in my classroom" and "I am more confident about teaching a Pathways to Success intervention after I watch my IC use it with my students in my classroom"), the combined mean score was 6.51. Similarly, on survey items assessing whether teachers believed they had learned other teaching practices from ICs during model lessons ("When I watch my IC, I learn other tricks teachers use in class" and "I pick up a lot of good ideas just watching my IC in my classroom"), the combined mean score was 6.13.

On survey items that asked whether ICs have enough content knowledge to teach all lessons ("There is some content in my class that my IC is not capable of teaching" and "My IC does not know all of my subject matter well enough to teach everything I teach), the combined mean score was 3.18. The data suggest that teachers clearly have opinions about model lessons. Model lessons helped them teach with fidelity to research-based practices, increased their confidence about new practices, made it easier to implement new practices, and provided an opportunity for them to learn other teaching practices.

Teachers also reported that they did not think ICs were ready to step in and teach all the content just because they were coaches. These results suggest that ICs should take care to limit their model lessons to teaching practices that they fully understand. When ICs demonstrate proven practices that they know extremely well, teachers see them as providing a very important service. If ICs try to take on all aspects of teaching a class, particularly on topics on which they may have limited content knowledge, teachers appear to be saying they are less helpful.

Teacher Interviews

Interviews conducted at Chase Middle School in Topeka supported the findings derived from the survey. Indeed, in each of the 13 interviews, the teacher stated that the model lessons were an essential part of the coaching process. Paul Gronquist's comments are typical:

> I think it was very important for her to come in and model it. I think the value of actually seeing it happen is you get to see how it works and how she interacts with certain kids that are real problems . . . It also instills confidence in myself. If we had just sat down and talked, I might have understood that, but seeing it in practice is a whole different thing. I think her value to me has been immense. I probably would have sunk without her.

Table 6.1   Survey Results

Question	Mean Score
Do teachers perceive that model lessons provided by ICs have increased their fidelity to research-based teaching practices?	6.40
Do teachers perceive that ICs have enough content knowledge to teach all lessons in the collaborating teachers' class?	3.18
Do teachers perceive that model lessons provided by ICs have increased their confidence with respect to implementing teaching practices?	6.22
Do teachers perceive that model lessons provided by ICs have made it easier for them to implement teaching practices?	6.51
Do teachers perceive that model lessons provided by ICs have enabled them to learn additional teaching practices?	6.13

Other teachers were just as clear about the value of model lessons. For example, Linda Lake said, "When she came into the classroom, that's what helped me the most." Hannah Waldy commented, "It's been very helpful to watch her," and Amber Sheritts noted, emphatically, "I could never have gotten that [teaching the Unit Organizer] if it hadn't been modeled, never." Teachers reported that watching a model lesson increased their confidence, and taught them many additional aspects of teaching. Vince Gregorio, for example, commented on how much he learned watching a model lesson:

In the tone of voice she uses, kind of the enthusiasm you need to put into it, all the way into the exact order things need to go, to how much repetition the kids can't handle. One thing I did appreciate was how she would involve the students, which she does a lot, how that would function, what her expectations were for the students to be able to function with that, answering, repeating, not just having the kids recall things, saying things back, repeating stuff. Actually, how to circulate the room, make sure you call on boys and girls evenly, and try to shift from one side of the room to the other, she really showed how to teach it as a complete lesson, not just a strategy.

The Light Just Went On

She came in and modeled after I tried the Unit Organizer once, and . . . it was funny because I could see the look on the kids' faces. It was as if they were saying, "This is so not what you had us do." So I was like, OK, I'm learning too. And it was wonderful.

Because she could bounce off math things to me that needed discussion as we did it, and I could bounce off the organizational stuff to her. The kids got the big picture.

I could never have gotten that if it hadn't been modeled for me. Never could have gotten it. I would have failed miserably at it and given it up, or I'd have done another unit, and if it had gone as bad as the first time I tried it on my own, I'd have never done it again. Because even when she and I just talked about it, I thought OK, I'll do it if they make me do it, but I'm not going to do it after this. Next year if we don't have to do this, I'm not going to do it, because I can't see any benefit to it—because I didn't know how to use it.

Then when I saw her... that was just like, wow! I look for that light in the kids' eyes. When Lynn came in and modeled for me, oh my God, the light just went on.

MODEL LESSONS AND TACIT KNOWLEDGE

One reason why ICs should consider including model lessons in their repertoire of coaching practices is that they provide a chance for teachers to learn many teaching techniques that are not written in teacher's manuals. If you reread Vince Gregorio's comments on the previous page, you'll see that what he appreciated about the model lesson was the opportunity to hear the IC's voice, and to note how she structured questions, and to see how she moved around the room. As Vince says, "She showed me how to teach it as a complete strategy."

Researchers and theorists who study the way adults learn would say that what Vince was responding to was the "tacit" knowledge held by the IC. Tacit knowledge, as authors Nonanka and Takeuchi (1995) have explained, "is hard to articulate with formal language. It is personal knowledge embedded in individual experience and involves intangible factors such as personal belief, perspective, and the value system" (p. viii). Nonanka and Takeuchi derive their definition from Michel Polanyi's pioneering writing about the tacit aspects of knowledge. As the authors explain,

> Polanyi contends that human beings acquire knowledge by actively creating and organizing their own experiences. Thus, knowledge that can be expressed in words and numbers represents only the tip of the iceberg of the entire body of knowledge. As Polanyi puts it [1966] "We can know more than we can tell" (p. 4). (Nonanka & Takeuchi, 1995, p. 60)

A simple example illustrates how tacit knowledge shapes our actions. My favorite car, looking back over the years, was a beat-up old 1984 Volvo station wagon that I drove until it wouldn't run any more. I'm not sure what I liked about the car, the front fender was dented, the back hatch was impossible to open, and the car broke down so frequently that my children gave it the ironic nickname "Old Reliable." One particularly annoying problem was that the driver-side speaker for the car's stereo cut out whenever I drove over a bump in the road. My wife, Jenny, who is especially wise in many ways, somehow learned and taught me that if I banged the door on a special spot, the speaker would kick back in. Before long, I developed a little ritual. Whenever I went over a bump, I got ready, clenched my fist, and banged the door the moment the speaker cut out so that it was back on in an instant. Eventually, I didn't even have to think about it. This just became a habitual thing for me to do when I drove my car.

Eventually I decided to fix the speaker, which meant I no longer had to clench my fist and bang the door. Yet, even though the speaker was fixed, after hitting a bump I still found myself clenching my fist to bang the door. My little ritual had become so ingrained that I kept doing it even though it was unnecessary. One sunny day, I was driving along Naismith Boulevard in Lawrence, and even though the speaker was working perfectly well, I clenched my fist just before I drove over a bump in the road. The noteworthy fact was that I was unconscious of the fact that there was a bump in the road. Obviously, in some part of my brain I was aware of the bump, but I didn't consciously know it was there, or even consciously know what was going on. That knowledge that I didn't have to know or think about is what we call *tacit knowledge*.

There is a tacit dimension to the work done by any skillful practitioner or artist, such as a teacher. Polanyi, remember, says, "We know more than we can tell," and that is certainly true of master teachers. There is the information in manuals and research articles, and then there are the artistic elements that outstanding teachers may not even realize they know or do. The art of teaching may involve a tone of voice, certain facial expressions, certain ways of moving about the classroom, and any number of ways of encouraging students that great teachers do without even knowing they do them. And that is one reason why ICs need to model teaching practices.

OBSERVE: I WATCH YOU

After the collaborating teacher has watched the coach provide a model lesson and then discussed her thoughts and questions about it with her IC, it is time for the IC to observe the teacher. While watching the teacher, the IC does the same as the teacher did while watching the model lesson: the IC watches for the critical teaching behaviors they identified using a copy of the co-constructed observation form that the teacher used to observe the coach when she did the model lesson. And, as the teacher did earlier, the IC watches the teacher carefully and checks off the form every time she sees the teacher perform one of the identified critical teaching behaviors.

Since teachers have already used the form to watch the IC's model lesson, they are usually quite comfortable with their IC's using the form in the classroom. However, ICs need to be careful to stress the informality of the observation, which is why we emphasize the idea of simply saying, "You watch me and I watch you." For some teachers, the very notion of "observation" is intimidating, and some ICs avoid using that term, choosing to say instead that they'll "visit" the classroom. If ICs are careful to watch for and record the many good aspects of the lesson they observe, however, teachers will become much less reticent about inviting them to watch lessons. As Tricia McKale explains, "They know I'm not coming in to catch them doing something they are not supposed to be doing. They know exactly what I'm looking for, and it's something they've agreed needs to be included so it gives them a lot more power and control over the lesson."

As an observer, the IC should try to remove his personal judgments from the activity of observing. Rather than seeing himself as evaluating the teacher, the coach should see himself as a second set of eyes in the room, using the observation form or other data-gathering methods as tools for recording relevant data about how the lesson proceeds. While observing, the IC should especially attend to the collaborating teacher's efforts to use the critical teaching practices. Whenever the teacher uses one of the critical behaviors, the IC should check the appropriate column of the observation form and write down specific data about how the teacher used the behavior. For example, if a critical teaching behavior is to explain expectations to students, the IC might jot down a quick summary of exactly what the teacher said when she clarified expectations.

What data the coach records during the observation varies, depending on what intervention teachers are learning to use. In many cases, the IC will only need to use the observation form to gather the necessary data. A teacher implementing Content Enhancement Routines (described in Chapter 7), for example, would be learning to use the steps of the "Cue, Do, Review" teaching routine, including "Cue," a way to provide students with an advance organizer, "Do" a way to involve students in a learning experience mediated by a visual device or graphic organizer, and "Review," a way to involve students in summing up the lesson. Each stage of the process involves critical teaching practices; thus the IC's job as an observer is to use the observation form to record when each teaching practice occurs. If the teaching practice doesn't occur, the IC leaves that part of the form blank.

Other interventions require other kinds of data gathering. For example, ICs who are coaching teachers to increase the number of high-level questions used (also described in the next chapter) might simply write down each question posed by the teacher so that the coach and teacher can review them later. ICs who are coaching teachers with respect to opportunities to respond (the number of times students are invited to speak or interact during a lesson) might simply keep a tally of the number of opportunities to respond provided during a lesson (samples of many of these forms are included in the Instructional Coach's Tool Kit at the end of this book). Thus, ICs may use the observation forms or other data-gathering methods depending on the teaching practice being learned.

While observing the lesson and gathering data, an IC has to be especially careful to note positive actions taking place in the class, such as effective instructional practices or positive student responses. While intuitively an IC might think that the most important part of observing a lesson is to find areas of weakness that need to be improved, in reality, the most important part of the observation may be to look for things the teacher does well. Seeing what needs to be improved or what has been overlooked is often quite easy; seeing and recording what went well sometimes requires extra effort.

ICs who are highly sensitive to the positive things that take place in the classroom can provide a great service to the teachers and the school. Too often, the challenges of being an educator and the emotional exhaustion that comes with trying to reach every child every day make it difficult for teachers to fully comprehend the good they are doing. Furthermore, the conversations in schools sometimes have a tendency to turn negative, perhaps as a defense mechanism for teachers who are frustrated that they cannot reach more students. Kegan and Lahey (2001), who have studied conversations in numerous organizations, report that people frequently under-communicate the positive aspects of their work:

> Nearly every organization or work team we've spent time with . . . astonishingly undercommunicates the genuinely positive, appreciative, and admiring experiences of its members. This . . . is a terrible deprivation of the vitality of the work setting. (pp. 91–92)

Thus, a very valuable service an IC can provide is to start to communicate the "genuinely positive, appreciative, and admiring experiences" of the teachers they observe in the classroom. Indeed, ICs should consider it one of their goals to change the kind of conversations that take place in schools.

EXPLORE: THE COLLABORATIVE EXPLORATION OF DATA

As soon as possible after observing a lesson, the IC should set up a follow-up meeting with the collaborating teacher so that they can discuss the data the coach collected while observing the lesson. This meeting, like other aspects of the instructional coaching process, is based on the mutual respect between professionals inherent in the partnership principles. The collaborative exploration of data taking place during this meeting is *not* an opportunity for the IC to share his "expert" opinion on what the teachers did right or wrong. More than anything else, it is a learning conversation where both parties use data as a point of departure for dialogue.

We can get a better understanding of what is meant by the collaborative exploration of data by clarifying what it is not. This meeting is not an opportunity for top-down feedback. Top-down feedback, as the figure below suggests, occurs when one person, an expert, watches a novice and provides feedback until the novice masters a skill. This might be a great way to teach some skills, but it is problematic as a model for interaction between professionals who are peers.

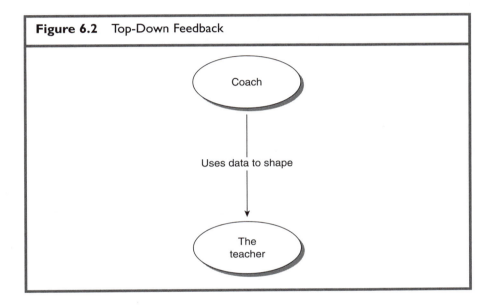

Figure 6.2   Top-Down Feedback

The problem with top-down feedback is that it is based on the assumption that there is only one right way to see things, and that right way is the view held by the feedback giver. Kegan and Lahey (2001) explain the assumptions of this approach:

> The first [assumption] is that the perspective of the feedback giver (let's call him the supervisor)—what he sees and thinks, his feedback—is right, is correct. An accompanying assumption is that there is only one correct answer. When you put these two assumptions together, they amount to this: the supervisor has the one and only correct view of the situation. (We call this "the super vision assumption"; that is, the supervisor has *super* vision.) (p. 128)

During top-down feedback, the feedback giver is prepared to "(1) say exactly what the person is doing wrong, (2) give the sense the criticism is meant to help, (3) suggest a solution, and (4) give a timely message" (Kegan & Lahey, 2001, p. 128). The person giving top-down feedback, in other words, working from the assumption that he is right, does all of the thinking for the person receiving the feedback. That is hardly the partnership approach, and the reason why Kegan and Lahey say, "many a relationship has been damaged and a work setting poisoned by *perfectly delivered* constructive feedback!" (p. 128).

An alternative to top-down feedback is the partnership approach, or the collaborative exploration of data. As depicted in the figure below, during the partnership approach, the IC and teacher sit side by side as partners and review the data that the IC has gathered. The IC does not withhold her opinion, but offers it in a provisional way, communicating that she is open to other points of view.

IC Tricia McKale describes how she conducts the collaborative exploration of data as follows:

> I turn it into a question first. I lay out my data, usually on an observation form, and say, "Well, here's everything that I saw. How do you think the lesson went? What did you think went really well in the lesson?" and they'll tell me. And then I'll say, "OK, now based on either your experience or this form we've got, what do you think were the components that made that go really well? That made the difference?" And then we'll see, does that match up with what I observed, because I may have missed something. And then I ask, "OK, what do you think some things were either according to your experience or what I have on this observation form, what are some things that we kind of still need to work on as a team?" And I let them come up with those answers.

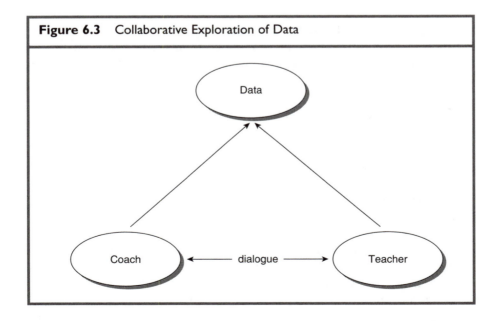

Figure 6.3   Collaborative Exploration of Data

A Language of Ongoing Regard

One important goal ICs should hold during the collaborative exploration of data is to communicate clearly the genuinely positive aspects of the lesson that was observed. I do not mean that they should be promoting thoughtless, vague, or empty happy words or phrases. A "language of ongoing regard" has specific characteristics. Kegan and Lahey (2001) stress that authentic appreciative or admiring feedback needs to be (a) direct, (b) specific, and (c) non-attributive. Most ICs recognize the importance of direct, specific feedback. Direct comments are spoken to a person in the first person, not about a person, in the third person. Thus, it is preferable to tell someone directly, "I appreciate your help," rather than saying publicly, "I appreciate Jean's help." Specific comments clearly explain the details of what we are praising, rather than offering general statements. Thus, it is preferable to say, "You asked 42 questions today during your class" in contrast to "you asked a lot of questions today in your class."

The importance of making nonattributive comments may be less obvious. Kegan and Lahey (2001) explain that our positive comments about others are more effective when we describe our experience of others rather than the attributes of others. For example, it is less effective to say to someone, "you're very patient" (describing an attribute that we judge them to have) than it is to say, "you waited 10 seconds for Alison to give her answer, and when she got it right, she lit up like a Christmas tree." Kegan and Lahey explain why nonattribute feedback is more effective:

> It may seem odd to you that we're urging you not to make statements of this sort: "Carlos, I just want you to know how much I appreciate how generous you are" (or: "what a good sense of humor you have" or "that you always know the right thing to say"), or "Alice, you are so patient" (or, "so prompt," "so never-say-die," "always there when you are needed,"), and so on . . . These seem like such nice things to say to someone . . . The problem we see is this: the person, inevitably and quite properly, relates what you say to how she knows herself to be. You can tell Carlos he is generous, but he knows how generous he actually is. You can tell Alice she is very patient, but she knows her side of how patient she is being with you. (p. 99)

Learning how to give direct, specific, nonattributive feedback is a skill that every IC should develop, and one that can be practiced and developed daily until it becomes a habit of thought. ICs can practice developing this "language of ongoing regard" at their workplace, but they can also practice it with their children, parents, spouse, or other people in their life. There is great benefit in practicing such feedback until it becomes a habitual way of communicating. Indeed, it seems strange that we often feel uncomfortable telling people directly and specifically why we appreciate them. Perhaps we're afraid our comments will seem to be insincere or self-serving flattery. Nothing could be further from the truth. As Kegan and Lahey (2001) state, "Ongoing regard is not about praising, stroking, or positively defining a person to herself or to others. We say again: it is about enhancing the quality of a precious kind of information. It is about informing the person about *our* experience of him or her" (p. 101).

Dialogue

Frequently, during the collaborative exploration of data, the IC and teacher swiftly move toward identifying next steps that they both agree will have the most positive impact on teaching. On other occasions, however, the IC and teacher hold different opinions about the significance of the data or what the teacher's next steps should be. The best route for the IC to take here is not to withhold her perspective, nor is it to push for her perspective. Partnership involves two equals sharing ideas, and this doesn't require one person to suppress or promote her ideas for another's. Rather, when the IC and the collaborating teacher see the data differently, the coach, acting on one of the partnership principles, can employ the tools of dialogue to foster an authentic learning conversation. When skillfully handled, a dialogue about differing perceptions of data can help both the IC and the teacher learn a great deal.

In his groundbreaking book *Dialogue and the Art of Thinking Together* (1999), William Isaacs describes dialogue as "a conversation in which people think together in relationship" (p. 19). Done well, a dialogue is a profound act of mutual learning during which two or more people suspend their personal opinions for the broader purpose of finding something closer to truth than they had before their conversation. At its best, as Daniel Yankelovich (1999) has observed, "in dialogue, we penetrate behind the polite superficialities and defenses in which we habitually armor ourselves. We listen and respond to one another with an authenticity that forges a bond between us" (p. 15). Tricia McKale observes that when an IC and coach engage in dialogue, both "stand to learn more from each other, and there's a better chance of implementing and sustaining change."

To become skilled at dialogue is no easy task, and there are no simple recipes for becoming a dialogical master. ICs can improve their ability to engage in dialogue by reading, learning, and practicing the skills described in several books about dialogue, three of which are described in the Going Deeper section of this chapter. To get started, ICs can use the following six strategies as ways to start to move toward more dialogical conversations.

Strategies for Promoting Dialogue

Learn, internalize, and practice the partnership principles.
Employ the partnership communication skills.
Suspend the assumption that you're right.
Respect your partner's opinion.
Balance advocacy and inquiry.
Ask questions that surface your assumptions and your partner's assumptions.

---

1. *Learn, internalize, and practice the partnership principles.* Developing a deep understanding of the partnership principles is one way to get better at opening up opportunities for dialogue. A partnership assumes equality—an openness between people—and dialogue is the natural mode of communication between partners.

2. *Employ the partnership communication skills.* ICs who would like to engage in dialogical conversation should commit to learning and using the partnership communication skills described in Chapter 4. This involves listening authentically and empathetically, recognizing and suspending the "stories" that might lead to preconceptions, and working to build an emotional connection and a trusting relationship with collaborating teachers. There can be no dialogue if we do not hear our partner in the conversation.

3. *Suspend the assumption that you're right.* ICs who want to engage in dialogue should suspend the notion that the purpose of the conversation is to prove that they are right. Frequently, conversation takes on the form of a debate, where two or more people strive to gain the upper hand and prove that their perspective is the one that others should hold. Both parties in the conversation wait anxiously while the other speaks until they can make their point and win the debate. Dialogue is a fundamentally different kind of conversation. To engage in true dialogue, ICs must let go of the desire to be right. Being right is irrelevant; what matters is to come to the right conclusion. That is why dialogue begins with our own reflection on how we communicate.

If we want to engage in dialogue, we need to pay attention to how we talk, to ensure that the purpose of what we say and think is to further communication and learning. As Isaacs says, dialogue "is not something you do to another person. It is something you do with people. Indeed, a large part of learning this has to do with learning to shift your attitudes about relationships with others, so that we gradually give up the effort to make them understand us, and come to a greater understanding of ourselves and each other" (1999, p. 9).

4. *Respect your partner's opinion.* To engage in effective dialogue, ICs must have a deep respect for others' opinions. For whatever reason, we are inclined to give our own ideas and opinions much more weight than those of others. Indeed, this frequently becomes a habit of mind, and without even thinking about it, we often assume our way of seeing things is the right way. In dialogue, ICs must perceive that the opinions and ideas of others have equal weight; otherwise, dialogue is impossible. In this sense, dialogue is an act of will, like listening: a determined effort to engage in conversations fully committed to hearing and respecting what others have to say. As Isaacs (1999) observed, "respect is not a passive act. To respect someone is to look for the spring that feeds their pool of experience . . . At its core, the act of respect invites us to see others as legitimate" (pp. 110–111).

5. *Balance advocacy and inquiry.* As Chris Argyris has explained (Argyris, Putnam, & Smith, 1985), ICs who wish to engage in dialogue need to skillfully balance advocacy and inquiry. Dialogue is not about withholding our thoughts and opinions. It is about sharing our thoughts and opinions in a way that doesn't silence the person with whom we're conversing. Of course, to advocate for a position, we need to have some clarity on what our opinion is. When we advocate from a dialogical perspective, our goal is not to push for our perspective, but to clearly understand and explain our perspective. This often involves clearly communicating the assumptions that we hold in support of our opinion.

Advocacy, by itself, does little to support learning; it leads to a competition of wills where the loudest or most aggressive arguer wins. Dialogue is a partnership activity in which two or more people communicate, not to win, but to achieve mutual understanding. We can encourage inquiry by asking our partners to explain the assumptions or the data that support their opinions, and we should hold our own opinions up to the same scrutiny. As William Isaacs summarized,

> *Advocacy* means speaking what you think, speaking from a point of view. *Inquiry* means looking into what you do not yet understand, or seeking to discover what others see and understand that may be differ from your point of view . . . balancing advocacy and inquiry means stating clearly and confidently what one thinks and why one thinks it, while at the same time being open to being wrong. It means encouraging others to challenge our views, and to explore what might stop them from doing so. (1999, p. 188)

6. *Ask questions that surface your assumptions and your partner's assumptions.* A shift to a dialogical conversation can also be enabled by asking questions that surface our own and our partner's assumptions. By asking questions that get to the heart of the discussion, we can redirect a conversation from debate to dialogue. ICs can ask simple questions that help uncover assumptions, such as, "What do you think the data suggests?" "What leads you to believe . . . ?" "What are some other ways we can look at that?" or "What do you think your students think about this?" Tricia McKale explains, "I use a lot of open-ended questions—very few yes and no. With my questions, I'm going after thoughtful responses."

Isaacs notes that "an estimated forty percent of all questions that people utter are really statements in disguise. Another forty percent are really judgments in disguise: 'Do you really think she deserved that raise?' Only a small percent of 'inquires' are genuine questions" (1999, p. 149). In dialogue, the goal of questions should be to move all partners further into the inquiry. Good questions should help partners learn together, and that, ultimately, should be the principal goal for both the IC and the collaborating teacher.

Support

The components of coaching discussed in this and the previous chapter (enroll, identify, explain, model, observe, and explore) are the primary activities carried out by ICs. Usually, most or all of these components of coaching are utilized, but the sequence in which the components have been described is not always followed. Sometimes the IC opens the door to a teacher's classroom by offering to model a lesson. Sometimes coaching begins with the IC observing. Sometimes the IC provides several model lessons. Sometimes the IC spends the bulk of time observing, sharing data, and conversing about the results. As Tricia McKale explains, "Each person is different because the needs of each class are so varied. There's no way to create a template that will work in every situation." Consequently, each coaching sequence must be tailored to the unique needs of each individual teacher.

During coaching, the IC provides as much support as necessary, but no more. In most cases, after a teacher has mastered a new teaching practice, the coach and teacher choose to move on to some other intervention. Teachers who enhance their ability to manage student behavior and who have worked with an IC might move on to explore teaching practices related to content knowledge, say, developing effective Unit Organizers that contain essential questions, a unit map, and a course schedule, or they might continue to work on behavior management by collaborating with the IC to increase the number of opportunities to respond that they provide for students. What matters is that the teacher and the IC keep learning together, working as partners to ensure that students receive excellent instruction. "My job," Tricia comments, "is to remove every barrier that might stand in the way of teachers implementing a new teaching practice."

Reflect

When an IC moves through the components of coaching with a teacher, both the teacher and the coach should be learning. The teacher is learning a new teaching practice. At the same time, the coach could be learning any number of new skills or insights related to working with students, providing model lessons, enrolling teachers in the instructional coaching process, building relationships, addressing teachers' core concerns, or any other aspect of instructional coaching. Every day provides numerous learning experiences for even the most experienced coaches.

To ensure that they do not forget what they learn along the way, many coaches keep journals, either on their computers or in handwritten notebooks, to record the important things they learn. ICs can also use a reflective practice developed by the U.S. Army: After-Action Review (AAR). According to *The U.S. Army Leadership Field Manual*, "An AAR is a professional discussion of an event, focused on performance standards, that allow participants to discover for themselves what happened, why it happened, and how to sustain strengths and improve on weaknesses" (U.S. Army, 2004, p. 6). Put another way, the AAR structures reflection on (a) what was supposed to happen, (b) what really happened, (c) why there's a difference between a and b, and (d) what should be done differently next time. Some ICs use an AAR, such as the one included below, to record their thoughts about what they learned while coaching with a teacher.

After-action reflection can be conducted in many different ways. For example, some coaches like to purchase a high-quality notebook and keep a journal in which they write down their reflections. Other coaches write their thoughts in a document on their computer. Coaches might also choose to go high-tech. Coaches who own iPods can purchase inexpensive microphones and record their thoughts on their iPod. Then, they can download their thoughts to their computer and keep an oral history of their experiences. These oral histories can even be burned to a CD and listened to periodically, say, on a car CD player, allowing an IC to look back over her learning experiences.

The AAR does not have to be a solo experience: indeed, it is often more effective when conducted with a group or team. For this to happen, a coach accepts responsibility for sharing his or her experiences with a collaborating teacher and, together with others, explores the four questions: What was supposed to happen? What really happened? What accounts for the difference? What should be done differently next time? The coach leading the discussion begins by providing a quick but complete answer to the first two questions, describing his or her expectations for the collaboration and the reality of what happened. Then, the other people involved in the conversation ask questions and offer their insights as the group collectively considers what really was different and what should be different next time.

Figure 6.4   After-Action Report

Instructional Coaching
Progress through Partnership

AFTER-ACTION
R E P O R T

School: _____   Strategy/Routine: _____

Teacher: _____   Unit/Content: _____

What was supposed to happen?

_____
_____
_____
_____
_____

What happened?

_____
_____
_____
_____
_____

What accounts for the differences?

_____
_____
_____
_____
_____

What should be done differently next time?

_____
_____
_____
_____
_____

Additional Comments? (Please use back of form)

When people choose to become ICs, they choose a profession where the learning experiences come fast and furious. Coaches need to learn teaching practices, communication strategies, and leadership tactics, while also learning how to respond effectively to each individual teacher. Every coaching relationship is unique, and we are not being rhetorical saying coaches learn something new every time they work with a teacher. What coaches do with that learning, of course, makes all the difference. If ICs do not take the time to stop, reflect, and record what they've learned, they run the risk of missing many learning opportunities. As Tricia notes, "We can miss the advantages of adequate reflection time because we're so wrapped up in action." However, if ICs pause to reflect, adjust their practices, and set new goals, they can make personal learning a central part of their coaching practice and quickly increase their effectiveness as leaders of change in school.

CORE CONCERNS

What if teachers don't want an IC in their classrooms? The instructional coaching process isn't very effective if ICs aren't able to go into teachers' classrooms, and as mentioned, not every teacher warms to the idea of a coach in the classroom, at least not right away. We have found that this resistance often has very little to do with the innovations ICs are offering. Often resistance arises because teachers do not like the way coaching has been proposed to them. Resistance, after all, as counselors have explained to us for some time, is not owned by one person—resistance requires at least two people: one to resist and one to propose whatever is being resisted. ICs can dramatically increase their effectiveness when they become more aware of how their actions might actually be encouraging teachers to resist coaching. Therefore, one of the most powerful tactics a coach can employ is to stop the behaviors that encourage others to resist change.

Encouraging teachers to invite ICs into the classroom involves skillful negotiation, and ICs can be more effective if they are aware of some of the basics of negotiation. In their exploration of the emotional aspects of negotiation, Fisher and Shapiro (2005), two internationally recognized leaders from the Harvard Negotiation Project, state that five core concerns stand at the heart of negotiations. According to Fisher and Shapiro, these core concerns are "human wants that are important to almost everyone in virtually every negotiation. They are often unspoken but are no less real than our own tangible interests . . . Core concerns offer you a powerful framework to deal with emotions without getting overwhelmed by them" (p. 15).

Fisher and Shapiro's Five Core Concerns for Negotiation	
Appreciation	Status
Affiliation	Fulfilling role
Autonomy	

ICs are well-advised to become familiar with the concerns identified by Fisher and Shapiro. "Because everyone has these concerns," the authors explain, "you can immediately utilize them to stimulate positive emotions" (2005, p. 16). If an IC is able to meet teachers' needs related to each concern (appreciation, affiliation, autonomy, status, role) she will have a much better chance of finding teachers who are excited about collaborating with her. Similarly, if an IC learns how to avoid behaviors that violate teachers' core concerns, there is a much greater chance that teachers will invite them into their classrooms.

The first core concern identified by Fisher and Shapiro is appreciation. This concern, the authors explain, "is not just a noun that labels a concern: it is also an action" (p. 27). People who are intent on expressing appreciation should (a) "understand each other's point of view," (b) "find merit in what each of us thinks, feels, does," and (c) "communicate our understanding through words and actions." ICs intent on meeting teachers' need for appreciation should employ all three strategies. The authors conclude, "when another person feels truly heard, you have valued not only the person's message but also the person as a individual" (p. 39). Tricia McKale also recognizes the importance of appreciation. As she explains, "I always start out with appreciation. That way, we're more likely to move forward, even if we start out at opposite sides of the table."

The second core concern, affiliation, the authors explain, "involves an *honest* connection. It only happens when someone has a true concern for our well-being" (p. 54). Fisher and Shapiro suggest several strategies, and each of these can be employed by ICs to build affiliation with collaborating teachers:

"Arrange to meet in an informal social setting" (p. 57)

"Introduce yourself informally, suggesting that they use your first name" (p. 57)

"Sit side by side, if that is reasonably possible" (p. 57)

"Refer to the importance of their interests" (p. 57)

"Emphasize the shared nature of the task you both face" (p. 58)

"Avoid dominating the conversation" (p. 58)

A third core concern is the need for autonomy. As the authors explain, "Each of us wants an appropriate degree of autonomy," (p. 72) and "we easily get offended when others limit our scope of autonomy beyond what we think is appropriate" (p. 74). Thomas Davenport, one of the nation's leading experts on knowledge workers, observes that a need for autonomy is a common characteristic of people "who think for a living" (people such as teachers or ICs).

Davenport states,

> One important aspect of knowledge workers is that they don't like to be told what to do. Thinking for a living engenders thinking for oneself. Knowledge workers are paid for their education, experience, and expertise, so it is not surprising that they often take offense when someone else rides roughshod over their intellectual territory. (2005, p. 15)

An IC who truly lives out the partnership approach should demonstrate an authentic respect for the independent decision making of collaborating teachers. If ICs fail to respect the autonomy of collaborating teachers, they often sow the seeds of resistance before they really ever even begin. In seven years of studying instructional coaching, I have found that our least effective interventions have been those where a person in authority tells a staff member that they must work with the coach. Not surprisingly, such misplaced administrative enthusiasm, which fails to take into account each teacher's need for autonomy, almost always makes the coach's job much more difficult.

Status, another core concern, Fisher and Shapiro (2005) explain, "refers to our standing in comparison to the standing of others" (p. 95), and "competing for status tends to induce negative emotions" (p. 96). ICs who treat others as inferior almost always encounter resistance, regardless of how valuable the knowledge and skills are that they have to share. For that reason, effective ICs go out of their way to respect the status of teachers. ICs often portray themselves as "a second set of hands," or as displaying what IC Devona Dunekack refers to as a "servitude attitude." The best ICs have extensive knowledge to share, but they don't make a show out of sharing. In fact, they are very careful to always to recognize a collaborating teacher's expertise and status as classroom leader.

The final core concern identified by Fisher and Shapiro (2005) is "having a fulfilling role." As the authors explain, "a fulfilling role can occupy an important place in our lives. Our identity becomes closely associated to the role and all that it brings—the status, power, the affiliation. Losing that role can feel like someone is cutting off a part of us. We may go to great lengths to resist being hurt" (p. 125). ICs need to communicate clearly that they are in no way interested in taking over any role held by collaborating teachers.

ICs can communicate that they are not a threat to a teacher's roles by ensuring that collaborating teachers realize that they are the driving force behind collaborative planning, and that every teacher is the ultimate decision maker for issues related to their classroom. "Once I work with a teacher," Tricia explains, "it always comes back to what do they want, where do they want to go. I can't drive the car from the back seat, and ultimately they're driving anyway."

Additionally, ICs must be sure not to interfere with a teacher's role as the leading mentor, supporter, and teacher in the classroom. At all times when they are in the classroom, ICs need to make it clear to students that their teacher is the person in charge. As heartwarming as it may be for a coach to hear a student say, "I wish you were my teacher," those words should be a sign to the IC that he needs to do a better job of supporting the collaborating teacher in her role as classroom leader. Finally, ICs also need to be sensitive to the roles held by others within the school. If ICs are reckless about assuming formal (head of the reading committee) or informal (staff lounge comedian) roles typically held by others in a school, they can inadvertently produce resistance from teachers, who in many cases could have been valuable allies down the line.

The best way to get around resistance to coaching is to act in a manner that significantly decreases the likelihood anyone might resist what we have to offer. By addressing teachers' core concerns for appreciation, affiliation, autonomy, status, and meaningful roles, ICs can increase the likelihood that teachers welcome them into their classrooms. If they violate one or more of the teachers' concerns, however, ICs can expect to be less successful, and unless ICs are in teachers' classrooms working in partnership, there is little likelihood that there will be any significant improvement in teaching practices.

GOING DEEPER

The Harvard Negotiation Project

Over the past three decades, researchers and authors at the Harvard Negotiation Project have produced a series of outstanding books exploring many aspects of interpersonal communication. *Getting to Yes* (Fisher, Ury, & Patton, 1991) is one of the most influential books written about the topic of negotiation and summarizes strategies that can be used to develop "win-win" negotiations. *Getting Past No* (Ury, 1991), a sequel of sorts to *Getting to Yes*, summarizes communication tactics that can be used to deal with people with more challenging personalities. *Getting Together* (Fisher & Brown, 1988) describes seven aspects of relationship building (rationality, understanding, communication, reliability, persuasion, and acceptance). *Getting It Done* (do you see a pattern here?) (Fisher & Sharp, 1998) provides suggestions on how to lead a team or organization when you have little or no formal power to lead the group. *Difficult Conversations* (Stone, Patton, & Heen, 1999) describes strategies to use to engage others in conversations about important topics they may not want to discuss—a very appropriate book for ICs. Finally, Fisher and Shapiro's *Beyond Reason* (2005), referenced at length in this chapter, extends the ideas in *Difficult Conversations* by exploring the emotional aspects of negotiation.

Dialogue

There are several excellent books on dialogue that any IC can benefit from studying. Perhaps the best place to start is David Bohm's short work *On*

Dialogue (2000). Bohm's book is wise, insightful, profound, and easy to understand, quite an accomplishment.

If you can only read one book on dialogue, I would recommend William Isaacs's *Dialogue and the Art of Thinking Together* (1999). The book is more challenging than the others, but Isaacs provides excellent strategies and, perhaps more important, numerous frameworks for better understanding dialogue. Daniel Yankelovich's *The Magic of Dialogue: Transforming Conflict Into Cooperation* (1999) is also an excellent introduction to dialogue, with many suggestions and strategies that ICs will find helpful.

Kegan and Lahey's *How the Way We Talk Can Change the Way We Work: Seven Languages for Transformation* (2002) provides, in addition to the communication strategy summarized above—enabling a language of ongoing regard through specific, direct, non-attributive feedback—valuable insight into how our own assumptions, and the assumptions of others, can sabotage our efforts to change. Also, the book provides a road map for leading cultural transformation in organizations, from a culture of complaint to a culture of commitment, and from blame to personal responsibility.

TO SUM UP

- Model lessons are an essential component of the instructional coaching process. Survey data and interviews suggest that teachers greatly benefit from watching ICs deliver model lessons.
- Model lessons provide a way for ICs to demonstrate, and teachers to learn, the tacit dimensions of teaching practices.
- Teachers' observations of model lessons, and ICs' observations of teacher lessons, can be given focus through the use of an observation form.
- To foster a language of ongoing regard, ICs should give feedback that is specific, direct, and non-attributive.
- The effect of top-down feedback is limited because it is built on the assumption that only one person has the correct view of events—the person giving feedback.
- During the collaborative exploration of data, ICs and teachers sit together as partners to interpret the data gathered by ICs during teachers' lessons.
- When teachers and ICs see the data differently, ICs can enable mutual understanding through dialogue.
- To decrease the likelihood of resistance, ICs should address teachers' core concerns for appreciation, affiliation, autonomy, status, and meaningful roles.

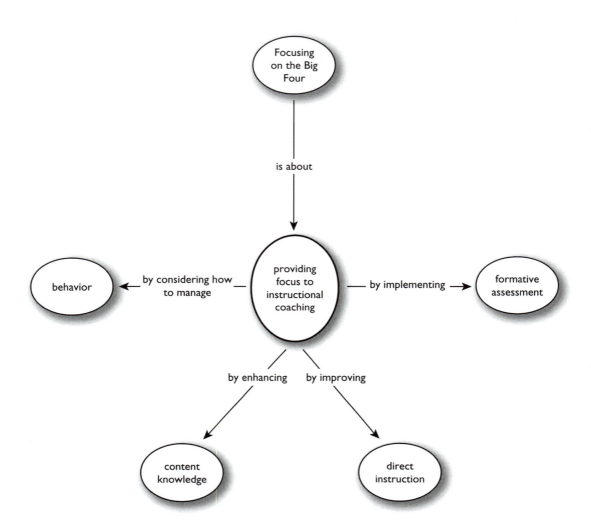

Chapter 7

Focusing on the Big Four

Behavior, Content Knowledge, Direct Instruction, and Formative Assessment

Teachers agonize when they feel that they're ineffective. They really want that to change even if they don't know how to change . . . That's why there is a tremendous need for the kind of work we do.

—LaVonne Holmgren, instructional coach,
Landon Middle School

CHAPTER OVERVIEW

Instructional coaches can easily feel overwhelmed when looking at the many teaching practices they could share with teachers and the many points of departure for coaching presented by the unique abilities of each teacher with whom they work. To help make this process easier, researchers and ICs associated with the University of Kansas Center for Research on Learning have developed the Big Four, a framework for organizing interventions and providing focus to coaching practice. The Big Four, described in this chapter, includes: behavior, content knowledge, direct instruction, and formative assessment.

THE POWER OF FOCUS

What does a good learning experience look like? There are probably as many ways to answer that question as there are people in schools. A good learning experience is motivating, challenging, meaningful, and inspiring. In a well-run classroom, students are focused on learning, they are respectful, and they are growing. Students learn from a teacher who is caring, compassionate, and clear, a teacher who knows what information is most important to teach and makes sure every student masters it. Students know their learning targets, and they receive useful feedback on their progress toward the target. Learning activities and reading materials are appropriate for each student's unique learning needs, and students learn about topics that are relevant to them.

ICs might use all of these aspects of good learning experiences as points of departure for collaborating with teachers. Indeed, there may be as many starting points for coaching as there are opinions about what constitutes good learning. To help sort through this jungle of possibility, ICs need to identify the teaching practices, learning strategies, tools, and other interventions that have the greatest likelihood of helping students. ICs affiliated with the University of Kansas Center for Research on Learning use the Big Four as a framework to help them with these tasks.

TWO DISCLAIMERS BEFORE WE BEGIN

Disclaimer 1: The Big Four Is Not Just for Weaker Teachers

When coaches collaborate with teachers on the Big Four, they are not simply there to help teachers remedy weaknesses in their teaching practice. Effective ICs help teachers grow by building on their strengths and helping them achieve potential they may not have realized that they had. Effective coaches help all teachers move forward. Elizabeth and Gifford Pinchot explain this facet of coaching when comparing executive coaches to therapists:

> Society often perceives therapists as working in the arena of the dysfunctional: therapists try to fix that which is not functioning. Such a view can lead to a belief that the client is "sick." But in coaching we are not therapists; we are peers working with admirable people who are often highly advanced in their understanding of themselves and how to get the most out of who they are. Our clients are certainly not sick; instead they are exceptional people eagerly striving to continually develop themselves—way up from already good. And the coach is there to facilitate and help. (Goldsmith, Lyons, & Freas, 2000, p. 46)

Disclaimer 2: This Is Just an Introduction

The many practices introduced in this chapter all can be studied in much greater detail. ICs affiliated with the University of Kansas Center for Research on Learning spend approximately six days over the course of the year developing their skills with respect to coaching classroom management, and they read the more than 350 pages of our book *Coaching Classroom Management* (Sprick, Knight, Reinke, & McKale 2007). Similarly, ICs learning to coach teachers to use Content Enhancement complete five days of intensive professional development, spread over a year, read more than 15 research articles, develop a deep knowledge of the 12 instructor's manuals for the 12 routines, and create an extensive portfolio to document their learning. The Big Four described here is just an introduction. Educational leaders who are interested in adopting the Big Four as a framework for improving instruction should plan to provide their ICs with extensive professional development. As is the case with any new model, for ICs to be highly effective, they must have a deep knowledge of whatever practices they share with teachers.

1. Behavior

2. Content

3. Direct instruction

4. Formative assessment

THE BIG FOUR

LaVonne Holmgren is an IC at Landon Middle School. When LaVonne works with teachers, she uses the Big Four as a framework for making sense of the opportunities and challenges her teachers face. The Big Four is a way for LaVonne and her teachers to decide where to start. If a teacher's students are off task, if classroom management seems to be an issue, then LaVonne might share interventions that assist with behavior. If a teacher is struggling to organize, prioritize, or understand content, then content interventions make sense. Similarly, if teachers might benefit from enhancing their instructional practices or from expanding their use of formative assessment, then LaVonne might employ other teacher tools. This chapter provides an overview of some effective practices an IC can use with teachers to address the concerns surfaced by the Big Four.

LaVonne Holmgren

LaVonne Holmgren has been an IC at Landon Middle School for six years. She is a certified Strategic Instruction Model Learning Strategies professional developer, and she has received extensive professional development in Content Enhancement, Randy Sprick's Safe and Civil Schools program, and Richard Stiggins's Assessment for Learning. Prior to becoming an IC, LaVonne was an elementary classroom teacher and a teacher of strategies for Grades K–4.

Behavior

Learning how to manage student behavior in the classroom is one of the most challenging and important skills teachers need to master. For that reason, ICs can provide a great service to collaborating teachers by empowering them to manage behavior in their classrooms. If students ignore their teachers' lessons, disrupt the flow of instruction, disturb other students, or act rudely, they inhibit the learning of every student in the classroom, including themselves. And the side effects of teaching a chaotic class can be devastating. Teachers can become physically exhausted from trying to find the self-control and emotional resilience necessary to teach a class that is out of control. Teachers can be even more taxed by the doubts and insecurities they feel when they are unable to create a safe and civil learning environment. Losing control of a class can be a recipe for disaster.

ICs like LaVonne can dramatically reduce teachers' anxiety and dramatically increase the amount of learning taking place in many classrooms by helping teachers manage classroom behavior. Consequently, behavior is often a starting point for ICs collaborating with teachers. There are many effective practices that ICs can use to help teachers with this very important part of instruction.

Resources and References

In this section, I use the approach to classroom management detailed in Randy Sprick's *CHAMPs: A Proactive and Positive Approach to Classroom Management* (Sprick, Garrison, & Howard, 1998) as my primary example. Most of the ideas summarized here are elaborated in much greater detail in *Coaching Classroom Management* (Sprick, Knight, et al., 2007). I am very grateful to my collaborators Randy Sprick, Wendy Reinke, and Tricia McKale, whose expertise greatly inform my discussion of behavior. Readers who are interested in deepening their understanding of behavior coaching might wish to look into that book.

There are several alternatives to CHAMPs and Coaching Classroom Management. One example is the Classroom Organization and Management Program (www.COMP.org) based on the research of Carolyn Evertson and her colleagues at Vanderbilt University (Evertson, 1995; Evertson & Harris, 1999). A book such as Robert Marzano's *Classroom Management That Works* (2003) can also be the basis for developing your own instructional coaching approach to address behavior.

When LaVonne Holmgren collaborates with teachers on issues related to classroom management, she uses a number of tools, many of which are described in more detail in *Coaching Classroom Management* and *CHAMPs*. The primary tools include (a) developing and teaching expectations, (b) ratio of interactions, (c) developing effective corrective comments, (d) time on task, and (e) opportunities to respond. Each of these is described here.

DEVELOPING AND TEACHING EXPECTATIONS

If teachers want their classrooms to be orderly, they must ensure that their students have a clear understanding of what is expected of them in all activities. In a recent conversation, Randy Sprick, a nationally recognized expert on classroom management, explained the importance of expectations: "If teachers are unclear about their expectations, the kids learn it's all a crapshoot, so you might as well do whatever you want." To create safe and civil classrooms, Randy suggests, "teachers need to clarify, activity structure by activity structure, exactly what is appropriate behavior and what is inappropriate behavior."

LaVonne Holmgren uses CHAMPs when she collaborates with teachers to develop expectations. She helps teachers write up exactly how they expect students to behave during all activities (such as direct instruction, group work, and independent practice), and all transitions (such as entering the room, taking out textbooks, gathering learning materials from various areas of the room, and leaving the room at the bell).

Among the CHAMPs tools LaVonne uses is a framework coaches can use to identify and explain what they expect from students in five important areas of behavior, encapsulated in the CHAMPs acronym. The areas of behavior are as follows: (a) conversation, what kind of conversation is acceptable; (b) help, how students should ask for help; (c) activity, what the student should be doing; (d) movement, what kind of movement, if any, is permitted; and (e) participation, what appropriate participation looks like. LaVonne views developing expectations as an important service she can provide to help teachers. "The teacher has to get crystal clear on what they expect students to do coming into the room, getting ready to do their work, and in all the various activities and transitions. All of these things need to have been thought through by the teacher and communicated to the students."

Ratio of Interactions

Another important service ICs can provide for teachers is to help them see how the way they praise and criticize students can have a significant impact on how students behave. Coaches can demonstrate that to encourage students to act appropriately, teachers need to encourage the behavior they want to see and correct the behavior they want to discourage.

Since many children consider attention the major reward in the classroom, particularly the teachers' attention, it follows that teachers should give more attention to the kinds of behavior they want to encourage than they do to the behavior they want to discourage. A common rule of thumb in the literature on classroom management is that to encourage positive behavior, teachers should pay at least three times as much attention to behavior they want to encourage as they do to the behavior they want to discourage.

The reality in many schools is that teachers pay much more attention to inappropriate behavior than they do to appropriate behavior. In one informal study that I conducted in approximately 50 classrooms in inner-city schools, we found that, on average, teachers were commenting on negative behavior about six times more frequently than they commented on positive behavior. We also found that the more frequently teachers paid attention to negative behavior, the more frequently they saw it manifested in their students.

ICs can help teachers increase the amount of attention they pay to behavior they want to reinforce. First, coaches can observe teachers and keep a tally of how often they attend to positive behavior and how often they attend to negative behavior. Such observation does not need to be sophisticated. An IC can simply draw a line down the middle of a page, and put a check mark on one side when the teacher attends to positive behavior and a check mark on the other side when the teacher attends to negative behavior. Then, the coach can meet with the teacher, share the data, and collaboratively, they can discuss the significance and implications of the findings.

ICs can also provide teachers with suggestions or model how to be more attentive to positive behavior. For example, coaches can show teachers how to give "noncontingent attention." According to Sprick, Garrison, and Howard (1998) this means "giving students time and attention not because of anything they've done, but just because you notice and value them as people" (p. 210). Similarly, coaches can demonstrate how teachers can keep their own tally of positive and negative attention and encourage them to plan to be positive with students, especially with students they have had to correct. Coaches can also guide teachers to scan their classroom to look for positive actions, heighten teachers' awareness of positive student behavior, and help decrease the frequency and intensity of corrective responses.

LaVonne believes that teachers need to communicate positively because she sees it as such an important part of each child's development.

> There are so many kids who are needy and all they get is negative interactions, in the home or in the community. I am just amazed at the number of students who pass me who never make eye contact. I think a lot of the interactions they have each day must be negative. Increasing the number of positive interactions we have with students is the one thing that, I think, teachers and kids can most benefit from.

Effective Corrective Comments

ICs can also empower teachers to manage classroom behavior by helping them learn how to correct inappropriate behavior effectively. If teachers are not careful, they can be drawn into a vicious cycle with students, and their criticisms of inappropriate behavior can encourage students to continue to be off task. Additionally, if teachers are too aggressive in their criticism of students, they can render students so self-conscious that they find it impossible to concentrate on learning. Indeed, poorly provided corrections can distract an entire class of students, take an entire class off task, or severely disrupt the flow of a lesson. Clearly, learning how to correct misbehavior effectively is an important skill teachers can benefit from mastering.

LaVonne Holmgren has observed that a teacher who is unable to correct inappropriate behavior effectively may find it increasingly more difficult to create a positive learning environment. "If teachers don't feel like they have control, they can start to do more and more sarcastic and downgrading things to try to control students. And if students don't feel respected, they are really not going to pay attention to what they are taught. So learning how to correct students is really critical if you are going to have learning occur."

In my conversations with Randy Sprick, he has emphasized the importance of teachers developing routine ways of correcting rule violations:

> The teacher needs to have developed a plan that allows them to be on automatic pilot when correcting those rule violations. So that when a rule violation occurs . . . [if I'm teaching] . . . I should be able literally to use a relatively few brain cells and immediately correct the behavior so that I can get my mental and physical energy back on a roll and momentum for instruction. If the teacher has to stop and think, "Well, what am I going to do now" when a kid misbehaves, that 30-second pause takes the teacher and the students away from the lesson.

There is much an IC can do to help teachers become masters at correcting unacceptable student behavior. First, an IC can simply keep a tally of the number of disruptions that occur during a lesson. Disruptions can be defined as any action by a student that interrupts the flow of learning during class. Coaches and teachers can then review the number of disruptions for a short sample of time, say a 10-minute period, to monitor how a class is progressing and plan strategies to decrease disruptions.

Randy suggests several additional tactics a coach can employ to help teachers improve their ability to handle rule violations. First, the IC and collaborating teacher can make a list of the most common rule violations that the teacher anticipates occurring in the classroom. Then, they identify exactly what the consequences will be for each rule violation. Following this, the coach supports the teacher as he learns to apply the consequences calmly, consistently, quickly, and with as little interruption to flow of the class as possible. ICs can support teachers by giving model lessons, observing teachers, or having collaborative conversations.

Time on Task

Another simple but powerful service that an IC can provide for teachers is to document students' time on task, that is, the percentage of time students are engaged in the learning task that has been set before them by their teacher. Research suggests that in an effective class, students should be on task more than 90% of the time. Coaches can gather data on time on task quickly and easily. Using a form such as the one included below, developed by Wendy Reinke (2005) from Johns Hopkins University, coaches can get a quick measure of what percentage of time students are engaged in learning.

The form is easy to use. Every five seconds, the coach glances at a student. If the student is on task at the moment the coach looks at her, the coach puts a plus sign (+) in the appropriate box. If the student is off task, the coach puts a zero (0) in the box. While observing the class, the coach moves attention systematically from one student to the next. Thus a coach might observe students in rows, by looking at each student in each row every five seconds, moving down each row student by student. If observing students in groups, a coach might move his attention from student to student, every five seconds, going in a clockwise motion around the room. Each box on the form represents each student observed.

The IC keeps observing students systematically until all 60 boxes contain either a plus or a zero. Once all the boxes are filled, the coach has spent five minutes observing the class. To calculate a percentage of time on task, ICs simply divide the total number of boxes that indicate a student was on task (the boxes with plus signs) by the total number of boxes. Reinke suggests that coaches visit at least three times (thus completing three forms) before they calculate time on task for a given class.

If a coach employs the tools and teaching practices described in this chapter to help teachers increase their classroom management skills, their collaborating teachers should see a significant increase in time on task. By recording time on task, ICs can give teachers a quick, broad measure of how much learning is taking place in their classroom, thereby providing a reality check or a measure of progress. For some new teachers, 90% may seem like a difficult target to achieve, but when teachers and ICs collaborate to make incremental improvements, developing and teaching expectations, increasing the positive ratio of interaction, improving the consistency and effectiveness of correction procedures, by making tiny steps they can make big improvements. When teachers and coaches work together step-by-step to develop practices that ensure that students are on task at least 90% of the time, they can do a lot to increase student learning and student achievement. After all, if students are on task 10% more, that means they are learning 10% more.

Opportunities to Respond

Another powerful way ICs can empower teachers to increase time on task is to guide them to increase the number of opportunities students have to respond or react to whatever learning activity is taking place in the classroom. Simply put, when learning is back and forth, students are more often on task; when learning is one directional, teachers giving lessons with little response, students frequently end up being off task. "Opportunities to respond" are ways that students might be prompted to react to any learning

Form 7.1   Classroom Academic Engagement Form

Classroom ID: _____   Date: _____

Observer: _____

Beginning Time: _____

(+) indicates engaged

(0) indicated not engaged

1	2	3	4	5	6	7	8	9	10	11	12
13	14	15	16	17	18	19	20	21	22	23	24
25	26	27	28	29	30	31	32	33	34	35	36
37	38	39	40	41	42	43	44	45	46	47	48
49	50	51	52	53	54	55	56	57	58	59	60

Comments: _____

_____

_____

_____

_____

_____

_____

_____

SOURCE: Developed by W. Reinke, 2005; reprinted with permission.

activity in which they are involved. During teacher-directed instruction, for example, students' opportunities to respond might include questions from the teacher; prompts to turn to another student to share an idea; prompts to use a whiteboard to write answers or questions or to work out problems; writing answers, ideas, or thoughts in a learning journal; or any of a myriad of other prompts to respond. Opportunities to respond should be part of all learning activities. Thus, during group or cooperative learning, students can also be involved in activities that prompt them to respond in multiple ways.

ICs can easily gather data on opportunities to respond. All it takes is to keep a tally of each opportunity to respond provided for students during a set period of time. Then, the coach should calculate the number of opportunities to respond per minute. Usually, it is easiest to record opportunities to respond during teacher's direct instruction.

Creating Respect

I think Maslow had it right. We have a basic human need for respect. And although I'm a coach, I'm a teacher first, and if I am not respectful in every one of my relationships, then no matter what rules or classroom management techniques I have, students aren't going to respond to me. If students don't feel respected by you, they are really not going to pay too much attention to whatever you want to teach them. They're always going to have their guard up, and they should if they don't feel safe.

As a coach, one of the first things I do is I help teachers use Talking Together, which is a series of lessons that talk about creating respect in a learning community, in the classroom. I help teachers do that first lesson about community, and one of the first things kids come up with about a good community is safety. So then we just flip it around and talk about emotional safety in the classroom. If students are not emotionally safe, they are not going to contribute, not going to say what they really think, not going to participate. When I help teachers start by talking about community and safety, it really sets a tone for what is acceptable and unacceptable behavior. Then the teacher can guide the students to talk about what rules they need in order to interact appropriately in a learning community.

I've seen it completely change a teacher's year. A lot of times in middle school, kids are testing social relationships, and one way they do that is by bullying or being disrespectful. In my first year as a coach, I worked with a teacher who couldn't get anything taught since the kids were so disrespectful—she had to constantly stop and take care of behavior. She was constantly putting out fires. We used Talking Together as a way to set group norms and get that clear. At the end of the year, she came up to me with her math book and said, "I finished the book. I wouldn't have gotten halfway through it if we hadn't done Talking Together."

Table 7.1   Behavior Coaching and Data Measures

Data to Be Gathered	Purpose
Time on task	Provides a reality check and progress measure of student engagement
Opportunities to respond	Provides a measure of a simple, powerful way to increase engagement
Ratios of interaction	Promotes a positive learning community and reinforces appropriate student behavior
Disruptions	Provides a reality check and progress measure of the effectiveness of the teacher's correction procedures

Content

A few years back, I had a week when I was particularly overwhelmed with demands on my time. Most people know the feeling—there was always one more thing to do. Each event in and of itself was worthwhile, and I had set up my schedule so that I could fit everything in, but my calendar was full to the brink. This balancing act came to a head in the middle of the week when I went to present at a conference in Wisconsin.

Early Wednesday evening, I found myself rushing to the airport to catch a plane. I knew that my travel arrangements called for me to catch a plane to Chicago and drive to the conference. I didn't have time to check my e-mails about my final destination or print off a map, but I was sure that once I got to Oshkosh, I'd find my way to the hotel without a problem.

On the plane, I hastily reviewed my notes and did some writing that had to be done that day. After arriving in Chicago, I quickly got a rental car and drove through the busy traffic until I got out on the highway and headed north. Eventually, about midnight, I found myself approaching Oshkosh. I've always felt that I have a sixth sense when it comes to directions, so when I saw a hotel on the outskirts of the city, I had a hunch that was my destination, and I turned off the freeway and swung right into the hotel parking lot.

Even though I trusted my special sixth sense had helped me find the conference location, I thought I'd better phone the hotel to make sure I was in the right place before I grabbed my bags and went up to the front desk. I was very disappointed to discover that I was indeed not at the right hotel. Not only that, I was in the wrong city! My presentation the next day was in Milwaukee, a town I had driven through more than two hours before. The Oshkosh presentation was scheduled for the day after.

Rushed for time, and trusting my hunches, I ended up two hours out of my way, actually wasting four hours since I had to turn around and drive back to Milwaukee that night before turning around to travel back to Oshkosh the following day. Too rushed to use a map or check my plans, I wasted a lot of time and found myself a long way away from where I really needed to be.

ICs inevitably work with teachers whose professional experiences are similar to my trip to Milwaukee, too rushed to plan out their instructional time. Teachers who feel the urgency to keep their students busy might be tempted to teach without a complete map of their content, or spend too much time on particular information, finding themselves rushing to get to where they need to be only to find that their class has arrived at the wrong destination. In some situations, the lack of a long-term plan for a class can mean that essential information is only superficially taught or missed completely. As one teacher, only half jokingly, once said, "If you're teaching the Pilgrims in May, you know you're in trouble."

Teachers frequently feel rushed; they face great pressure to accomplish numerous tasks, and they feel the weight of the moral imperative behind what they do when their students fall behind. Faced with such challenges, they may not know where to begin when it comes to developing their content knowledge and making decisions about what content to teach. Many teachers face additional challenges: they may be teaching a course or subject area for the first time, or be new to the profession of teaching. Challenges like these can make planning even more difficult—while also more important. Clearly, ICs can provide a very valuable service by helping teachers sort through, prioritize, plan, and differentiate the content they teach in their classes.

Resources and References

IC LaVonne Holmgren helps her teachers focus on the content that matters most through use of Content Enhancement, the example I will use primarily as an example in this section. Content Enhancement is the product of more than two decades of research (e.g., Bulgren & Lenz, 1996; Lenz & Deshler, 2004; Schumaker, Deshler, & McKnight, 1991). Content Enhancement Routines are sets of procedures teachers use to introduce bodies of content, to teach major concepts and vocabulary, and to help students remember information. ICs who help teachers deepen their knowledge can employ Content Enhancement Routines to (a) focus their courses on the most important information; (b) create course, unit, and lesson plans for instruction; (c) identify and explain foundational structures for content to be taught in a course; and (d) identify and explain essential concepts that are foundational for a course.

Coaches could use other resources to focus on enhancing teachers' understanding of the content they teach. Grant Wiggins & Jay McTighe's *Understanding by Design* (2nd ed., 2005), mentioned throughout this chapter, provides ICs and collaborating teachers with useful guidelines for what they refer to as "backward design," a curriculum planning procedure that prompts coaches and teachers to (a) identify the most important information students will learn (enduring understanding), (b) develop essential questions, (c) describe assessment evidence, and (d) develop a learning plan. Carol Ann Tomlinson and Jay McTighe's *Integrating Differentiated Instruction and Understanding by Design: Connecting Content and Kids* (2006), as its title suggests, integrates understanding by design, "predominantly . . . a curriculum design model" (p. 2), with differentiated instruction, "predominantly . . . an instructional design model" (p. 3). Heidi Hayes Jacobs's publications related to curriculum mapping, especially *Mapping the Big Picture: Integrating Curriculum and Assessment K–12* (1997) and *Getting Results With Curriculum Mapping* (2004), though focused on curriculum mapping that takes place at the department, school, or district level, provide many useful suggestions for developing essential questions, content to be covered, skills to be taught, and assessment to be employed.

CONTENT COACHING

When IC LaVonne Holmgren sits down to collaborate with teachers on their content, she likely will not be an expert in every subject matter taught by her collaborating teachers. For that reason, coaches like LaVonne need proven planning and teaching tools that, by design, compel teachers to make smart decisions about what content they will teach. When discussing content, LaVonne addresses four major aspects of curriculum design: (a) developing essential questions; (b) mapping content; (c) identifying and teaching content relationship structures; and (d) identifying, defining, and teaching concepts. Each of these is described in the section below.

Developing Essential Questions

One important support LaVonne Holmgren provides is to help teachers use essential questions to align their lesson plans with state standards. "In Kansas," she reports, "we are very much mandated to follow the curriculum standards for the course content that the state has established at the Board of Education." One way in which LaVonne has supported teachers so that they can accomplish this goal is that she has helped them write critical questions for their courses. "What I've helped teachers do this year is to actually take their state's standards and write key questions for their units."

Wiggins and McTighe, in their book *Understanding by Design* (2005), stress the importance and benefits of developing essential questions:

> The best questions point to and highlight the big ideas. They serve as doorways through which learners explore the key concepts, themes, theories, issues and problems that reside within the content, perhaps as yet unseen: it is through the process of actively "interrogating" the content through provocative questions that students deepen their understanding. (p. 106)

"The best questions," Wiggins and McTighe say, "push us to the heart—the essence" (p. 107). In many ways, enduring questions are a way teachers outline the intellectual legacy that a teacher leaves with a student. When composing critical questions, teachers and coaches might be wise to simply ask themselves, what is the legacy I want to leave with my students? Fifteen years from now, if I bump into a student during a vacation at Disneyworld, what do I want him to remember that I taught him?

To assist teachers in developing essential questions for courses, units, and lessons, LaVonne utilizes scientifically proven routines that have been created to organize courses (Lenz, Schumaker, Deshler, & Bulgren, 1998, *The Course Organizer Routine*), units (Lenz, Bulgren, Schumaker, Deshler, & Boudah, 1994, *The Unit Organizer Routine*), and lessons (Lenz, Marrs, Schumaker, & Deshler, 1993, *The Lesson Organizer Routine*). In *Teaching Content to All: Inclusive Practice in Middle and High Schools*, Keith Lenz, along with coauthors Bulgren, Kissam, and Taymans (2004), makes several excellent suggestions about writing effective questions. I have modified Keith's suggestions slightly and put them into a checklist (see Table 7.2) for use by ICs who are collaborating with teachers to develop effective questions.

Mapping Content

Once critical questions have been identified, LaVonne collaborates with teachers to develop a map that describes the most important content to be taught in a course, unit, or lesson, similar to the map on the Unit Organizer included below. The map is a word web that depicts and connects all the information to be learned in a course, unit, or lesson. While the vertical organization of the web is hierarchical, placing the big ideas above supplementary ideas, the horizontal organization is chronological, showing the sequence in which the content will be taught. The web provides students with a map for the content they will be studying, and provides teachers and coaches with an overview of the content to be taught so that they can make decisions about where to use inclusive teaching practices or where to differentiate instruction.

Keith Lenz et al.'s *Course Organizer* (1998), *Unit Organizer* (1994), and *Lesson Organizer* (1993) incorporate both content webs (referred to as *maps*) and critical questions. Unit Organizers like the one included below can be employed by an IC and teacher to help the teacher identify "enduring

Table 7.2 Critical Questions Checklist

Questions About Critical Questions	Yes or No?
Are the questions written in a form that requires an extended verbal explanation?	
Have I written "how" or "why" questions rather than objectives or commands?	
Do the questions identify ways in which students should understand the information to be learned?	
Do the questions communicate how students should learn the content?	
Do the questions help students think not only about the content but also about how the content is meaningful or important?	
Do the questions prompt students to relate learning to their lives or other learning?	
Do the questions help students organize information to be learned?	
Do the questions include expectations for learning how to use the content as well as what content to learn?	
Do the questions help students identify the critical content structures, concepts, or ideas to be learned?	
Have I limited my number of questions to 10 or fewer?	

SOURCE: Keith Lenz.

understanding," write critical questions, map out the unit content, include a schedule for content, and record the content structures. Having a device such as a Unit Organizer also helps both the IC and the teacher focus and document their conversations about content. Additionally, once completed, the Unit Organizer can be shared with students over the course of a unit so that they have an overview of the content to be covered, a place to record important information as they learn it (the expanded organizer included), and a brief study guide to use to check and solidify their understanding and prepare for evaluations.

LaVonne Holmgren uses Content Enhancement Routines to help her collaborating teachers clarify exactly what content they will teach in a course, unit, or lesson. "Content Enhancement gets the teacher, first of all, very clear on the knowledge and metacognitive processes that students need to be able to do in order to be successful. After developing a Unit Organizer, for

Figure 7.1 Unit Organizer

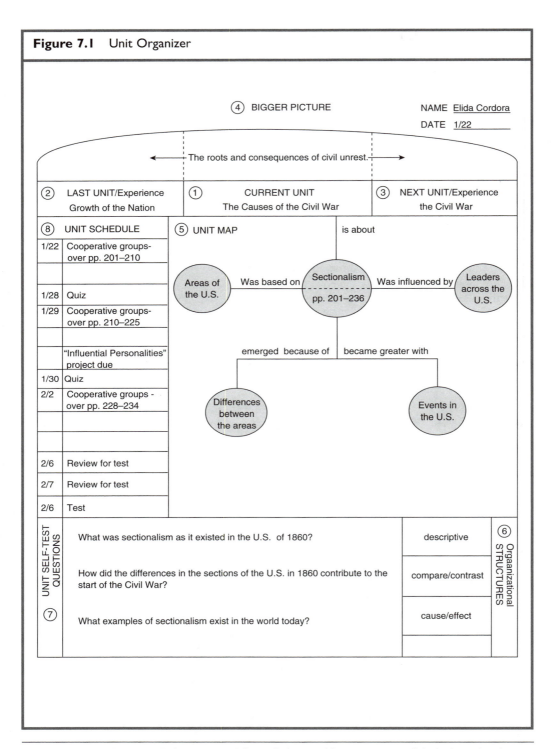

SOURCE: From Lenz, B. K., Bulgren, J. A., Schumaker, J., Deshler, D. D., & Boudah, D. (1994), *The Unit Organizer Routine.*

Figure 7.2 Expanded Unit Organizer

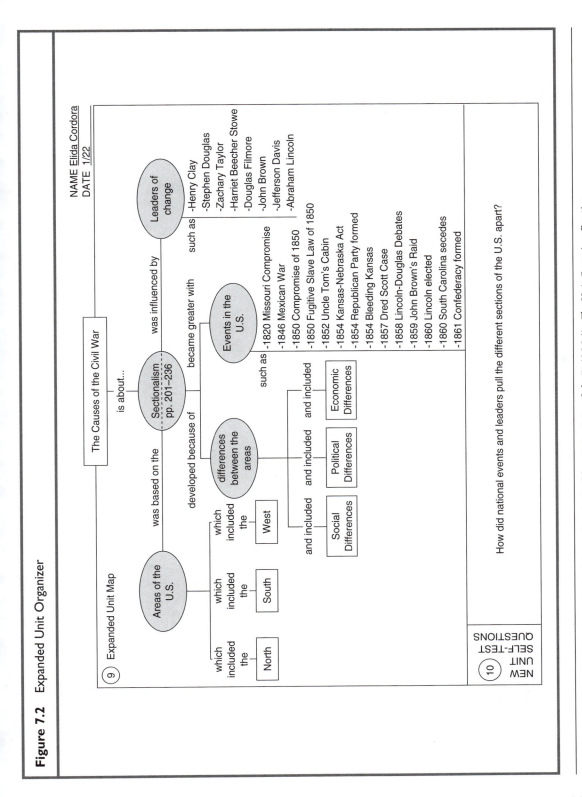

SOURCE: From Lenz, B. K., Bulgren, J. A., Schumaker, J., Deshler, D. D., & Boudah, D. (1994), *The Unit Organizer Routine.*

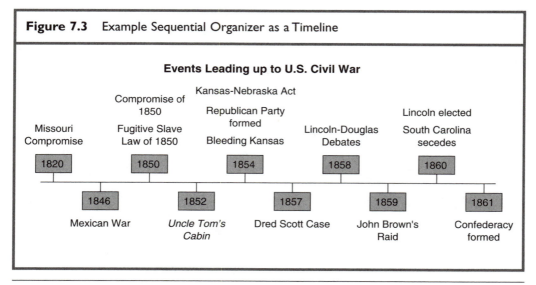

Figure 7.3   Example Sequential Organizer as a Timeline

Events Leading up to U.S. Civil War

SOURCE: Keith Lenz.

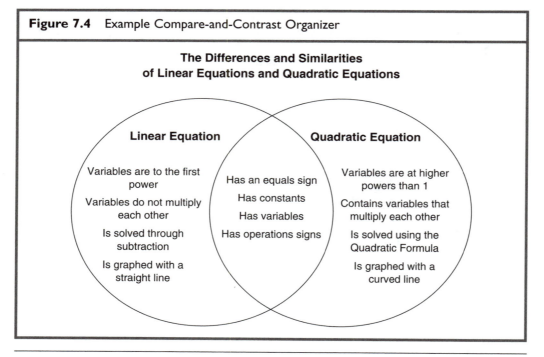

Figure 7.4   Example Compare-and-Contrast Organizer

The Differences and Similarities
of Linear Equations and Quadratic Equations

SOURCE: Keith Lenz.

example, teachers have a very clear perspective going into the unit on what they're going to teach, how they're going to move students to success."

Developing content maps has another important benefit. When teachers are able to see an entire unit or course laid out visually, they are better able

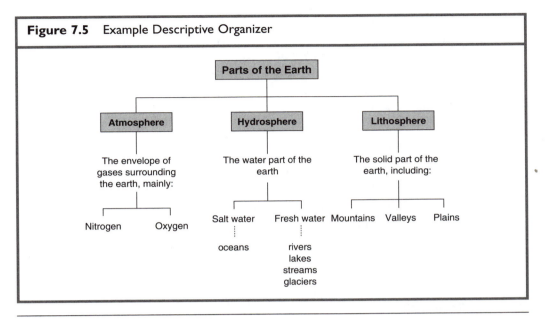

Figure 7.5 Example Descriptive Organizer

SOURCE: From Scanlon, D., Deshler, D. D., Schumaker, J. B. (2004). *The Order Routine.*

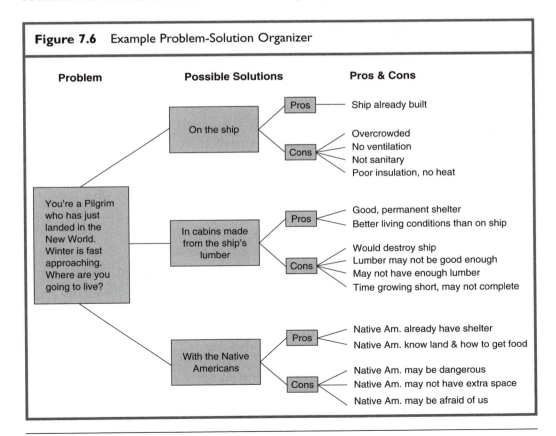

Figure 7.6 Example Problem-Solution Organizer

SOURCE: From Scanlon, D., Deshler, D. D., Schumaker, J. B. (2004). *The Order Routine.*

to make decisions about how to differentiate instruction so that they can reach more students. As LaVonne says, "When teachers see the unit laid out in front of them, they can better choose activities that zone in on how to get students to learn that knowledge." Furthermore, the Unit Organizer helps students. "The students really like seeing right on their Unit Organizer, the first day, what will be expected of them at the end of the unit."

Content Structures

Another way that LaVonne helps teachers deepen their understanding of content is by sharing the Order Routine (Scanlon, Deshler, & Schumaker, 2004), another Content Enhancement Routine designed to help teachers recognize and teach the organizational structures that underlie the content they are learning. Content structures are the patterns that reveal how various parts of the content relate to other parts of the content. Thus, for example, in the Civil War Unit Organizer above, the information related to events follows a chronological pattern, whereas the information students would learn and discover related to comparing the North, South, and West would be organized according to comparison and contrast.

By collaborating with teachers to identify the key content structures that are embedded in the content their students will be learning, ICs can help teachers gain a deeper understanding of what they teach. Once teachers recognize these structures, they can teach students to identify and recognize them in the content. When students are able to recognize these patterns, they will be better able to organize, remember, and apply content. In the same way that understanding text structures can help students comprehend texts, understanding content structures can help students better comprehend content.

David Scanlon, the author of *The Order Routine* (Scanlon, Deshler, & Schumaker, 2004), identifies four content structures as most important for comprehending content: sequential, compare and contrast, descriptive, and problem-solution. Examples of diagrams for each of the structures are included below.

Identifying, Defining, and Teaching Concepts

If you are a parent, then you know the importance of having a shared understanding of the meaning of concepts. Many an argument between a parent and a child has arisen because the two had different understandings of a concept. Let me give you an example using a concept that is near and dear to the heart of most parents: clean. Just about any parent has at one time or another, sometimes daily or even hourly, it seems, used this concept with his or her children—as in "make sure the dishes are clean, your clothes are clean, your room is clean, your language is clean." When parent and child have the same understanding of the concept, then communication can proceed smoothly. Unfortunately, when parent and child have different understandings of the concept, conflicts can arise.

I had this problem with my son Ben when he was 12 years old, after I explained that he had to clean his room, or he would not be able to go a movie that night. Just before it was time for Ben to go to the movies, he told me his room was clean, and I, of course, went to check. Ben had indeed spent some time working on the room but what he had done was pile up all of his dirty and clean clothes, garbage, half-eaten food products, dirty dishes, and other unsavory items in a corner of his room, and covered them with one of the sheets from his bed. True enough, the room was tidier, but it was far from clean. In fact, my guess was that it would only take a day or two before a science project would spontaneously break out in the pile under Ben's sheet.

"Ben," I said, "that's not clean; that's disgusting! You're not going anywhere until you clean up that mess." I left Ben to his room, where he was, no doubt, furious that he wouldn't be able to go to the movie. A dark cloud settled on our family that night, and in a stroke of inspiration, I decided I'd better check with Ben. What I learned in an ensuing conversation was that Ben was not the least bit interested in skipping work. In his 12-year-old mind, he really thought that his room was clean. Ben's concept of clean was clearly different from mine. Once we had a shared understanding of the concept, we were able to communicate much better. The fault in this conflict wasn't really with Ben, the fault was with me: I had failed to adequately explain the concept, which ended up causing problems.

When teachers and students do not have a shared understanding of concepts, it can cause problems in the classroom. For example, if students have an imprecise understanding of literary terms, they may struggle, not enjoying or appreciating a literary work. Interpreting a short story, for example, is easier for readers who understand the meaning of concepts such as symbol, metaphor, theme, and characterization. A student who has a full understanding of those concepts can begin to recognize those literary features and thus deepen his or her experience of literature. If a reader doesn't understand those concepts, however, reading a great work of art may be no more rewarding that filling in boxes on a work sheet. Concepts are windows that can open up any discipline.

Jan Bulgren, who has studied concepts for more than a decade, defines a concept for me as "a category or class into which events, ideas, or subjects can be grouped." Jan explained that "all members of the same concept class must possess all of a set of critical characteristics." The online encyclopedia *Wikipedia* on January 27, 2006, offered a similar definition: "A concept is an abstract, universal idea, notion, or entity that serves to designate a category or class of entities, events, or relations."

To assist teachers in defining and teaching students' concepts, Jan has developed the Concept Mastery Routine (Bulgren, Deshler, & Schumaker, 1993). Built around a device such as the one included below, this routine serves at least two purposes. First, it guides teachers to develop precise, correct, and teachable concept definitions. Teachers who plan to use this device must think carefully about the meaning of the concept they plan to teach, and identify the *always*, *sometimes*, and *never present* characteristics. In the device included below, for example, a teacher read reference documents and thought carefully before identifying that the always present characteristics in the concept of democracy are that leaders are accountable by election, citizens have civil rights, individuals can oppose the government, and there is a statement of civil and political rights.

After developing concept diagrams, teachers use them to ensure that students master concepts. Starting with a blank diagram, a teacher co-constructs the diagram with students to ensure that they master the concept. Then, the teacher asks the students to think through several potential examples and nonexamples to ensure that they have a deep and solid knowledge of the concept.

Concepts are important for several reasons. First, concepts often represent foundational knowledge that students need to know in order to master content. For example, students who do not understand the concepts of subject and verb are likely unable to learn other grammatical terms and concepts, such as subject-verb agreement, sentence structure, and punctuation, simply because understanding those concepts requires an understanding of subjects and verbs.

Second, concepts are important because they can open students up to entirely new ways of interpreting, understanding, and knowing. For example, when a student learns the concept of supply and demand in a business math course, she can begin to see the world from a new perspective. Similarly, when students learn the concept culture in a social studies class, or congruence in geometry, they can begin to understand information and relationships in their courses in much more meaningful and interesting ways.

Direct Instruction

If ICs are working with teachers who have a deep understanding of their content and who manage classroom behavior effectively, they can shift their focus to collaboratively exploring how to enhance instruction so that more students master content. Indeed, some instructional coaching programs focus only on this aspect of coaching. In our experience over the past 10 years, however, coaching that ignores other aspects of the Big Four may miss opportunities to strengthen teachers' practices.

Resources and References

I use several sources as references for this section, including Lenz, Alley, and Schumaker's (1987) research on Advance Organizers, Anita Archer's ideas regarding modeling in the classroom ("I Do It, We Do It, You Do It"), Benjamin Bloom's *Taxonomy of Educational Objectives* (Bloom, Englehart, Furst, Hill, & Krathwohl, 1956), and Joyce Rademacher's *Quality Assignment Routine* (Rademacher, Deshler, Schumaker, & Lenz, 1998).

Figure 7.7 Concept Diagram

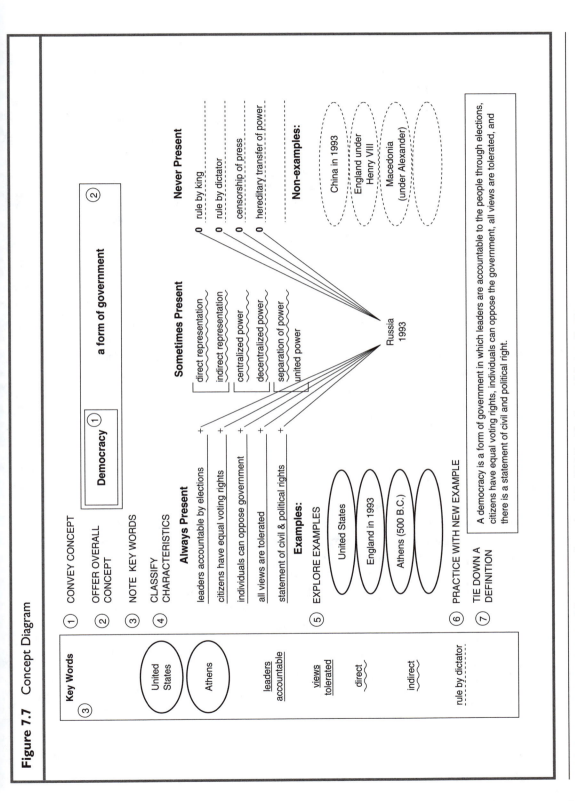

SOURCE: From Bulgren, J. A., Deshler, D. D., Schumaker, J. B. (1993). *The Concept Mastery Routine.*

> There are numerous other resources coaches might use to enhance teachers' instructional practices. Madeline Hunter's *Mastery Teaching: Increasing Instructional Effectiveness in Elementary, Secondary Schools, and Colleges and Universities* (1982) has been so influential that a friend of mine refers to her, only half-facetiously, as the woman who invented teaching. Hunter's material, although now somewhat dated, still remains a resource that coaches can use to teach or reinforce such teaching practices as writing objectives, beginning a lesson with an anticipatory set, modeling, checking for understanding, and using guided practice. Charlotte Danielson's *Enhancing Professional Practice: Framework for Teaching* (1996) is also used by ICs as a resource for guiding teachers to improve their teaching in the four broad domains of Danielson's framework: (a) planning and preparation, (b) the classroom environment, (c) components of instruction, and (d) professional responsibilities.

COACHING INSTRUCTION

When she coaches teachers on instruction, LaVonne Holmgren focuses on a few teaching practices that are particularly important for teaching for understanding, specifically (a) advance and post organizers, (b) modeling, (c) high-level questioning, and (d) quality assignments. Each of these is described below.

Advance and Post Organizers

ICs guide teachers to use advance organizers for a simple reason: advance organizers set up learning activities effectively for students, so students will get more out of them. Specifically, advance organizers provide students with a context for learning, guide students to review prior knowledge, prepare students for activities, and increase students' enthusiasm for learning. Advance organizers are especially helpful for students who traditionally struggle to master content (Lenz, Alley, & Schumaker, 1987).

ICs should ensure that effective advance organizers have at least four components: First, the teacher provides a brief overview of the lesson, describing the various learning activities students will be experiencing. This overview should take less than a minute. Second, the teacher explains what students will be doing during the activities. Third, the teacher reviews content that students must keep in mind as they take part in the day's learning and previews the new content students will be learning. On some occasions teachers may briefly reteach content students do not have but that they need in order to master the new learning. Fourth, the teacher explains why the learning activity is important and communicates rationales for why students are doing the learning activities. An effective advance organizer shouldn't take more than two or three minutes to conduct, but it should significantly increase what students get out of their learning.

In some classrooms, the last three minutes of a class can have next to no impact on student learning as students restlessly wait for the end of the period. This is a terrible waste of instructional time and a valuable teaching opportunity. Psychologists tell us that the two most powerful impressions are made on our memory at the start and the end of an experience, the so-called primacy and recency effects. It follows, then, that those last three minutes are some of the most important parts of a day's instruction, and teachers can help their students get the most out of a class by using post organizers to sum up the day's activities.

Like advance organizers, effective post organizers consist of four components. First, the teacher asks students questions that allow them to summarize and clarify key learning. Second, the teacher helps students organize and synthesize the key learning. Third, the teacher provides an opportunity for students to ask any questions they have about what they have learned. Fourth, the teacher prepares students for the next day's lesson, explaining how what they have learned is connected to what will be coming in the future, and getting students excited about the learning they will be doing next.

I taught myself how to use advance organizers when I taught at Humber College in Toronto, Ontario. At the start of my class, I would explain the four parts of advance and post organizers, prompting my students to write notes about each of the parts. Then, I told my students that they should watch each class very carefully for each part of the advance and post organizers because if I skipped any part of them, I would put a dollar into a pot to buy treats for an end-of-the-course celebration. In this way, I ensured that my students watched carefully for each component of the advance and post organizer (which they certainly did), and I got immediate feedback every day on how effective I had been. I must admit that having to put a dollar away every time I skipped an organizer quickly sharpened my ability to use all components of advance and post organizers.

A less expensive way for teachers to master this teaching practice is to work with an IC. IC LaVonne Holmgren considers advance organizers to be an important tool she can share with her teachers. "Giving an advance organizer sets the tone; it just gives students a mind-set up front to construct meaning as we go through the lesson. If I do that, my students are a lot more willing to go through the lesson and follow through with it . . . they know that they can count on me."

Modeling

When LaVonne Holmgren works with teachers, she teaches them a simple, yet powerful way to learn how to model during teaching—"I Do It, We Do It, You Do It"—an approach to instruction I first learned from Dr. Anita Archer. "I Do It, We Do It, You Do It" is a simple way of helping teachers structure instruction so that students see a model, get a chance to test their knowledge, and then have a chance to practice their new knowledge. This instructional approach is especially powerful when teachers are teaching students how to perform tasks, skills, or strategies such as completing a mathematics calculation, breaking up a big word, or linking new information to known information.

During the "I Do It" part of instruction, teachers demonstrate exactly how to complete a task, skill, or strategy. For example, during the "I Do It" phase, a math teacher demonstrating how to perform a calculation carefully walks through all steps of the calculation, showing students exactly how she would "do it." During this phase of instruction, teachers are very explicit about all aspects of what they are doing. Teachers show, not tell, and this usually means that teachers "think out loud" while they are demonstrating— indeed, this aspect of instruction is frequently referred to as a "think aloud." What matters during the "I Do It" is that teachers are deliberate enough so that students can follow along with the model. Teachers should demonstrate how to problem solve, how to make metacognitive decisions and choices, and how to maintain focus leading to a successful outcome. Inexperienced teachers sometimes rush through this phase of instruction and that can make it difficult for their students to follow the model. Masterful teachers almost put on a kind of performance during the "I Do It" so that students get a clear picture of how to act and think when they "do it."

During the "We Do It" phase of instruction, the teacher and student interact, with the teacher guiding students as they learn how to complete a task, skill, or strategy. A teacher instructing students in how to use visual images to increase reading comprehension, for example, might ask various students to describe possible images for the setting and characters in a story. During the "We Do It" phase, teachers must be careful to challenge and support students while at the same time clarifying their understanding. Thus, teachers should choose questions carefully. If questions are difficult, they'll confuse rather than clarify, but if questions are too easy, they'll bore students. The goal of this phase of instruction is for teachers to practice with the students until the teacher feels students are ready to practice independently.

During the "You Do It" phase of instruction, students practice on their own. If students are learning how to write topic sentences, for example, they would write topic sentences. During this phase, teachers provide students with an opportunity to practice whatever it is they're learning, and the teacher circulates around the room to provide individual support to students who are momentarily struggling. After students complete their practice attempts, teachers can take up the practice attempts with students, gather the attempts, score all of them or a sample of them, and use them for formative assessments of student progress, or have students peer-review each other's work.

Ed Ellis, at the University of Alabama, has an interesting twist on "I Do It, We Do It, You Do It." Before students start independent practice—"You Do It," Ed has students practice with a partner. Ed, taking full advantage of his southern dialect, refers to this phase as "Ya'll Do It." Having students do the "Ya'll Do It" provides just one more opportunity for them to deepen their understanding before they have the opportunity to demonstrate mastery of their newly developed skills.

LaVonne Holmgren relates the "I Do It, We Do It, You Do It" phases of instruction to her personal experience learning to play the piano. For LaVonne, modeling, guided practice, and independent practice are important because they help students get very clear on whatever it is they are learning.

When I practiced piano, my music teacher said, "Use the right fingers, use the right fingers, use the right fingers!' However, being a kid, I thought, 'I really don't need to do that.' Well, after about three years I couldn't go any further, and I had to unlearn my bad habits and then learn to use the correct fingering after all. If we don't do enough of the "We Do It," the students will practice wrong. By the time that the teacher figures that out, a whole lot of unlearning has to be done. A lot of times teachers want to do a quick model and then get to the "You do it," but I think the "We Do It" step is a really critical one.

High-Level Questions

In 2005, we conducted a study of the kinds of questions teachers ask during instruction in typical classrooms. Eight ICs went into classrooms and observed teachers, writing down each question they wrote. In total, we gathered more than 1,000 questions. When we categorized those questions, using the *Taxonomy of Educational Objectives* developed by Benjamin Bloom and his colleagues (1956), we found that more that 75% of the questions teachers asked were the lowest-level, knowledge-related questions. These are troubling data. If teachers do not ask higher-level questions that prompt students to apply or synthesize their new knowledge, they cannot be sure that their students are fully internalizing what they are learning.

Figure 7.8 Bloom's Taxonomy of Educational Objectives

1. Knowledge	4. Analysis
2. Comprehension	5. Synthesis
3. Application	6. Evaluation

To support teachers who want to ask more high-level questions (HLQs), we used Bloom's taxonomy as a starting point for conversations with teachers about their questions. Specifically, ICs helped teachers to understand and use Bloom's taxonomy as a tool for developing and asking questions.

Bloom and his colleagues, after much deliberation, identified six levels of educational objectives (1956):

Knowledge "involves the recall of specifics and universals, the recall of methods and processes, or the recall of a pattern, structure, or setting" (p. 201).

Comprehension "represents the lowest level of understanding . . . a type of understanding . . . such that the individual knows what is being communicated" (p. 204).

Application refers to "the use of abstractions in particular and concrete situations" (p. 205).

Analysis is "the breakdown of communication into its constituent elements or parts . . . [so] that the relative hierarchy of ideas is made clear and/or the relations between the ideas are made explicit" (p. 205).

Synthesis refers to "the putting together of elements or parts so as to form a whole."

Finally, *evaluation* is "judgments about the value of materials and methods for given purposes" (p. 206).

ICs can use the taxonomy (or variations on the taxonomy) in simple, but powerful ways. First, they can observe teachers and note each question they hear them ask during their classes. A sample of the observation form we have used to coach teachers to develop HLQs is included. Then, ICs can explain the six levels of the taxonomy, and together with the teacher, they can identify the level of all of the questions asked during the class. In most cases at the beginning, most questions are knowledge or comprehension questions. Following this, the coach and teacher can write several higher-level questions to be used in a future lesson, during which the IC observes again to record the level of questions. The teacher and IC continued to collaborate in this way until the teacher is satisfied with the number of HLQs being asked in the class.

Quality Assignments

One powerful way that ICs can also enhance the impact of instruction is by improving the quality of the activities students experience. LaVonne Holmgren uses Joyce Rademacher's *Quality Assignment Routine* (Rademacher et al., 1998) to help teachers plan assignments that are interesting, engaging, and meaningful. Rademacher suggests using the following components when developing quality assignments (summarized in the acronym *PLAN*).

First, teachers and coaches need to *plan* the assignment with care to ensure that they reflect on and explain the purpose, guidelines, and rationales

Form 7.2   Question Chart

Question	Level

1. Knowledge	2. Comprehension	3. Application
4. Analysis	5. Synthesis	6. Evaluation

for the assignment they will be sharing with students. Second, ICs and teachers need to *link* the assignment to student needs, considering what modifications, accommodations, and differentiations to include. Rademacher suggests that teachers use the HALO effect while addressing student needs, referring to the importance of considering the needs of *h*igh-achieving, *a*verage-achieving, *l*ow-achieving, and *o*ther students (English-language learners, students with physical disabilities, and so on). ICs and teachers should also consider the options for format, content, location, resources, and the obstacles that might interfere with students' performing a given task successfully. Third, ICs and teachers need to *arrange* clear directions, which means they must clearly articulate the steps students have to take and the resources students need in order to complete the assignment, the grading criteria, and the due date for the assignment. Finally, ICs and teachers should *note* when they will evaluate the effectiveness of the assignment and reflect on what changes they can make to improve the assignment.

Figure 7.9   Creating Quality Assignments

Plan the purpose of the assignment.	Arrange clear student directions.
Link assignments to student needs.	Note evaluation date and results.

Formative Assessment

> *You can't tell me that kids don't want to learn. Some times they don't want to learn the things that adults say they should, . . . but once they begin to experience success that target becomes a whole lot more attractive. . . . We've got to find a way to turn them on to the possibility of their own success.*

—Richard Stiggins (personal communication)

I learned the power of formative assessment one Christmas holiday. Like many parents, I spent a fair bit of the holiday watching my children play the video games they received for Christmas. They loved their games, and they were determined to play, it seemed to me, all hours of the day or night. Every time I checked the TV room, children were wrapped up in a video hockey game or in moving Super Mario to another level.

As I watched everyone playing, I couldn't help but notice something interesting: the kids were learning. Each time they played, their skills improved, they learned new information, and they were able to play better and go further. What they were learning was not particularly useful, perhaps, but they were improving their skills at a ridiculously rapid pace. If only, I thought, students could embrace their learning in school with the same enthusiasm they show for video games.

Not too long after that holiday, I gained some insight into why children are so engaged by video games when Mihaly Csikszentmihalyi, the author of *Flow: The Psychology of Optimal Experience* (1990), came to the Center for Research on Learning to meet with our staff to discuss student learning. During his visit, Dr. Csikszentmihalyi explained that a key to happiness is engagement. When we are fully engaged in an activity, we are happier. Furthermore, he explained, engaging activities, which he refers to as *flow experiences*, usually include the same structural elements. Among other things, flow experiences provide the right kind of challenge for our personal experience. That is, flow experiences are not so difficult that they frustrate us or so easy that they bore us. Add to that, Csikszentmihalyi explained, flow experiences are goal-directed activities for which we receive extensive feedback on how close we are to our goal. If we enjoy playing golf or a video game, for example, we likely enjoy it because we experience the right kind of challenge for our skill level and because the game provides immediate feedback on how we are progressing.

What Csikszentmihalyi says about happiness has also been said by Richard Stiggins about the role of assessment in student motivation. Dr. Stiggins is one of the nation's leading experts on formative assessment and the author of numerous books and articles about formative assessment, including the classic text *Classroom Assessment for Student Learning* (Stiggins, Arter, Chappuis, & Chappuis, 2004). In an interview I conducted with Dr. Stiggins at the ETS Assessment Training Institute in Portland, Oregon, he echoed Dr. Csikszentmihalyi:

> When the feedback suggests to me that I'm not making it, leading me to an inference that I'm incapable of making it, then I give up in hopelessness and I stop trying . . . I've got to get them [students] to somehow believe that effort is of value, that there is some relationship between effort and their level of success. If I can't get them to believe that, then I can't help them.

When ICs introduce teachers to formative assessment, they begin the exciting work of empowering teachers to help their students see the relationship between effort and success—in other words, to help teachers help their students have hope.

Resources and References

Many of the ideas in this section were influenced by Dr. Stiggins's *Classroom Assessment for Student Learning* (2004). More information about the Assessment Training Institute, which he directs, is included at the end of this chapter in the Going Deeper section. Other resources coaches might consider reviewing include Black, Harrison, Lee, Marshall, and Wiliam's *Assessment for Learning: Putting It Into Practice* (2003), which provides an overview of the meta-analysis the authors conducted on assessment for learning, a summary of the assessment principles derived from that research, and a description of how they "went about putting ideas into practice with six schools and the forty-eight teachers of English, mathematics, and science" (p. 4). James H. McMillan's *Essential Assessment Concepts for Teachers and Administrators* (2001), as its title indicates, offers accessible definitions for concepts such as validity, reliability, and fairness, as well as discussions of how teaching, learning, and assessment are integrated, and suggestions for how to understand and use numerical data and how to interpret standardized assessments.

INSTRUCTIONAL COACHING AND FORMATIVE ASSESSMENT

IC LaVonne Holmgren employs six different strategies to help teachers begin to develop "assessment literacy." Those strategies—(a) identifying the type of assessment; (b) developing course maps, unit maps, and essential questions; (c) answering essential questions; (d) developing quality assessments; (e) providing feedback; and (f) involving students—are described in this section.

Figure 7.10   Formative Assessment

Identify the type of assessment.	Develop quality assessments.
Develop course and unit maps and questions.	Provide feedback.
	Involve students.
Answer essential questions.	

What are the different types of assessment? The starting point for ICs is to identify what kind of assessment a teacher has to create. Assessment usually takes one of three forms:

1. Diagnostic

2. Formative

3. Summative

Jay McTighe and Ken O'Connor (2006) distinguished between these forms of assessment in a recent article in *Education Leadership*. Diagnostic assessments, they explain, "typically precede instruction. Teachers use them to check students' prior knowledge and skill levels, identify student misconceptions, profile learners' interests, and reveal learning style preferences. Diagnostic assessments provide information to assist teachers planning and guide differentiated instruction" (p. 11). Formative assessments "occur concurrently with instruction. These ongoing assessments provide specific feedback to teachers and students for the purpose of guiding teaching to improve learning" (pp. 11–12). Finally, summative assessments "summarize what students have learned at the conclusion of an instructional segment. These assessments tend to be evaluative, and teachers typically encapsulate and report assessment results as a grade" (p. 11).

Developing Course and Unit Questions

ICs and teachers must develop a clear sense of what the class will be covering. ICs who have worked with teachers to develop Course and Unit

Organizers (described previously in this chapter) have, for all intents and purposes, completed this first task. The Course, Unit, and Lesson Organizers provide tools ICs can use to help teachers develop essential course, unit, and lesson questions; identify core concepts; map units; identify content relationships; and develop a detailed schedule of instruction.

The development of long-term course and unit plans, of course, is tightly integrated with the development of assignments (perhaps utilizing the Quality Assignment Routine (Rademacher et al., 1998) and formative and summative assessments. Indeed, it is a wise practice for a teacher to plan her instruction keeping the idea of the final and ongoing assessments in mind. Nothing is more frustrating for learners than to face a final assessment that bears little resemblance to the learning activities they completed as they moved toward the final assessment. Therefore, ICs and collaborating teachers must work together to ensure that learning activities prepare students for the final assessment, and that the final assessment effectively reflects the learning that took place in the school.

In the midst of mapping out a long-term plan for a course, the IC can assist teachers in the clarifying exactly what it is that students need to learn during the class. State and national standards provide a starting point for this, but standards in and of themselves may not be enough. In my conversation with Richard Stiggins, he explained that "what we need is to help people re-center away from the standards themselves and practicing old state assessments to the enabling proficiencies that underpin the standards and over time build things that bring kids up the scaffolding to a place where they are ready to demonstrate their mastery of those standards."

In looking at the standards, Tom Guskey suggests teachers reconsider the categories in the *Taxonomy of Educational Objectives* (Bloom, Englehart, et al., 1956). Guskey states that the "categories that teachers in a wide variety of subject areas find most useful" are knowledge of terms, knowledge of facts, knowledge of rules and principles, knowledge of processes and procedures, ability to make translations, ability to make applications, and skill in analyzing and synthesizing.

Stiggins identifies five categories for achievement targets: knowledge, reasoning, performance skills, product development capabilities, and dispositions. According to Stiggins, well-designed targets should be specific, should be clearly stated, should center on what's truly important, and should fit into the broader context of a teacher's unit or course. When teachers have a clear understanding of learning targets, they can focus their lessons on the most important learning that should be taking place in class. When students have a clear understanding of learning targets from the beginning, when they come to see learning goals as their goals, they are more likely to be engaged and motivated in their classes. Effective unit questions should lead students to hit all of the targets identified in a course.

Creating Answers for Unit Questions

When the IC and teacher have identified all the unit questions for all the units, the complete set of questions should lead students to every important form of learning to be assessed. Thus, if a student can thoroughly and correctly answer each unit question, that student should receive an A in the course.

However, the questions don't help if they are not complete, comprehensive, and easy to use. ICs should guide teachers to write complete answers to all of the questions.

One way ICs and teachers can work through answers to unit questions is to use Jan Bulgren's *Question Exploration Routine* (Bulgren, Lenz, Deshler, & Schumaker, 2001). This Content Enhancement Routine is built around a device that guides teachers to break down and unpack unit questions. As the example Question Exploration Device below shows, the device has six sections or boxes. In the first box, the teacher writes the unit question. In the second box, the teacher notes and defines key vocabulary that students will need to understand in order to answer the question. In the third box, the teacher writes smaller questions that might lead students to the bigger understanding required to answer the questions. In the fourth box, the teacher writes a complete, concise answer to the question. In the fifth box, the teacher notes how the new knowledge can be applied to other learning experiences in the teacher's class. Finally, in the sixth box, the teacher notes how the new knowledge can be applied in other courses or applied to real-life experiences.

After completing the Question Exploration Device, teachers can use it with students in their classrooms to guide them through the construction of their own answers to unit questions. Teachers would start with a blank device and involve students in co-constructing an answer. Teachers should have completed a version of the device prior to sharing it with students, but should be open to new ideas, new knowledge that might be included on the device when it is rewritten with students.

Developing Appropriate, High-Quality Assessments

ICs can assist in the development of high-quality assessments by guiding teachers to create a complete picture of what it is that they wish to assess. This picture begins when teachers write complete answers to their unit questions. Answers should be written as brief, clear statements that capture each essential component. In some cases, completing a Question Exploration Device might provide all the information that a teacher needs. On other occasions, teachers might choose to write propositions, "clearly stated sentences that reflect important elements of the content and stipulate the kind of cognitive operation respondents must carry out" (Stiggins, et al., 2004, p. 133). LaVonne Holmgren uses a simple form, like the one included below, to guide teachers to record propositions and identify the methods they will use to assess student learning.

Providing Constructive Feedback

I learned about the negative power of feedback one day when my son Ben brought home an essay he had written while he was in middle school. If you are a parent and a teacher, you know how interesting it can be when your child

---

Figure 7.11   Question Exploration Guide

---

① What is the critical question?
   Why is conflict important to the plot in a narrative?

---

② What are the key terms and explanations?

Conflict?	A struggle between people or within a person
Plot?	Connected events in a narrative
Narrative?	A story with an introduction, high point, and resolution
Resolution?	How the conflict is ended

---

③ What are the supporting questions and answers?

Who has a conflict?	A main idea has a conflict.
Why is conflict important in the introduction?	It grabs the reader's interest in the main character's problem.
Why is it important at the high point?	The main character must make an important decision.
Why is it important in the resolution?	We see the solution and learn the author's message.

---

④ What is the overall idea answer?
   The conflict gets us interested to see the main character's decision about a problem and learn the author's message.

---

⑤ How can we use the main idea again?
   Select a narrative we've read, describe the conflict, and explain how the author uses conflict as described in the main idea.

---

⑥ Is there a main idea? Is there a real-world use?
   Select a real-life conflict shown on TV, or described in a newspaper or magazine. Explain how the storytellers have kept you involved in the conflict as described in the main idea and what, if any, message has been delivered.

SOURCE: Bulgren, J. A., Lenz, B. K., Deshler, D. D., Schumaker, J. B. (2001).

brings work home that he's done in school. This particular day, Ben brought home an essay he'd been asked to write about how "kindness unites us." I assumed that the teacher had chosen this topic to inspire and interest students, and I thought it was a great topic. However, Ben wasn't very excited about his essay, and when he showed me his paper, I understood why. It was covered in red, critical comments. I counted over 30 critical words on the first page, written in large, aggressive handwriting. There was not one positive word. After getting the paper back, Ben had completely lost interest in writing anything further on the topic.

The feedback that Ben's teacher gave him on his paper is pretty much the opposite of what good feedback should be. With so much negative feedback, Ben was de-motivated, and didn't know where to start. As classroom management expert Randy Sprick likes to say, "no one was ever motivated

Table 7.3   Proposition Form

Unit Question:		
Proposition #	Proposition	Assessment

by punishment," and this teacher's feedback certainly felt more like a punishment than a learning opportunity.

Feedback can have a positive or a negative impact on learning. Walberg (1984) ranked feedback third on a list of the 26 most effective instructional variables affecting student achievement. Unfortunately, teachers providing feedback often make one of two errors. First, like the teacher who graded Ben's paper, they provide too much feedback, especially too much negative feedback. Even if students are able to get beyond the negative psychological impact of so much criticism, they often struggle to process and act on too much specific detail. Other teachers err in the other direction by providing too many general comments and too little useful, specific information.

Educational researcher Frank Kline (Kline, Schumaker, & Deshler, 1991) found that feedback is most effective when teachers lay out the criteria explicitly before students begin to practice. Following this, feedback should be specific; should be provided as soon as possible; should identify one or two larger categories of error, rather than every single error made by a student; and should be mostly positive. Additionally, teachers should explain what students need to do to improve, and then check to make sure that students comprehend the feedback. Ben's teacher, for example, would have provided more effective feedback if he had explained exactly what the criteria were for the assignment, had made several positive comments about

Ben's efforts, had zoned in on one or more broad categories of error, and had ensured that Ben knew how to act on the feedback. Elaborated feedback of that sort can have a significant, positive impact on student learning.

Effective feedback does not need to take a great deal of time. ICs can show teachers how to use what I refer to as "feedback on the fly," quick feedback given in less than 30 seconds, to ensure that students are motivated and still on track. Feedback on the fly is a quick way to encourage students with authentic praise while also providing them with practical suggestions on how to get around roadblocks that might keep them from progressing.

Involving Students

ICs can also help teachers significantly increase the impact of formative assessments by guiding teachers to ensure that students are deeply involved in the assessment process, from the development of assessments and criteria to peer evaluation of products, peer feedback, and monitoring of progress. The more students are involved in assessment, the more meaningful it is for them.

ICs like LaVonne Holmgren can help teachers find many ways to involve students in assessment. For example, teachers can ask students to propose unit questions and involve students in creating propositions that answer the questions. Teachers might post unit questions around a room and then have students post answers right beneath the questions, just as students discover answers. Teachers can also involve students in developing grading criteria by sharing samples of products with students, asking students to identify the differences between high-quality and low-quality writing. By deeply involving students in developing grading criteria, teachers can make it much easier for students to understand and meet that criteria.

Students can also be involved in peer review and providing feedback. This can be a powerful way, when managed effectively, to create a culture of support in the classroom, while also increasing student "buy-in" and student engagement. Another way to involve students is to provide them with opportunities to monitor their progress toward their goals. The learning strategies developed for the Strategic Instruction Model all provide progress charts so that students can see precisely where they are on their journey toward mastering skills and strategies. Such progress monitoring may not be as much fun as a video game, but when students are able to frequently update their progress toward their goals, that experience can be highly motivating.

When ICs work with teachers on formative assessments, it is important that students know what the targets are that they are trying to hit and that they get very clear feedback, on high-quality assessments, on how well they are progressing toward their targets. Stiggins's suggestions (2004) to teachers regarding assessment nicely make this point:

> I urge that you specify clear expectations in your classroom. Do so in writing and publish them for all to see. Eliminate the mystery surrounding the meaning of success in your classroom by letting your

students see your vision. If they can see it, they can hit it. But if they cannot see it, their challenge turns into pin the tail on the donkey—blindfolded of course. (p. 83)

GOING DEEPER

Behavior

Randy Sprick and his colleagues at Safe and Civil Schools have developed several interventions for increasing positive behavior schoolwide and for improving classroom management and positive behavior. For more information, visit their Web site: www.safeandcivilschools.com. Additionally, Randy Sprick, Wendy Reinke, Tricia McKale, and I have coauthored *Coaching Classroom Management* (2007), which provides a comprehensive description of the activities ICs can employ to empower teachers to manage their classrooms effectively.

Content Knowledge

A series of twelve Content Enhancement Routines have been published to help teachers plan and teach more accessible classes. In addition to the Course, Unit, and Lesson Organizer planning routines and the Concept Mastery, Question Exploration, and Order Routines, all described in this chapter, there are routines that assist teachers in comparing concepts, guiding students through difficult texts, teaching vocabulary, and other essential teaching practices. More information may be found at www.kucrl.org. Additionally, Wiggins and McTighe's *Understanding by Design* (2nd ed., 2005) offers resources for teachers and ICs intent on ensuring that they identify and emphasize "enduring understanding." More information about understanding by design can be found at http://ubdexchange.org.

Direct Instruction

Since 1977, educational researchers at the Center for Research on Learning at the University of Kansas have been conducting research on effective instructional practices. Many of the direct instruction effective practices described in this chapter are embedded in the Learning Strategies Curriculum studied and published by the center. More information on the center's research on instruction may be found at: www.kucrl.org. More information and tools ICs can use to enhance teachers' direct instructional practices can be found at www.instructionalcoach.org.

Formative Assessment

Richard Stiggins and his colleagues at the ETS Assessment Training Institute have developed many professional development tools and publications to support teachers' learning about assessment for learning. In addition to *Classroom Assessment* for *Student Learning* (2004), the EB/ATI Training Institute has produced DVDs, videotapes, and other training materials to support professional learning.

TO SUM UP

- ICs run the risk of being inefficient if they don't have a repertoire of effective practices to share with teachers.
- ICs can use the Big Four (behavior, content knowledge, direct instruction, formative assessment) to focus their efforts with teachers.
- To improve teachers' classroom management skills, ICs can gather data on (a) time on task, (b) the ratio of interactions, (c) disruptions, and (d) opportunities to respond.
- ICs can use all the components of coaching to empower teachers to increase time on task, effective corrections, and to develop and teach behavioral expectations.
- To help teachers place proper emphasis on "enduring understanding," ICs can guide teachers to create course, unit, and lesson questions, to develop content maps, identify content structures, and to identify, define, and teach essential concepts.
- Content Enhancement is one approach ICs can take to help make content more accessible to more students.
- ICs can help teachers improve the effectiveness of direct instruction by coaching teachers with respect to (a) advance and post organizers; (b) the "I Do It, We Do It, You Do It" approach to modeling, guided practice, and independent practice; (c) high-level questions; and (d) quality assignments.
- Teachers can increase student motivation by ensuring that students know the targets they are aiming for, by developing better assessments, by providing effective extended feedback, and by involving students in the process of assessment.
- ICs can help teachers improve their formative assessments by guiding them to develop unit questions, answers for the questions, and quality assignments.

NOTE

1. The Content Enhancement devices included in this chapter are instructional tools developed and researched at the University of Kansas Center for Research on Learning (Bulgren, Schumaker, Deshler, 1988). It is one of a number of teaching devices designed for teachers to use as they teach content information to classes containing diverse student populations. It is a data-based teaching instrument that has been found effective when used with a planning routine as well as a teaching routine that combines cues about the instruction, specialized delivery of the content, involvement of the students in the cognitive processes, and a review of the learning process and content material (Bulgren, Deshhler, & Schumaker, 1993). It has not been shown to be an effective tool if it is simply distributed to students.

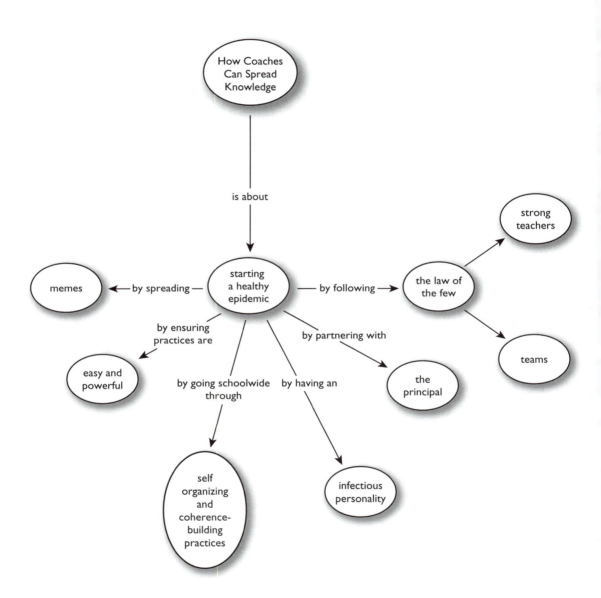

Chapter 8

How Coaches Can Spread Knowledge

At first, people were unclear about what I was doing, and teachers were reticent and apprehensive. I felt I had to keep clarifying what was going on . . . now, less than a year after I started, every single person on the freshman team is doing something with our project. There are times when I'm really busy, but I feel incredible seeing this happening for other teachers.

—Shelly Bolejack, instructional coach, Pathways to Success

CHAPTER OVERVIEW

This chapter describes issues that ICs should consider if they wish to spread ideas in their schools or districts, including, (a) understanding memes and the spread of healthy viruses, (b) ensuring that practices shared are easy and powerful, (c) employing self-organizing and coherence-building practices to go schoolwide with instructional coaching, (d) having an infectious personality, (e) partnering with the principal, and (e) following the Law of the Few.

HOW IDEAS SPREAD

In 1334, in the Hopei province of China, a terrible virus, *Yersinia pestis*, began to infect the province's inhabitants. In very little time, the disease infected the vast majority of the population, killing more than 90% of the residents in Hopei and more than two-thirds of the citizens of China. From China, the disease spread to Kaffa, a Genoese trading community on the Black Sea, and from there it was carried to Europe on ships to Genoa. Once in Europe, the virus proceeded to devastate the continent. In the four years between 1347 and 1351, the Black Plague killed one-third of Europe's population, more than 25 million people. In four years, the plague spread from one person to another across the entire continent of Europe, touching every person's life and profoundly altering the course of history.

A much more rapid virus covered most of the world on May 4, 2002. On that day, many people woke up to find a message in their e-mail in-box with the simple heartwarming message "ILOVEYOU." Those who opened that e-mail found a note saying "kindly check the attached LOVELETTER coming from me." Those unfortunate people who clicked on the supposed love letter, maybe hoping for a little joy in their lives, unleashed a worm virus that deleted files on their computer and sent the virus to everyone in their computer's Outlook address book. In a few hours, the virus, which originated in the Philippines, traveled across the United States, Britain, Hong Kong, Europe, Asia, and North America. In a flash, thousands of businesses across the world were brought to their knees by the ILOVEYOU virus.

What do these two events have to do with professional development in schools? As it turns out, quite a lot. As Malcolm Gladwell (2000) has explained, "ideas and products and messages and behaviors spread just like viruses do." The way ideas spread can be "textbook examples of epidemics in action . . . clear examples of contagious behavior" (p. 7). Furthermore, as Seth Godin (2001), the former marketing director for Yahoo! adds, "An idea that just sits there is worthless. But an idea that moves and grows and infects everyone it touches . . . that's an idea virus" (p. 19).

Shelly Bolejack, the IC at Highland Park High School, is a lot more pleasant than cholera or an Internet virus, but her goal, nonetheless, is to create an epidemic. Shelly has something to share—research-validated instructional practices—and she wants to "infect" the teachers in her school. But Shelly likes to think of herself as a healthy virus; she has ideas, strategies, and routines that will help teachers be more effective. "I just want to help teachers become the best teachers they can be," she says.

Shelly started out as an IC with the explicit purpose of spreading her ideas to (or infecting) the educators in her school. And that is what has happened with the Freshman Academy at Highland Park High School, says Shelly.

> Once somebody tries it, the next teacher tries it, and another teacher talks to another and so on. . . . Since I'm in the school every day, I can show them what it looks like. I gather materials, explain how it works, answer questions, model it, listen to their issues. Teachers have to see that it works. And because the strategies are research based, since they work, they sell themselves. Even teachers who have felt like they haven't been successful can be successful since the strategies are so complete. When teachers see that success, it makes them want to continue.

Shelly Bolejack

Shelly Bolejack, for the past five years, has been an IC on the Pathways to Success program at Highland Park High School, the school she attended as a student growing up. Prior to being a coach, Shelly taught middle school for 15 years. Shelly is an expert in the University of Kansas Center for Research on Learning's Content Enhancement and Learning Strategies Instruction and Randy Sprick's CHAMPs program. During the two years she taught Pathways to Success writing strategies, her students led all other students in the district on the Kansas State Writing Assessment.

UNDERSTANDING MEMES

So what is this idea virus we're talking about, and how does it spread? Maybe an example would be helpful. Do you remember the Macarena? That simple song and dance built around four or five notes and five or six moves (including, as one Web site said, "moving your rump to the left, the right, and the left") became so ubiquitous that it's hard to imagine anybody in the Western world not having heard it. I was introduced to the Macarena when three students in a college course I was teaching taught it to the class as a kind of end-of-semester activity.

After that, for a while, the song kept popping up in various ways, as between-period entertainment at a hockey game, as the centerpiece of a skit in my son Ben's kindergarten class, until it seemed like the Macarena was everywhere. This simple dance tune, released by two Spanish flamenco artists in 1993, soon seemed to blare out of every speaker in every store or shop I visited. The Macarena was in TV commercials, was taught to robots at the University of Southern California, and was danced by Madeleine Albright with the representative from Botswana during a break at the United Nations. "Macarena fever," as CNN described it, even swept India, where music videos showed groups of happy men in turbans dancing to that hypnotic beat. The song became inescapable, and the way the song spread across the world exemplifies how a human creation (in this case a song) can spread in a fashion very similar to how a virus spreads.

I first learned to think about ideas spreading like viruses from Csikszentmihalyi's book *The Evolving Self* (1993). Csikszentmihalyi suggests that the theories people apply to the evolution of the species can also be applied to the evolution of ideas and technology. He explains that ideas are shared through what evolutionary theorist Richard Dawkins has called *memes*—"patterns of behavior, values, languages, and technologies"

(Csikszentmihalyi, 1993, p. 7). The term *meme* refers to "a unit of cultural information comparable in its effects on society to those of the chemically coded instructions in the gene on the human organism" (Csikszentmihalyi, 1993, p. 120). An opera, a Nobel Prize–winning novel, and the Macarena are all memes. So are scientifically proven effective teaching practices.

The information in memes is not passed on through chemical instructions or chromosomes, but through imitation and learning. When you learn the tune of "Happy Birthday," how to skate backward, or the words to a prayer, you are part of a process of selection that transmits memes through time. Teaching practices are passed on or rejected in just the same way. Like all other memes, the instructional practices ICs share compete for the teachers' attention. When those ideas are adopted, in a small way, intellectual evolution takes place in schools.

This way of understanding organizational learning is important for understanding professional development because intellectual evolution happens both in the collective minds of a civilization and in the individual minds of teachers. By coming to understand the attributes of memes that catch on, we can learn how to create our own healthy epidemic in our schools.

RESILIENT VIRUSES

Whenever a person decides to adopt something new, that decision always involves a choice. A teacher who decides to use the Paragraph Writing Strategy, for example, has to decide to use it rather than some other approach to instruction. "Competition," says Csikszentmihalyi (1993), "is the thread that runs through evolution" (p. 21). But when we talk about the evolution of ideas, we're not talking about "the selective survival of dinosaurs or elephants, but of information. What counts is not the external, material shape of the organism, but the instruction it bears" (p. 21). And some information is much more likely to survive, to spread, to infect others, than other information.

Ideas are most likely to survive and spread if they are easier to use and more powerful than the memes they are replacing. Csikszentmihalyi (1993) explains,

> generally memes that do the job with the least demand on psychic energy will survive. An appliance that does more work with less effort will be preferred . . . The way this development occurs is always the same: an older viable meme generates in the mind of a person a new meme that is more attractive and has an even better chance of surviving in the human mind because it is more powerful, more efficient, or cheaper. (p. 123)

Simply put, ideas or technologies that catch on are easier to use and more powerful than the ones they replace.

This has significant implications for sharing ideas in schools. An idea will catch on much quicker if it is (a) powerful and (b) easy to use. Both of these attributes are essential. An intervention that is easy to implement but has no positive impact on student achievement or teacher's professional life most likely won't be adopted by many people in a school. If it doesn't really work, why would someone implement it? At the same time, an intervention that is effective but extremely difficult to learn and use will also have few takers. If it's difficult to use, where will a teacher find the energy and time to implement it? Interventions that are difficult to implement or that have little impact in the classroom will likely end up collecting dust on someone's shelf in a classroom.

Born Again

When I heard about Pathways to Success, my first reaction was, I don't want to try anything new. I went on with my life and teaching, did what I normally did, and that whole year went by and I stayed out of it. My mind was set.

Devona, our school's IC, would just darken my door and say, "Hey, let's talk." There was never any pressure; I never felt forced. It was friendly harassment. Every three or four weeks she'd ask if I wanted to give Paragraph Writing or some other strategy a shot. She kept saying "You're going to love it." I think she said that about 25 times, and I kept thinking, "I'm not going to love this."

When I finally said OK, Devona said, "I'll get all your materials." That was the first thing I wanted to hear because I was thinking in my head, "I don't want to have to do one more thing." She got all the materials together for me, made my copies and overheads; she also went over the manual with me. She planned the days that she was going to model, and then she came in and did it. I was sitting there learning along with the students. Once you see it and understand how it works, it's a lot easier to go on—just hitting the book cold and trying to do it wouldn't work for me.

More than anything, Devona just gave me moral support. I was kind of learning it right before the kids learned it, and as I had questions about little things or nuances, she was there to help me. When I didn't feel effective, she would step in, give me suggestions and moral support, and come back and model. I could sit there and have an epiphany and think, "Oh yes, I understand now."

Pretty soon I realized that the kids were getting it! I could see the difference in how their papers were organized, in their word choice and sentence structure; and they had strong beginnings and endings, and they used transitions effectively. When I saw the state writing scores, it really hit me that the Paragraph Writing Strategy was incredibly effective. I marveled at how effective it really was, and how simple, and how easily kids picked it up.

> *Most people in the school knew that I had been opposed to trying the strate-gies, so when I did try them, it was like I had been born again. There's nothing that's a greater motivator than an excited teacher. I was pretty established at the school, I had a good reputation, and I was kind of one of the leaders. People listened to what I had to say because they figured, "Hey, if it can work for her, it can work for me." Pretty soon our department was teaching all the writing strategies in all the language arts classes.*

ENSURING THAT PRACTICES SHARED ARE EASY AND POWERFUL

ICs can do a lot to ensure that an intervention is powerful. First, they must ensure that the intervention will work, that it is scientifically based, and that it responds to a teacher's most pressing needs. Also, ICs should focus their efforts on enabling teachers to use the materials in the most effective way. As explained in more detail in Chapters 5 and 6, ICs must use instructional methods, model practices in teachers' classrooms, observe teachers, and collaboratively explore data they gathered while observing. If an IC can find an intervention that will really make a difference for the students in a teacher's class, he is halfway there.

Once a coach introduces a powerful intervention, he also has to do everything possible to make it easy for the teacher to use it. Thus, an IC might prepare handouts or overheads, highlight key sections in a teacher's manual, prepare checklists or short lists of key practices, and provide feed-back and moral support. Many of the activities an IC undertakes to increase the power of intervention, such as modeling in the classroom, also make it easier for teachers to implement. "I never would have mastered the Paragraph Strategy," says Shelly Bolejack, talking about her days as a teacher, "if it hadn't been successful, if it hadn't been easy to use, if I hadn't had somebody there showing me how to do it. There were times when I thought, I can't do this, but there was always someone there ready and willing to help me. They'd always say 'this is no big deal; we'll get through this."

"The most important thing," says Shelly, "is that I make it easier for people to use the materials. With No Child Left Behind, and all of the stress and strain that teachers are going through now, there's a lot they have to do, and they're mentally exhausted. The easier it can be for them to slip into something new, the better." Shelly has a unique way of describing how ICs work with teachers: "It's like we're caterers. We bring the meal in, we help them, and we pick up afterwards. I look at myself as catering to whatever the teachers' needs are at the time."

EMPLOYING SELF-ORGANIZATION AND COHERENCE-BUILDING PRACTICES TO GO SCHOOLWIDE WITH INSTRUCTIONAL COACHING

Our belief that ideas proliferate through word of mouth and the collective power of individual teachers has challenged us to rethink how interventions are implemented across teams and schools. We recognize that the most powerful professional development brings teams and schools together to pursue specific targets and goals. Stephanie Hirsch, Director of the National Staff Development Council, who has studied several effective coaching programs, has made the point to me in conversation that "the coach's job is to get [each learning team] to a point where it is a high-functioning team without the coach, and then . . . move on to another team." She adds, "you have greater impact when you're very deliberate about what the coaches will do and the role they will serve within the school, and how their time will be used."

While ICs and other change agents must be deliberate about what they do, they also have to let go of the notion that they can arrive at a school with preconceived, tidy, inflexible, five-year plans for school reform. Real life in schools has shown us for a long time that, as Michael Fullan has observed, "the direct approach of naming the goal and mobilizing to achieve it does not, and cannot work in something as complex as change agentry" (2001, p. 1). You need to "resist controlling the uncontrollable . . . you need to tweak and trust the process of change while knowing that it is unpredictable" (Fullan, 2003, p. 21).

The challenge, then, is "to be deliberate" at the same time as you resist "controlling the uncontrollable," but is that possible? Educational leaders can meet this challenge by utilizing a self-organizing approach to organizational learning. What we mean by self-organization can be illustrated by a simple example.

In the 1960s, when architect Ronald J. Thom was drawing up the designs for the beautiful Trent University campus in Peterborough, Ontario, he wanted to create a campus that, among other things, allowed pedestrians to move from building to building in the easiest and most natural manner. Mr. Thom came up with a design plan that was as innovative as it was obvious. He first had grass planted all over campus, and waited to put in the sidewalks and pathways. After a few weeks, students walking around the university had created paths in the grass along all of the easiest walking routes. Once students' footprints had marked the most natural routes, the builders constructed the sidewalks right there.

This story exemplifies the self-organizing approach to sharing ideas taken by some educational leaders and their ICs. They do not come to school with inflexible, preconceived notions of exactly what their school needs. Rather, they engage in a process of building coherence after they arrive at the school, maybe starting with only a few interested teachers. Each IC's goal is to build widespread interest in research-validated interventions by starting out one-to-one, working with teachers who choose to work with them. Once a critical mass of teachers is committed to the project, they begin to facilitate the development and growth of professional learning communities, the standardization of curriculum across grade levels and across the district, the teaching of strategies across grade levels, and the development of a consistent districtwide scope and sequence. Metaphorically speaking, these coaches and leaders build the sidewalks of the program *after* everyone has communicated where they want and need to go.

One advantage of this approach is that it is a coherent, deliberate way of improving schools that engenders in teachers a deep and authentic commitment to the initiative. In most cases, the best a strictly top-down approach can hope for is what Chris Argyris refers to as "external commitment [which] is triggered by management policies and practices that enable employees to accomplish their tasks."[1] A self-organizing approach engenders what Argyris refers to as "internal commitment." This deeper form of commitment "derives from energies internal to human beings that are activated because getting a job done is intrinsically rewarding."

ICs believe in and respect the professionalism of teachers, and their experience has shown that if you provide teachers with something that works in the classroom, and you make it easy to implement, almost all teachers in a school will make an "internal commitment"; that is, they will choose the program because on their own they have concluded that it is good for them and their students. As Argyris has observed, "when someone else defines objectives, goals, and the steps to be taken to reach them, whatever commitment exists will be external."

We can understand this distinction between external and internal commitment by reflecting on drivers' commitment to keep driving within the speed limit. Consider the habits of drivers sailing along the highway at 15 miles above the speed limit, who suddenly notice a police car's flashing red lights up ahead. Almost at the moment they see the flashing red lights, they hit the brakes and drop their speed to the legal limit. No doubt, also, when they are out of the sight of the police car, they step on the gas and increase their speed back up to where they were before they saw the lights. That is an example of external commitment; it works so long as the external pressure exists, but once the external pressure is gone, the new behavior is usually gone as well.

Internal commitment works differently. To return to our example, let's say that our drivers were home one night watching PBS and they saw a powerful documentary on the importance of driving safely. While watching the documentary, they decided that as a parent and a community leader they really should drive safely. From that day forward, they made it a habit to drive cautiously, within the speed limit, regardless of whether there was a police car on the horizon or not. That is internal commitment, and that is the kind of commitment that ICs seek when they work with teachers.

HAVING AN INFECTIOUS PERSONALITY

A critical part of an approach to change designed to engender internal commitment is the person who is responsible for making that change happen, the IC. We often underestimate just how much impact we can have on others. A person with an infectious personality can profoundly affect others, and simple actions can have far-reaching implications. In my life, the person who turned me toward the professional road I've been following for most of the past 20 years has such an infectious personality that she changed my life without even trying. Dee LaFrance is a kind-hearted, extremely effective teacher whom I met during my first year teaching at Humber College in Toronto, Canada. A certified professional developer for the Strategic Instruction Model, Dee was hired by the college to teach students with learning disabilities and to provide professional development for college teachers working with these students. Dee took me under her wing and showed me how to teach several very powerful writing and reading strategies developed at the University of Kansas Center for Research on Learning. Thanks to Dee, the learning strategies course she helped me develop ended up winning an award at the college, and I went from being a sessional teacher to being a full-time permanent teacher.

Dee won me over to teaching learning strategies by example more than anything else. She was a master teacher. She was warm, in control, highly organized, and a great motivator of students. Dee taught students who, in many ways, were the most challenging, students who had failed the college writing courses at least three times, and some who had never learned how to get along socially. Nevertheless, Dee was able to motivate her students to work harder than they may have ever worked in a classroom before. I remember once watching petite Dee, gently leading a group of challenging students working feverishly for the chance to win a spelling dictionary. I'm sure they weren't interested in the dictionary; the prize they wanted was to succeed in Dee's classroom.

Dee had a full repertoire of teaching practices, but what won her students over wasn't a technique that could be learned from a manual. Dee was an optimist about her students. She really did believe *each* student she taught would succeed, and every day in every little interaction, she communicated that to them all. She had waltzed them around many roadblocks, and she made sure her students knew that the roadblocks they were facing were temporary, and that they too could become capable, effective readers and writers who would eventually graduate from college. When Dee told her colleagues that she believed all students could learn, she wasn't uttering a popular cliché, she was describing her way of life.

Inspired by Dee, I began to gather information about learning strategies, became a professional developer, and eventually moved from Canada to study strategies and professional development at the University of Kansas University Center for Research on Learning. Twenty years later, as I'm writing these notes, sitting in my office at the Center for Research on Learning (where the strategies Dee taught were developed), I've learned that Dee's optimism is an important characteristic of most instructional leaders. People who make a difference have to, like Dee, learn how to waltz around roadblocks. Michael Fullan suggests that Dee's personality is a characteristic of many effective leaders:

> Effective leaders make people feel that even the most difficult problems can be tackled productively. They are always hopeful— conveying a sense of optimism and an attitude of never giving up in the pursuit of highly valued goals. Their enthusiasm and confidence (not certainty) are, in a word, infectious. . . . (Fullan, 2001, p. 7)

Martin Seligman's well-known research on optimism provides some insight into the specifics of what optimism is. Seligman found that people with optimistic habits of mind were happier, more persistent, and consequently, more successful professionally and personally than their more pessimistic counterparts (Seligman, 1991). What matters, according to Seligman, is how people think and talk themselves through difficulty, failure, and frustration. Optimists talk themselves through challenges and remain hopeful and energized when they encounter roadblocks. Seligman explains,

> The skills of optimism do not consist in learning to say positive things to yourself. We have found over the years that the positive statements you make to yourself have little if any effect. What *is* crucial is what you think when you fail, using the power of "non-negative thinking." Changing the destructive things you say to yourself when you experience the setbacks that life deals all of us is the central skill of optimism. (Seligman, 1991, p. 15)

In *The Tipping Point*, Malcolm Gladwell observes that when it comes to sharing ideas, the way people talk is as important as what they have to say. "Persuasion," Gladwell suggests, "often works in ways that we do not appreciate" (2000, p. 79). Persuasive people are sensitive to the nonverbal cues of those with whom they interact and the impact of their nonverbal cues. More important, highly persuasive people have a special talent or learn to interact in ways that are in harmony with the speech patterns and gestures of those with whom they interact. Persuasive people "can build a level of trust and rapport in five minutes that most people take half an hour to do" (2000, p. 84). Describing Tom Gau, a highly persuasive financial planner, Gladwell observes,

> He seems to have some kind of indefinable trait, something powerful and contagious and irresistible that goes beyond what comes out his mouth, that makes people who meet him want to agree with him. It's energy. It's enthusiasm. It's charm. It's likability. It's all those things and something more. (Gladwell, 2000, p. 6)

Like Tom Gau, Shelly Bolejack's infectious personality has helped her be an effective IC. In less than a year, Shelly was able to bring on board every teacher in the Freshman Academy at Highland Park High School. Like the other successful ICs, Shelly has an optimistic, engaging personality that draws in teachers. She smiles frequently; laughs with teachers, students, and everyone else around her; and refuses to let the inevitable frustrations of life in a school destroy her commitment to improving instruction. Describing other successful ICs, Shelly observes that "ICs have to be gregarious, extroverted people. They have to really like talking to people. They have to like making connections, and it has nothing to do with teaching strategies. Once you've made that emotional connection with another person, it's easier for them to come and see you because they don't see you as a threat; they see you as a friend."

ICs have to enjoy making the extra effort to involve others in the change initiative. Shelly observes that, "You have to be able to put yourself out there—sit in the lounge and talk to anybody that walks in. You have to enjoy working with others—many times you have to go out and seek teachers; they don't necessarily come to you. It's almost like being a missionary. You preach your stories and your strategies and you hope people will follow."

Additionally, ICs have to approach their task and their role in the school with humility. An arrogant coach will likely be an unsuccessful coach. A more effective coach usually approaches teachers by offering support, help, and service. Says Shelly, "ICs really need to have a desire to see that their teachers are successful. They have to want to put all the glory on the teacher."

PARTNERING WITH THE PRINCIPAL

The principal is not the only person who bears responsibility for change efforts in school, but she or he can have a big impact on how well any kind of reform or professional development program is implemented (DuFour, 1998). For that reason, ICs need to work in harmony with their school principal.

Shelly Bolejack felt it was very important for her to work in partnership with her principal, Vicki Vossler. "I just felt," said Shelly, "that in school there's the trickle-down effect, and if the principal isn't on board, the staff often won't be on board." For that reason, one of Shelly's first actions at the Freshman Academy was to make a connection with Vicki and explain what Pathways to Success could offer the school. "I made sure I talked with Vicki and explained in as great a depth as I possibly could, what some of the strategies were. I gave her a list of the strategies we offer, and I explained exactly what they do." Once Shelly explained the potential of Pathways to Success, Vicki accelerated the spread of ideas in school.

Some principals will have a deep understanding of the interventions and what they should look like in the classroom; they may even be the primary movers behind the change initiative being implemented by the IC. In other cases, the principal is one of the first people a coach educates. Working with the Freshman Academy at Highland Park, Shelly is fortunate that her principal, Vicki Vossler, is very supportive. "Vicki," Shelly reports, "made a commitment to the strategies and decided right away that the Freshman Academy was going to do it."

ICs use many different tools to educate the principals in their schools about the many different interventions available. Some ICs have prepared one-page summaries (called "Strategies at a Glance") of the teaching practices they share to make it easier for people to learn quickly about the interventions. Additionally, ICs can share checklists with principals that summarize the critical teaching behaviors in the teaching routines and learning strategies that teachers might be using. Some coaches have a variety of DVDs that they share with principals that provide a brief video snapshot of some of the materials. Finally, one of the most powerful ways that ICs can educate principals is by inviting them to observe classrooms where the interventions are being used. Just like teachers, principals sometimes learn best by watching the interventions being used.

The IC should be the right-hand person of the principal when it comes to instructional leadership in schools, but the principal must remain the instructional leader. No matter how effective an IC is, the principal's voice is ultimately the voice that is most important to teachers. For that reason, coaches must understand fully what their principal's vision is for school improvement, and principals must understand fully the interventions that their coach has to offer.

One way to ensure that ICs and principals are on the same page is to meet one-to-one for approximately 45 minutes each week. When Shelly meets with her principal, the meetings usually follow the same format. First, she asks the principal to discuss her most pressing concerns; the issues discussed are usually a blend of long-term and short-term issues. Second, Shelly and Vicki solve problems together. Third, Shelly reports on what she has done since the previous week's meeting. Fourth, Shelly and Vicki discuss teaching practices they would like to share with each other. In this way, both Shelly and Vicki fully understand all the tools they have at their command.

Shelly believes that Vicki's leadership style has increased teachers' interest and acceptance of her. "With Vicki, there's clear-cut leadership; she knows the strategies, she wants the school to be successful, and she knows the strategies are a way to achieve that." As a leader in the school, Vicki was very skilled at finding respectful and validating ways to encourage teachers to participate in the program. Shelly reports, "She was very positive—she didn't force it on anybody—she let them find their own way to the strategies. It may have taken a little coercing, but she was careful that teachers felt like the overall decision was theirs, and that meant they felt more successful."

Vicki encouraged teachers to attend summer workshops and to participate in any of the more formal professional development offered by Pathways to Success. Additionally, Vicki matched Shelly with teachers who had an urgent need for professional development assistance. Because Shelly was able to provide practical suggestions that addressed real problems, teachers started talking about the materials, and, as Shelly reports, "word of mouth is really how it spreads through a school."

FOLLOWING THE LAW OF THE FEW

Malcolm Gladwell (2001) comments that social epidemics spread because of the actions of a few factors:

> Economists often talk about the 80/20 Principle, which is the idea that in any situation roughly 80 percent of the work is done by 20 percent of the participants. In most societies, 20 percent of criminals commit 80 percent of crimes. Twenty percent of motorists commit 80 percent of all accidents. Twenty percent of beer drinkers drink 80 percent of all beer. When it comes to epidemics, though, this proportionality becomes even more extreme: a tiny percent of people do the majority of the work. (p. 19)

The same rule seems to apply to the spread of ideas in schools. Effective ICs realize that there are particular individuals whose involvement in the project can make a real difference to the development of the project. We have found that ideas spread much quicker if the principal and the leading teachers, those with informal power, are on board and support the project.

Strong Teachers

ICs have found that working with those few teachers who are the informal leaders in the school is almost as important as working with the principal. In any organization, there are a few people with informal power, people who have authority by virtue of their personal characteristics rather than their position. When it comes to change in schools, teachers with informal power are very important because they can sway the opinions of many in schools. Shelly refers to these teachers as "strong teachers."

> I usually go for the strongest people . . . once you get your strongest teachers on board, it's smooth sailing because other teachers are aware of who the strongest teachers are. They are more apt to listen to their teachers than an IC or the principal.

Identifying who the strong teachers are is a critical strategy for ICs. To identify who holds informal power in the school, ICs can talk with department chairs and engage in one-on-one conversations in the staff lounge. Sometimes the most important information is gathered through informal observation. For example, ICs should join staff meetings and sit in the staff lounge, watching all interactions with great care. Paying attention to nonverbal communication can be tremendously helpful. Coaches should watch to see which teacher's comments are listened to most attentively, who attracts eye contact, whose comments seem to have the greatest ability to turn the course of conversation in one direction or another. All of this can take time, sometimes one or two months.

Shelly's strategy sounds a lot like Core Group Theory, described by Art Kleiner in *Who Really Matters: The Core Group Theory of Power, Privilege, and Success* (2003). Kleiner contends that within every organization, there is a core group of people who define what the organization stands for and who, either directly or indirectly, shapes all of the organization's major decisions. "The Core Group won't be named in any formal organization chart, contract, or constitution. It exists in people's hearts and minds. Its power is derived not from authority, but for legitimacy" (p. 7).

Kleiner (2003) argues that understanding who the Core Group is and what they stand for is a central task for any leader. "If we want to live not just within society, but establish ourselves as leaders and creators, then we have to understand the dynamics of the Core Group" (p. 6). Kleiner adds, "If you remain unaware of the nature of an organization's particular Core Group, then the organization will be opaque, ungovernable, and dangerous to you—even if you are ostensibly the person in charge" (p. 9).

For ICs to be successful at spreading a healthy virus in schools, they need to identify, understand, and align themselves with the Core Group. You can't "change or influence an organization . . . unless you understand which aspects of the core group are open to change, in what ways, and by whom" (Kleiner, 2003, pp. 8–9). Shelly Bolejack may not have used the term Core Group, but she understood the importance of getting the right people on board quickly. "If you pay attention," Shelly says, "you get a pretty good understanding of who's strong, who's weak, who's struggling. You hear about the strong teachers through the grapevine from everyone; the administrators, counselors, teachers, and even students. Once the strong teachers start saying 'these strategies really work, you should try them,' it just spreads like wildfire."

Learning Teams

Almost immediately after they start working at schools, ICs on the Pathways to Success team start building networks for change in their schools. An IC's goal is to make sure that as many people as possible know about the program, the results that are being achieved, and the teachers who are getting on board. As teachers hear about others who are using strategies or routines, they are often curious and start to think about using the materials.

Shelly spreads the word about what is happening in the school in many ways. Every two weeks, she sends out a newsletter that explains who is doing what with the Pathways to Success project. The newsletter contains stories and pictures of teachers who are implementing the strategies, descriptions of strategies and routines, and information about the results that have been achieved. She reports, "I make myself visible. I spend a lot of time talking with teachers in empty classrooms. I always try to keep in contact one-to-one, through e-mail, or through my newsletter."

Ideas spread faster when there is a community of people sharing them. As Seth Godin observed, "Once your idea starts coursing through a [community] again and again and again, you'll have a piling on effect. People will want to be exposed to your idea just because everyone else . . . they respect is talking about it" (2001, p. 14). For that reason, even though ICs usually start out working one-to-one with teachers, their ultimate goal is to reinforce, and in some cases create learning teams so that ideas can be shared across grade levels and in some cases across schools. Gladwell, again, sees learning communities as an essential part of creating an epidemic:

> If you wanted to bring about a fundamental change in people's beliefs and behavior, a change that would persist and serve as an example to others, you needed to create a community around them, where those new beliefs could be practiced and expressed and nurtured. (2001, p. 173)

A great deal has been written about how effective learning teams or professional learning communities can accelerate professional learning in schools (DuFour, 2000), and more needs to be studied and written about the role of ICs on teams. This much is clear, however: ICs can use teams to spread ideas rapidly in their school. If a coach has the ear of a team or a learning community, he can enroll a large number of teachers quickly and can explain how coaching can support improvement efforts in the school.

If coaches are on the school improvement team or other important decision-making teams in a school, they can ensure that the widest number of people know about what they have to offer. By being on the team, the IC can also decrease the likelihood that schools embrace new practices that replicate or even interfere with the practices the IC already has to offer. Finally, since ICs spend so much time in conversation with so many teachers in the school, they frequently have a good idea of the hearts and minds of the staff. Consequently, they can provide a great service to teams by sharing what they know about the concerns of the staff.

Shelly Bolejack believes that ICs should keep their eyes open for opportunities to work with any group of teachers. Shelly sees herself as having an important role, not just as a professional developer, but as a leader of teams. Thus, she suggests that one goal ICs should hold is "to get a group of teachers working with you, and once they're working with you, to guide them to work together as a team." When people work together as a team," says Shelly, "they can have a lot of empathy for what they're going through. They muck through the same problems, talking together and understanding that we're all in this together—there's a lot of strength and power in that."

When working with teams, ICs can play an important role in shaping the direction of professional learning in a school. This may occur because an IC knows more about interventions than individual teachers and can help teachers make decisions about such issues as scope and sequence of instruction. For example, Shelly Bolejack's deep understanding of the Writing Strategies that are a part of the Strategic Instruction Model offered within the Pathways to Success program helped her assist the language arts team at Highland Park High School when they created their plans to institutionalize a sequence of writing strategies to be taught in ninth and tenth grade. When she enables this kind of teamwork, Shelly sees herself leading a "constant reevaluation process . . . tweaking, always tweaking what you've done for the best results."

Intellectual Evolution

The notion that ideas are shared in the same way that viruses are spread brings to light just how significant each of our individual choices and actions can be. Epidemics, like those mentioned at the opening of this chapter, start out small before they reach epidemic status. The Black Plague started in a single Chinese province and eventually spread across most of Europe; the ILOVEYOU virus started on a single computer in the Philippines and quickly spread across much of the world.

Epidemics grow and spread in unpredictable, irrational ways, and they grow or die based on the choices we make. Every time we choose, implement, or share an innovation that improves student achievement or school life, we are accelerating the improvement of schools in some way. We can never predict how significantly we will affect the evolution of ideas, but always, in some way—by choosing a more effective instructional practice (a meme) over another, less effective one—we are a part of the ongoing evolution of ideas in our schools and our world. I wrote this book, in part, because Dee LaFrance's teaching practices made an indelible impact on my life. Your actions and choices have the potential to affect those around you in exactly the same way.

GOING DEEPER

The Healthy Virus

Malcolm Gladwell's *The Tipping Point* (2000) is a popular and accessible description of the concept that ideas spread like a virus, but others have written commentaries on the same ideas. Csikszentmihalyi's *The Evolving Self* is also accessible, interesting, and also offers insights into how human consciousness evolves. Seth Godin's *Unleashing the Idea Virus* (2002) is a short but useful book that focuses on the marketing implications of recognizing that ideas spread like a virus. All three of these books contain valuable information for people interested in leading system change.

Martin Seligman

Seligman, perhaps most famous for coining the phrase "learned helplessness," has also authored *Learned Optimism: How to Change Your Mind and*

Your Life (1998), likely his best known work. *Learned Optimism* provides a compelling argument for the importance of optimism, along with assessment measures and suggestions for self-regulation strategies that people can employ to control helplessness and maximize their own optimism.

Michael Fullan

No author has influenced my thinking (and the thinking of many educators) more than Michael Fullan. His books offer profound insights into the tortuous challenge of leading change. Dr. Fullan's *The New Meaning of Education Change* (3rd ed., 2001) provides a comprehensive overview of current thinking with respect to change in schools. Fullan's trilogy, *Change Forces: Probing the Depths of Educational Reform* (1993), *Change Forces With a Vengeance* (2003), and *Change Forces: The Sequel* (1999) offer a comprehensive overview of many issues related to leading change in school, with a particular emphasis on the implications of new science thinking in the way we understand change. Recently, Fullan's works have focused on leadership, including *Leading in a Culture of Change* (2001) and *Leadership and Sustainability* (2005).

TO SUM UP

- Ideas spread just like viruses, and in many ways, an IC's main task is to help create an intellectual epidemic in his or her school.
- Ideas that spread quickly are those that are powerful and easy to use.
- ICs can ensure that interventions are powerful by sharing scientifically proven, effective strategies and by helping teachers implement them in ways that are close to the research-validated methods.
- ICs can make it easier for teachers to implement interventions by preparing materials, modeling in the classroom, coaching teachers, and helping teachers see how articles and other research-based materials can be translated into real practices in the classrooms.
- ICs who have infectious, optimistic personalities, who make many connections with others, are more successful than coaches who are not "people people."
- ICs should be strategic about partnering with and educating the principals in their schools.
- ICs can accelerate the proliferation of ideas in their schools if they involve their schools' strong teachers early on in their project.
- ICs will accelerate the spread of ideas if they help build networks for change within their schools.

NOTE

1. These quotations from Chris Argyris are taken from Michael Fullan's *Leading in a Culture of Change* (2001, pp. 8, 9).

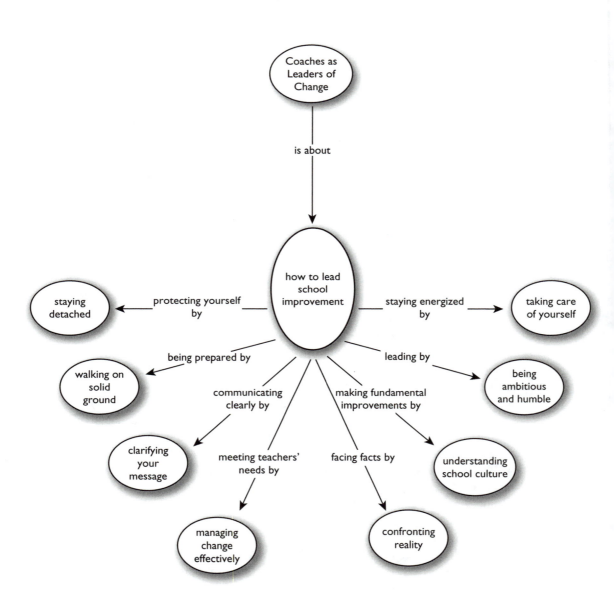

Coaches as Leaders of Change

Chapter 9

I think that most teachers see their teaching as an art and when you're messing with their art, they can become really angry. And it's really hard not to take it personally. But I keep moving forward because I'm bringing better methods, and once I've given lots of backup, once they've started using it, once they see growth in their kids, they're OK.

—Jean Clark, instructional coach,
Bohemia Manor Middle School

COACHES AS LEADERS OF CHANGE

The temptation is to avoid the leadership challenge altogether. Isn't it enough, we might ask, if ICs perform all the components of coaching (enroll, identify, explain, model, observe, explore, support, and reflect) in efficient and validating ways? Certainly a coach who does each of those tasks well is doing important and valuable work. The problem is that the complex challenges that require leadership refuse to leave coaches alone. ICs, sometimes on a daily basis, are thrown into situations where they will not be effective unless they lead. ICs need to shape team norms, facilitate schoolwide implementation of interventions, promote more constructive styles of professional discourse, motivate unmotivated teachers, raise thorny issues, negotiate resolutions to the conflicts that those thorny issues stir up, and stand in opposition to any action or attitude that is not good for children. Whether they like it or not, effective coaches must be effective leaders.

The concept of leadership carries with it many preconceptions. When we think of a leader, we often conjure up Hollywood images of men (usually) who exhibit heroic fortitude, courage, discipline, determination, and focus as they whip a bunch of losers into shape and overcome obstacles to fight the battle, take the flag, score the points, win at all costs, and beat the enemy. Clearly, that notion of leadership is at odds with the partnership approach proposed for ICs.

When it comes to instructional coaching, a different concept of leadership is more appropriate. In line with recent studies of leadership,

ICs need a paradoxical mix of humility and ambition (Collins, 2001), a desire to provide service that is at least as powerful as the drive to succeed (Greenleaf, 1998), a deep understanding of the emotional components of leadership (Goleman, Boyatzis, & McKee, 2002), and a recognition that a good leader must first be an effective teacher (Tichy, 2002). The reality is that instructional coaching usually demands leadership. The good news is that there are tactics (strategies or methods) that coaches can learn and employ that will increase their ability to lead change. This chapter focuses on seven high-leverage leadership tactics that coaches can employ to lead change in schools.

TACTIC 1: STAY DETACHED

Before she became an IC at Bohemia Manor Middle School in Cecil County, Jean Clark, one of the first winners of the Cecil County Teacher of the Year Award, was respected as a highly successful teacher. In fact, she was brought to Bohemia Manor by her principal, Joe Buckley, because he had personally experienced how effective she was. Nevertheless, despite her personal warmth and professional pedigree, Jean's first year at her new school was not all smooth sailing.

Jean came to Bohemia Manor excited about introducing Content Enhancement Routines and other research-based teaching practices to her teachers. An energetic and driven professional, she found it difficult to hide her enthusiasm for the teaching practices, and she fully expected her colleagues to see the value of focused planning and explicit teaching. Unfortunately, some teachers were not so quick to catch Jean's enthusiasm. In fact, not long after she started talking with staff, Jean observed that teachers were starting to avoid her in the halls, disparage her in the staff lounge, and going to great lengths to get out of her way. This wasn't easy for Jean to accept.

Talking about her experiences, Jean observed that "The decision to step forward and become a leader can be difficult because both professionally and personally you're moving away from your colleagues, and that's a very difficult thing—there's a lot of self-doubt and fear."

Jean Clark

Jean Clark is an IC at Bohemia Manor Middle School in Cecil County, Maryland. She became an IC in 2004, but she says that she feels she has been a change agent for most of her professional life. Jean taught English for many years, and was one of the first Cecil County Teachers of the Year. Jean is a certified Strategic Instruction Model Content Enhancement Professional Developer, a writer, and a poet.

Unfortunately, the resistance and personal attacks that Jean experienced are not uncommon. Ronald Heifetz and Marty Linsky, in their book *Leadership on the Line: Staying Alive Through the Dangers of Leading* (2002), observe that

> adaptive [complex] change stimulates resistance because it challenges people's habits, beliefs, and values. It asks them to take a loss, experience uncertainty, and even express disloyalty to people and cultures. Because adaptive change forces people to question and perhaps redefine aspects of their identity, it also challenges their sense of competence. Loss, disloyalty, and feeling incompetent: That's a lot to ask. No wonder people resist. (p. 30)

When people are nervous about change, they can feel compelled to resist, and can give voice to that resistance by attacking the person promoting the change. By standing for a new vision of what a school or individual can be, by standing for change, ICs can inadvertently put themselves in the line of fire. And attack can be a very effective way to resist change. According to Heifetz and Linsky (2002),

> Whatever the form of attack, if the attackers can turn the subject of the conversation from the issue you are advancing to your character or style, or even the attack itself, it will have succeeded in submerging the issue. (p. 41)

Jean Clark found that teachers were inclined to attack her even after they had seen success. In her role as an IC, Jean reminded teachers of how they were falling short in their commitment to help children. Jean explains,

> Teachers might be using the Unit Organizer and the course map and starting to see kids that normally don't respond, responding. Even with that, they'll use it for a while and then stop using it because they need a lot of support or because they're very busy at home, and eventually they revert to the old way of take out your book and let me do round-robin reading. Then they become angry because I suspect they know that's not what they really want to be doing. And here comes Jean Clark and I'm going to throw a pallet at her.

If coaches aren't attacked personally, they may find that their interventions come under attack. Even when programs are going well, when results are unmistakable, people in a school may find reasons to criticize a program. Unfortunately, what frequently occurs in schools is a vicious cycle that ensures that new teaching practices never get implemented—an "attempt, attack, abandon cycle" that prevents any real change from taking hold in schools. During the "attempt, attack, abandon cycle," someone introduces a new practice into a school, and teachers make a half-hearted *attempt* to implement it. Then, before the program has been implemented effectively, and before it has been given sufficient time to be fully implemented, various individuals in the school or district begin to *attack* the program. As a result, many of the teachers implementing the program now begin to lose their will to stick with it. Inevitably, even though the practice was never implemented well, leaders in the district reject it as unsuccessful, and *abandon* it, only to propose another program that is sure to be pulled into the same vicious cycle, to eventually be attacked and abandoned for another program, and on and on. Thus, schools stay on an unmerry-go-round of attempt, attack, abandon, without ever seeing any meaningful, sustained change in instruction taking place (Knight, 2006).

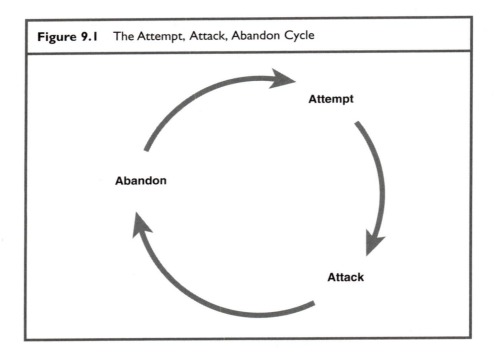

Figure 9.1   The Attempt, Attack, Abandon Cycle

The Attempt, Attack, Abandon Cycle

What should coaches do when they come under attack? Jean Clark is unequivocal about how difficult it can be to encounter resistance: "I've been really depressed at times because I can't stand being the enemy." After interviewing Jean and other ICs across the nation and observing many coaches in action, I've come to believe that ICs have to "stay detached" to stay effective. If coaches become too personally involved in their change initiatives, if they see every attack on their program as an attack on themselves, they may find the personal consequences devastating. Jean says that she's "getting tougher" and learning to detach herself from each teacher's individual struggle to change and improve. "I'm getting tougher to where I can say, hey, let them go, this is the change stuff that you're seeing; you're seeing them blow up, it's a loss right now and they're grieving over a lot of stuff. Just get out of the way."

I suggest four strategies ICs can employ to maintain a healthy distance when they are leading change.

1. *Use partnership communication.* This suggestion may seem paradoxical, or even contradictory. If partnership communication is all about building an emotional connection, how can ICs stay detached while also staying connected? In reality, it is paradoxical. As we saw in Chapter 4, the partnership approach grounds any act of communication in the belief that everyone's point of view should be listened to because everyone is equally valuable. Partnership communication helps us listen more effectively, empathize, and rethink communication from the perspective of the listener as opposed to our own point of view. ICs taking the partnership approach consciously build relationships by extending and turning toward others' emotional bids, and they are very aware of how their personal stories or the stories held by a listener can interfere with and sometimes stand in the way of any effective communication.

By taking the partnership approach, ICs can detach themselves by, first, proactively eliminating many of the time bombs that can blow up during interpersonal communication. Simply put, when teachers feel respected, when they are aware that their IC listens authentically, and when they feel an emotional connection with their IC, they are much less likely to attack the coach or the program. Paradoxically, therefore, the first step in staying detached is to reduce the number of attacks you might experience by taking the partnership approach.

2. *Change your thinking to create distance.* When Linda Stone, a former senior Microsoft executive, wrote out the most important lessons she'd learned in her life, she offered advice that seems highly pertinent to coaches trying to stay detached. Stone wrote, "Whenever we feel defensive, hurt, personally attacked, confused, or afraid, we have a choice—we can get very curious. Rather than saying, 'I never would have said that,' we can say, 'I wonder what these people heard me say? I wonder what their perception is?'" (Jensen, 2005, p. 63). Coaches can stay detached by reconceiving the attack as an opportunity to learn and better understand the people with whom they work.

3. *Keep it from being personal.* Perhaps the chief strategy ICs can use to stay detached is to be sensitive to the emotional undercurrents at work in any interchange. Then, if they notice an interaction turning

negative, they can stay detached by recognizing what is happening and by telling themselves to keep their distance. William Ury, more than two decades ago, referred to this tactic as "going to the balcony" (Ury, 1985). He suggested that whenever we feel a conversation turning negative and personal, we can detach ourselves by imagining that we are watching the interaction from a balcony. Ury describes "going to the balcony" as follows:

> When you find yourself facing a difficult negotiation, you need to step back, collect your wits, and see the situation objectively. Imagine you are on a stage and then imagine yourself climbing onto a balcony overlooking the stage. The "balcony" is a metaphor for a mental attitude of detachment. From the balcony you can calmly evaluate the conflict almost as if you were a third party . . . Going to the balcony means distancing yourself from your natural impulses and emotions. (1985, pp. 37–38)

The simple trick of imagining that we are physically distanced from the conversation can help us feel psychologically distanced from the interchange and help us avoid responding in ways we will later regret. One IC stays detached when things get heated simply by thinking, "Wow this looks like one of those conflict situations; I wonder if I can use my communication techniques to keep this from escalating." The simple act of naming the situation as one with potential for conflict somehow provides the distance necessary for this coach to stay detached.

Coaches also need to ensure that their program or activities are not seen as their personal pet project. An additional part of "keeping it from being personal," then, is to ensure that we keep the focus on instruction and students and not on us. Although we want to build an emotional connection and want our colleagues to enjoy working with us, we do not want them to work with us out of personal obligation. If teachers try our practices merely because they feel they owe it to us, rather than because they believe it is good for kids or for them, eventually, they will grow tired of spending their energy pleasing us. Coaches must resist the temptation to use their friendship as a leverage point for motivating colleagues, and continually turn the focus of conversations to how strategies or teaching practices can help students.

4. *Take the long view.* Staying detached is not synonymous with being apathetic about results. In truth, it is just the opposite. If ICs are too personally involved in their project, they may find the unsuccessful days emotionally devastating. Furthermore, if the teaching practices proposed are tied too closely to the IC, that perception can further inhibit the spread of ideas in schools.

We believe that by staying detached, ICs increase the likelihood that interventions will catch on in a school. To effectively lead change, ICs sometimes need to consciously stand back from the potentially distressing moments of resistance that might keep them up late into the night. A better strategy is to take the long view, recognizing that research is quite clear that a well-organized coaching program should lead to widespread implementation and improvements in student achievements. By staying detached, by seeing beyond the momentary lapse and keeping the long-term goals in view, ICs can be more effective leaders of change.

TACTIC 2: WALK ON SOLID GROUND

ICs who are uncertain of their principles, goals, priorities, or practices may be unprepared for the turbulence and waves of resistance they may encounter in a school. ICs must be clear on what they stand for, if they want others to stand with them in improving instruction for students. Henry Cloud, in his book *Integrity: The Courage to Meet the Demands of Reality* (2006), writes about the importance of being clear on who we are and what we stand for:

> People who do best in life have a well-defined *identity* on a number of fronts. They are secure in their boundaries, they know what they like and don't like, what they believe in and value, and they love and hate the right things. They are not wishy-washy and what psychologists call identity diffused, wondering who they are or what they are about, or thinking that they are everything. You get a good definition of who they are just from being around them. (p. 144)

A starting point for walking on solid ground is for ICs to work out their beliefs about the partnership principles of equality, choice, voice, dialogue, reflection, praxis, and reciprocity discussed in Chapter 5. ICs need to deeply understand these principles, first, so that they can decide whether or not they will ground their actions in them. If they do not agree with some of the principles, ICs should reflect and determine the principles that they will use as a foundation for action. Inevitably, ICs will be called upon to act in ways that are inconsistent with these principles (leading a change initiative that doesn't allow any room for teachers' choices, for example), and if they are unsure of their principles, they will have a harder time resisting such suggestions. They may also act in ways that will end up unsuccessful.

Jean Clark experienced the importance of walking on solid ground firsthand. When the program Jean was leading at Bohemia Manor Middle School began to gain momentum, administrators and teachers around the district started to ask her for the quick-fix version of Content Enhancement. She was invited to give a one-hour presentation to large groups of teachers, and to send materials to teachers without providing any kind of follow-up professional development. Jean's clarity about what she stood for, and her commitment to praxis and dialogue, helped her to say no. Because she knew what she stood for as a leader of professional learning, Jean was able to advocate for more effective forms of professional learning and keep the "attempt, attack, abandon cycle" from occurring, at least for the moment.

To stay grounded, coaches also need to stay fully conscious of the moral purpose that is at the heart of the work they do. As Michael Fullan observed, "Moral purpose, defined as making a difference in the lives of students, is a critical motivator for addressing the sustained task of complex reform. Passion and higher order purpose are required because the effort needed is gargantuan and must be morally worth doing" (2003, p. 18). One way for coaches to walk on solid ground is to remind themselves—perhaps every day, hour, or minute—that the primary purpose of their work is to make life better for children.

To stand on solid ground, coaches also need to understand fully their long-term and short-term goals. Lynn Barnes, a coach at Jardine Middle School, sets goals for every week, making plans, for example, to speak briefly to three non-implementers every five days. A useful practice for ICs before any meeting with a teacher or administrator is to ask, "What are my short-term goals for this interaction?" An IC's short-term goal with a teacher might be as simple as trying to enhance a relationship or as ambitious as getting someone on board to help lead a schoolwide reading program. When meeting with an administrator, a coach might set the short-term goal of always explaining a research-based teaching practice or explaining what someone should watch for while observing a teacher implement a new teaching practice.

As important as short-term goals are, an IC's long-term goals are even more important. Long-term goals provide focus and help ICs set priorities. Coaches who take the time to set long-term goals, and who monitor their progress, are better prepared to use their time efficiently. Simply put, coaches will lead change more effectively if they know their top priorities and have a clear understanding of the outcomes they hope to achieve. To lead teachers and schools in a given direction, coaches need to be clear on their destination.

Let me add a final word: being sure of what you stand for is an essential part of being a leader, but steadiness is not the same thing as stubbornness. In our studies of ICs, we have found that having too firm a ground to stand on can be problematic if coaches become impervious to new ideas. Michael Fullan offers some excellent advice: "beware of leaders who are always sure of themselves" (2001, p. 123). Coaches need to remain open to new ideas, to learning from the teachers and administrators with whom they collaborate, or their lack of flexibility may keep others from working with them. Indeed, when coaches have reflected on and clarified what it is that they stand for, they may actually find it much easier to open their mind to other ways of understanding.

TACTIC 3: CLARIFYING YOUR MESSAGE

In addition to being clear about short- and long-term goals, ICs also need to be clear about the information and vision they want to share with teachers. Noel Tichy, whom *BusinessWeek* has rated as one of the "Top-Ten

Management Gurus," considers such clarity to be an essential attribute of effective leaders. "Leaders," Tichy observes, "must be able to share their experience. And in order to do that, they must externalize the tacit knowledge within them. They must draw lessons from their experiences, and then convey those lessons in a form so that others can use it" (2002, pp. 74–75). Leaders intent on creating such learning conversations require what Tichy refers to as a *Teachable Point of View* (TPOV). A TPOV is a "cohesive set of ideas and concepts that a person is able to articulate clearly to others" (2002, p. 74). Roger Enrico from PepsiCo has said that "A Teachable Point of View is worth 50 IQ points" (Tichy, 2002, p. 97).

Tichy describes four basic building blocks of a TPOV. First, a TPOV is built on central ideas. Ideas "enable the leader to create dynamic and engaging stories that detail where the company is, where it is going, and how they will get there" (p. 75). Second, a TPOV must include values that leaders can articulate explicitly to shape support for ideas. Third, a TPOV must be energizing, including "a clear set of beliefs and actions for motivating others" (p. 76). Finally, a TPOV involves what Tichy describes as "edge," "facing reality . . . and making tough decisions" (p. 76).

When Jean Clark began as an IC, she spent a great deal of time developing her own TPOV—though she likely wouldn't have used that terminology. Jean was determined to find effective ways to explain Content Enhancement—and that took time. "In the beginning," Jean said, "this stuff didn't make any sense." So, to "make sense" of Content Enhancement, Jean spent many hours reading through instructor's manuals, paraphrasing materials in her own mind, drawing semantic maps, and taking notes until she felt she knew the material. Jean also practiced teaching routines in the classroom so that she was fully aware of how it felt to teach students how to master concepts using the Concept Mastery Routine (Bulgren, Schumaker, & Deshler, 1993) or how to organize their units using the Unit Organizer Routine (Lenz, Bulgren, Schumaker, Deshler, & Boudah, 1994).

Jean found that "the smartest thing" was to take time to learn "a piece at a time." According to Jean, "You can't take this really quickly, you have to think about it." However, Jean's determination to get clarity about Content Enhancement is paying off: "I'm definitely changing as a result of this, and I'm really starting to get the big picture with Content Enhancement and the whole model, the whole Strategic Instruction Model." As she gets clearer, Jean finds she has become more capable of getting other teachers to implement the model. Jean reports, "Other people are having 'aha's'! All you need is one person to have an 'aha' every now and then; that's enough."

TACTIC 4: MANAGING CHANGE EFFECTIVELY

Buckingham and Coffman (1999), who studied more than 80,000 managers from different industries, suggest that a large part of effective leadership is effective management. These researchers sifted through literally millions of data sets, sorting and resorting until they synthesized the essence of effective management into six critical questions. These questions help us understand how ICs can perform many management tasks of leading change.

The Big Six

1. Do I know what is expected of me?

2. Do I have the materials and equipment I need to do my work right?

3. At work, do I have the opportunity to do what I do best every day?

4. In the past seven days, have I received recognition or praise for doing good work?

5. Is there someone at work who cares about me?

6. Is there someone at work who encourages my development?

Let's take a look at each of these questions as they apply to instructional coaching.

Do I Know What Is Expected of Me?

Teachers who do not understand what they have to do to implement a teaching practice may be quick to drop that practice when they find out it is not what they expected. Consequently, if ICs are unclear about what teachers need to do in order to implement practices, they run the risk of severely damaging a relationship they may have spent months or years developing. For example, a teacher trying out a new approach she learned from a coach who is blindsided by a time-consuming demand to grade learning sheets may quickly reject the approach or, perhaps even worse, reject the coach when she realizes the additional grading is more than she can handle.

To be effective, ICs have to be careful to explain exactly what teachers can expect why they try something new. Among other concerns, ICs should explain (a) what additional demands, if any, will be made on teacher time; (b) how much class time a given teaching practice will take; (c) how students might be expected to respond; (d) how the intervention fits with the district or state curriculum; and (e) what else may have to change for the practice to be implemented.

Do I Have the Materials and Equipment I Need to Do My Work Right?

Teachers tell us that one of the main reasons why they often do not implement new teaching practices is that they do not have the time or desire to put together all the materials necessary to try something new. ICs in Topeka and Baltimore have gotten around this barrier to implementation by giving teachers a cardboard box called "strategy in a box," filled with every item a teacher might need to implement a strategy or routine, including printed overheads, handouts or learning sheets for students, reading materials, or whatever else might be necessary for implementation. As IC Irma Brasseur has commented, "Part of our goal is to release teachers from burdensome, mundane things so they can spend time thinking about being a learner, to make changes to bring out critical teaching behaviors."

At Work, Do I Have the Opportunity to Do What I Do Best Every Day?

Although coaches usually have little or no say in who teaches what classes, an IC can collaborate with teachers to make it possible for them to do their best every day. Most important, when coaches and individual teachers work together to identify instructional practices, they must be careful to identify interventions that build on the teacher's unique strengths. Teaching practices are not generic; what works well for one teacher might not work as well for another. The art of coaching is working together with a teacher to identify interventions that respond to the teacher's most pressing need while also taking advantage of the teacher's greatest strength.

In the Past Seven Days, Have I Received Recognition or Praise for Doing Good Work?

Recognizing and praising each teacher each week may be a stretch goal for some ICs, but that doesn't mean that it isn't a worthy one. As we've explained throughout this book, a coach is often much more effective if she can build an emotional connection with fellow teachers, and this includes recognizing, praising, and supporting teachers whenever possible. For Jean Clark, recognizing teachers also provides an opportunity for follow-up and dialogue: "If you don't have the follow-up and you don't have the opportunity to continually reuse it and talk about it and dialogue about it, it's not going to stick."

Is There Someone at Work Who Cares About Me?

Can a coach be successful if he doesn't care about fellow teachers? I don't think so. Coaches who are truly collaborative can't help but find themselves in caring relationships with collaborating teachers. Interviews I've conducted with coaches across the nation have shown again and again that an important aspect of coaching is simply being available as a listener or a friend to fellow teachers. As IC Devona Dunekack has observed, being a coach is "more than PD [professional development]. Every week, several times, people come and see me, shut the door and let go. They might talk about something personal, or something in the school. I'm just a good listening ear, and after we've talked, they can get up and do the job that is extremely important to do."

Is There Someone at Work Who Encourages My Development?

Ultimately, this is what an IC's primary work is, to continually encourage each teacher to develop, to be a better professional, to reach and encourage and support more children. As such, an effective IC contributes in immeasurable ways to the continual progress of the school. By facilitating the professional growth of their colleagues, coaches help teachers stay alive, stay growing, and stay effective shapers of children's lives.

Buckingham and Coffman's questions bring into focus some of the tactics, strategies, and perspectives an IC should employ, and the questions also demonstrate that having an IC in a school can be a powerful way to accelerate professional learning and, indeed, enable people to realize their potential and live meaningful lives. But managing is only part of leadership. To really lead change, you need to go further.

TACTIC 5: CONFRONTING REALITY

The most obvious leadership challenge may also be the most difficult: confronting reality. According to Bossidy and Charan (2004), who literally wrote the book on this topic, *Confronting Reality: Doing What Matters to Get Things Right*, "to confront reality is to recognize the world as it is, not as you wish it to be, and have the courage to do what must be done, not what you'd like to do" (pp. 6–7). But, recognizing and acting on the world as it is, is not always easy for ICs. When working one-to-one with teachers, for example, coaches may find it difficult to candidly discuss instructional practices since the way people teach is so intertwined with the way they define themselves. As a result, if I present an unattractive picture of the way a teacher delivers a particular lesson, for example, I may be criticizing an act that is at the heart of who that person is. To talk about teaching practice is to talk about one of the most personal parts of a teacher's life.

Recently, flying home from a work visit in Michigan, I had an experience that brought home to me just how difficult it can be to confront reality with others. When I sat down on the plane, I found myself sitting beside a fascinating man from the east coast. We quickly found ourselves talking about his work and his life, and I was impressed by the man's intellect, sense of humor, and wisdom. There was just one problem. His breath was terrible. Even though I really wanted to listen to this interesting man, I just couldn't get past the fact that his breath was so bad.

Always the coach, I began to be concerned about the many problems his breath might be causing. "I wonder," I thought, "if I should tell him about his problem. If this breath is a common problem, I wonder if this fellow is losing customers just because they can't stand the aroma emanating from his smiling face? I wonder what impact it has on his marriage and family? What does his wife think about this? I really should tell him about this problem so he can do something about it!" But I didn't say anything. The risks of upsetting this nice man, or getting him angry with me, seemed too great, and I just sat there listening—more concerned with getting along with him or avoiding conflict than I was with giving him some information that might have been very important.

My challenge on the plane is the challenge coaches face every day. ICs struggle to share information that is unpleasant at the same time that they work to maintain a healthy relationship with collaborating teachers. What is difficult one-to-one, where we are able to build strong, supportive bonds with individuals, is even more difficult at the group level. When we surface difficult truths in larger organizations like schools, not only do we have to address the personal issues that are an unavoidable part of confronting reality, we also have to deal with the other contingencies of life in organizations, such as incomplete data sources, misinformation arising from failure of internal communication, individuals who hide from their own professional failures, and so on. It's no wonder that Bossidy and Charan (2004) conclude that "Avoiding reality is a basic and ubiquitous human tendency" (p. 26).

Despite the seductive appeal of avoiding the truth, the fact is that schools won't move forward, and students' lives won't improve, unless ICs and other educational leaders ask some core questions about the teaching and learning that occurs in every classroom:

- What is it like to be a student in this classroom or school?
- How do the students feel in this class?
- Is this teacher using "hi-fi" teaching practices?
- Does the teacher appreciate, enjoy, and respect students?
- Are students engaged in this class?
- Are students experiencing meaningful learning experiences or are they simply completing tasks that fill the time?
- Does this class increase or decrease students' love of learning?
- Will students remember this class?

Along with questions about individual classes, coaches and educational leaders can confront reality by asking questions about the school and school culture:

- Are our teachers focused on becoming better teachers or are they focused on making excuses?
- Is our school improving or declining?

- Do our teachers focus on students and teaching during team meetings, or do they focus on blaming, excuse-making, or finger-pointing?
- Are our leaders supportive and positive?
- Do our leaders encourage our teachers to meet high standards?
- Do our leaders walk the talk?

Confronting reality in most schools is tough, but failure to confront reality is much worse because it ensures that no meaningful improvement takes place. ICs can help a teacher or school face facts by asking some or all of these truth-seeking questions.

TACTIC 6: UNDERSTANDING SCHOOL CULTURE

More than two decades ago, researcher Susan Rosenholtz made the rather startling (to me at least) claim that "reality is socially constructed and maintained through everyday organizational life" and that "teachers shape their beliefs and actions largely in conformance with the structures, policies and traditions of the workaday world around them" (1989, pp. 2–3).

Rosenholtz identified shared goals, teacher collaboration, teacher certainty, learning enrichment opportunities, and teacher commitment as important attributes of effective schools. She adapted organizational theorist Rosabeth Moss Kanter's description of "stuck" and "moving" institutions to distinguish between effective and ineffective academic social organizations:

> The stuck feel no sense of progress, growth or development and so tend to lower their aspirations and appear less motivated to achieve. They shy away from risks in the workplace and proceed in cautious, conservative ways. The moving, by contrast, tend to recognize and use more of their skills and aim still higher. Their sense of progress and future gain encourages them to look forward, to take risks, and to grow. (Rosenholtz, 1991, p. 149)

The implications of Rosenholtz's research are provocative, suggesting that a teacher's effective or ineffective teaching practices result as much from where the teacher teaches as much as they do from who the teacher is. Thus, if you moved teachers from a stuck school to a moving school, just by virtue of where they worked, Rosenholtz suggests, they would in many cases become better teachers. When I share this research with educators, 25 years after Rosenholtz conducted it, these ideas still ring true.

Whether they fully agree with Rosenholtz or not, ICs need to attend to Rosenholtz's lesson: school culture can accelerate or inhibit change in numerous ways in schools. In a sense, culture functions like gravity, no one can see it, but it keeps things in place. In workshops, I often talk about the culture of the elevator. Somehow, most people in North America have mysteriously learned that that there are certain rules to being in an elevator. You know the rules: (a) don't talk, (b) face the door with your back to the wall, (c) look at the numbers. When I was an undergraduate student at the University of Ottawa in Canada, a young poet purposefully broke these rules, by standing with his back to the door, facing the other passengers in the elevator. Usually some people riding along became genuinely uncomfortable just by the way he stood in the elevator. It was as if these people were thinking, "Doesn't he know what the rules are?"

Such is the hold that culture can have over us. We come to act in regulated ways without really being aware that there are any regulations. When cultural norms are good for students, such as norms that say we never talk disrespectfully about children, we believe that all children can succeed, and we support professional learning, cultural norms can be positive. However, when cultural norms are not good for students, such as norms that say we blame the children and their parents for our unsuccessful students, we bully children, and we ridicule professional learning, then they can be very destructive.

One important leadership tactic, then, is for ICs to be sensitive to the cultural norms in a school and to work to change norms that are not good for students. By doing that, coaches function similarly to a group of leaders Debra Meyerson (2001) refers to as *tempered radicals*. "Tempered radicals are people who operate on a fault line. They are organizational insiders who contribute and succeed in their jobs. At the same time, they are treated as outsiders because they represent ideals or agendas that are somehow at odds with the dominant culture" (p. 5).

One of the most important ways in which ICs can lead is by shaping the kinds of conversations that take place in schools. A coach intent on changing school culture must be what Kegan and Lahey (2001) refer to as "a discourse-shaping language leader" (p. 20). That is, he or she must stand for a new kind of conversation while at the same time staying a part of the school culture. Deborah Kolb and Judith Williams (2000) suggest that we redirect conversation away from unhealthy topics, like gossip, by using communication maneuvers they call *responsive turns*. Responsive turns are communication tactics ICs can use to redirect potential unhealthy conversations. I've included four responsive turns suggested by Kolb and Williams, along with my definitions and some examples.

TACTIC 7: BEING AMBITIOUS AND HUMBLE

When the teachers at Jean Clark's middle school resisted her suggestions and criticized her methods, Jean was tempted to return to the classroom and a simpler life. "I've always got one foot out the door," Jean said. But Jean did not give in to the seductive promise of a less stressful life. Rather, she stayed the course with the partnership approach. Jean employed a wide variety of

Table 9.1   Responsive Turns

Tactic	What It Is	Example
Interrupt	Cutting off the negative conversation before it begins	"Oh crap, I'm late; I've gotta go."
Name	Describing what's going on so everyone can see it	"I just feel that if we keep complaining about kids, we're never going to come up with anything useful."
Correct	Clarifying a statement that is not true	"I was at the meeting, and Mr. Smith was actually opposed to the plan."
Divert	Moving the conversation in a different direction	"Speaking of Tom, when does the basketball season start this year?"

relationship-building and communication strategies. She took time to meet one-to-one with teachers, talked with her colleagues about their day-to-day lives inside and outside of school, and listened authentically and with empathy.

At the same time, Jean refused to drift into the background. She was determined and driven—she sought out opportunities to bring together collaborating teachers to do co-planning with her, focusing on teachers who had informal power in her school. Jean also worked with her principal to set up afterschool professional development sessions and to encourage him to apply pressure on some teachers whom she thought might particularly benefit from instructional support. And she was also a voracious learner—attending courses, reading articles and books, and learning as much as she could, as quickly as possible, so that she had valuable, up-to-date knowledge to share with teachers. In short, Jean took a partnership approach with her teachers, but at the same time, she was willful, deliberate, and driven as she led change at her school.

Jean's combination of leadership and partnership slowly began to pay off, and she started to see improvements in the way teachers taught and students learned in her school and in her district as a result of her efforts. Indeed, in a matter of months, Bo Manor Middle School began to attract the attention of educators throughout Cecil County, and the impact of Jean's willful and respectful approach began to extend across the county.

Jean's approach is one that I have seen employed consistently by effective coaches in schools across America. To really make change happen, ICs employ the respectful, patient, and dialogical methods of the partnership approach. At the same time, they are driven, almost obsessive, about making significant changes happen. In his book *Good to Great* (2001), Jim Collins has identified the same kind of paradoxical attributes in leaders of great organizations. When he looked for common traits among great companies, Collins explains, he was taken aback by what he found:

> We were surprised, shocked really, to discover the type of leadership required for turning a good company into a great one. Compared to high-profile leaders with big personalities who make headlines and become celebrities, the good-to-great leaders seem to have come from Mars. Self-effacing, quiet, reserved, even shy—these leaders are a paradoxical blend of personal humility and professional will. They are more like Lincoln and Socrates than Patton or Caesar. (p. 13)

Effective leaders, Collins reports, "are ambitious first and foremost for the cause, the movement, the mission, the work—not themselves—and they have the will to do whatever it takes . . . to make good on that ambition" (2005, p. 11). Much the same can be said about effective ICs—they are very ambitious, but their ambition is for improvements in instruction and in the experiences of children in schools. "Success," Jean reports, "brings success . . . and it's starting to stick. There's a bunch of us doing it; we're becoming partners."

TACTIC 8: TAKING CARE OF YOURSELF

Being a leader is emotionally challenging, and thousands of change agents have found it difficult to remain optimistic, energetic, and enthusiastic. When we are marginalized, attacked, or silenced, when our successes are downplayed and our contributions are overlooked, it is difficult to remain optimistic. As Heifetz and Linsky explain:

> When you lead people, you often begin with a desire to contribute to an organization or community, to help people resolve important issues, to improve the quality of their lives. Your heart is not entirely innocent, but you begin with hope and concern for people. Along the way, however, it becomes difficult to sustain those feelings when many people reject your aspirations as too unrealistic, challenging or disruptive. Results arrive slowly. You become hardened to the discouraging reality. Your heart closes up. (2002, p. 226)

Too frequently, as the table below suggests, professionals in schools find it too difficult to maintain their own innocence, curiosity, and compassion.

For ICs to remain emotionally healthy, given the challenges that can confront them in a school, they must take time to keep themselves healthy.

Table 9.2 Hope and Hopelessness When Leading Change

Quality of Heart	Becomes	Dressed Up As
Innocence	Cynicism	Realism
Curiosity	Arrogance	Authoritative knowledge
Compassion	Callousness	The thick skin of experience

SOURCE: Heifetz & Linsky (2002, p. 226).

Distinguish Your Role From Your Self

Frequently, the kind of people who choose to become ICs are precisely those who are deeply invested in their role. Thus, coaches may tie their own sense of worth directly to their success or failure with teachers in school. When a teacher chooses to use a new practice that helps students be successful, these ICs may have a momentary blissful sense that they are competent, making a difference, and living a life that counts. Then, when teachers stop implementing change, resist change, or attack interventions or, even worse, ICs may feel a deep despair, questioning whether or not their work, or even their life, matters. Such profound emotional upswings and downturns can take a real toll on a coaches' well-being.

Heifetz and Linsky (2002) explain that leaders need to be careful to separate their "role" from their selves: "when you lead, people don't love you or hate you. Mostly they don't even know you. They love or hate the position you represent" (p. 198). To remain healthy, coaches need to remember this.

Find Confidants

Finding someone or a group of people to confide in is a positive way ICs can protect themselves and remain healthy. ICs, by virtue of their role, are often on their own in a school. They are often unable to immerse themselves completely in a school, simply because they are always trying to change it. Coaches are in the school, but not of the school. As a result, they sometimes find themselves on the outside of the in-group, when the in-group is intent on gossiping, complaining, or blaming. For that reason, finding someone to confide in outside the school can be very helpful.

When Jean Clark was considering going back to her first love—the classroom—what kept her committed to being an IC was the development of a collaborative friendship with Sherry Eichinger, a special education teacher at Bohemia Manor Middle School. As the vignette below illustrates, Jean became an emotional and intellectual partner with Sherry. As is the case with true partnerships, Jean, the coach, gained from collaborating with Sherry as much or more as Sherry, the teacher, gained from Jean.

Faith

In the years previous, I was training to be a professional developer. But I had this fear that maybe I don't have good people skills, perhaps I shouldn't be doing this. I kept running into these adults who were getting really ticked off at me. I kept thinking, "Well, you know, I'm just getting more and more awkward here as I'm aging and I'm not able to get these folks to work with me as I used to." So I was just about ready to get out of this field and go back to the classroom.

But what I've been discovering is that I can do this really, really well as long as I have partners. I see that when I have a partner like Sherry. She was a Christi McCollum scholar. She has a master's in special ed and in transitions, and she will not back off for those kids—she will do lots of work. I gained a great deal to suddenly be around someone who works like that. She started coming to me and asking, "Well, how would you teach a kid that really didn't understand how to read?" and "I don't understand how to do this," and every time she asked me a question, I had to think about it, and as soon as I started to think about it, I started thinking about how I learned.

The two of us work so well together. We disagree with one another at times, but we're both working for the same thing; we're both working for the kids and an understanding with the kids. I can't do it by myself, and I see that she can't do it by herself. We support one another. She supports me emotionally when I'm really depressed; she tries to keep me up. And when she's really depressed, thinking, "OK, I'm not going to do this another year, everybody's at my throat," I talk to her about it and remind her how far we've come. So we support one another both cognitively and emotionally. Because it's hard to do this work without a partner.

Being a change agent, you can weather it, you can weather what happens to you if you have enough folks talking to you—not just talking to you, but giving you things to think about, and letting you see their growth, like I've seen her growth. Having her there, it has given me faith.

Find Sanctuary

The need to build in a time and place to recharge your batteries is not a new idea. In as ancient a document as Genesis in the Bible, we were advised to ensure that we take one day off from all of our work. Researchers studying top athletes have found that that biblical advice still holds true for active athletes. Loehr and Schwartz (2003), for example, have conducted studies of the attributes of great athletes. When they compared great athletes with good athletes, they found that great athletes don't try any harder or, in many cases, aren't any more skilled than good athletes, but they are much better at building variety into their training routine.

I believe that ICs can take a page from the great athletes that Loehr and Schwartz describe. Coaches, like athletes, need to be sure to build in opportunities to relax, refresh, and recharge. Jean Clark reports that she's fully aware that she does need to take care of herself, and she has her ways to relax and renew herself that work best for her. "I'm a writer; I write constantly. I read all the time, I go to counseling. I'm in 12-step meetings, you name it . . . I go to church . . . I do everything to stay emotionally healthy."

One simple way to recharge is to find a place where you are able to relax and cool your heels, so to speak. Your own personal sanctuary might be your favorite coffee shop downtown, a park bench, a quiet out-of-the-way corner in the library, or the swing on your front porch. What matters is that you find a place where you feel free to relax and let your mind stand at ease for an hour or two. I don't own a condo by the ocean or a cabin by a mountain stream, but I have found my own way to find sanctuary. In Lawrence, Kansas, where I live, there is a five-mile concrete trail that provides bikers, runners, and Rollerbladers with a quick route out of town and into a beautiful, wide prairie meadow. My sanctuary is to tie up my old pair of Rollerblades, program my iPod to play whatever music suits me on a given day, and roll out into the valley. For an hour or so with my Rollerblades, music, and the nature trail, I'm able to put the pressing deadlines and other challenges I face on hold, and simply rest and relax. Indeed, many of the ideas that have found their way into this book first flew into my consciousness when I was far away from my computer, blading through the valley just outside of Lawrence.

THE FINAL WORD ON JEAN CLARK AND BOHEMIA MANOR MIDDLE SCHOOL

During the last weeks of Jean's first year at Bo Manor, I was sitting in my office at the University of Kansas. When my phone rang, I picked it up and heard the voice of Joe Buckley, Jean's principal, on the other end of the line. Joe had never called me; in fact, I had never given him my telephone number, but he told me that he had gone out of his way to get it from Jean. "Jim," he said, "we've just gotten our test scores, and let me read some of them to you." Joe quickly rattled off some scores that, I learned, showed that in each grade, the number of students who were proficient in math and reading had doubled. Bohemia Manor School, it turns out, was the only school in Cecil County in which a majority of students were proficient in all subjects and all grade levels. The results, were, as Joe said, "amazing." "Jim," he concluded, "I just had to call you to thank you for your work supporting Jean. These scores just show how important she is to this school. She's done an awesome job this year."

Throughout that year, I had worked with Jean, and I knew what struggles she had gone through to win over her school and to make meaningful improvements in instruction to take root. When I heard how genuinely grateful and excited her principal was, I felt a deep sense of satisfaction. Jean had stuck it out, weathered the attacks, and led her school forward, and in the end, her school's students were clearly better for her work. Working as an IC, Jean had had an unmistakable, positive impact on the teachers in her school, and consequently, the students in her school were learning more and performing better. What could be better than that?[1]

GOING DEEPER

Reading about leadership is a bit like reading about surfing, I imagine. Books might help, but you really have to dive in and get wet to truly benefit from your readings. Most readers of this book, I suspect, are already confronting leadership challenges. In that case, the following sources should prove helpful.

Michael Fullan's books, described in the Going Deeper section of Chapter 8, are a great starting point for the study of leadership.

Heifetz and Linsky's *Leadership on the Line: Staying Alive Through the Dangers of Leadership* (2002), accurately summarizes many of the emotionally taxing challenges a leader might face and offers practical strategies people can use to overcome those challenges. Heifetz and Linsky also explain how and why leaders should distinguish between technical and adaptive challenges.

Goleman, Boyatzis, and McKee's *Primal Leadership: Learning to Lead With Emotional Intelligence* (2002) applies the concept of emotional intelligence, first introduced by Daniel Goleman, to leadership. The authors contend that a leader's most important task, the primal task, is to address the emotional needs of those being led. Leaders who are astute enough to guide their teams to experience positive emotions are referred to as *resonant leaders*. The model of leadership they propose is consistent with the partnership principles, and the book's description of the relationship-building skills, leadership styles, and strategies necessary to create resonant leadership are very useful. The book also contains some excellent non-examples.

When I heard Dennis Sparks speak in 2005, he held up a copy of *Primal Leadership* and said, "If there is one book on leadership that educators should read, this is it." Some might make a claim that the same could be said for his book, *Leading for Results: Transforming Teaching, Learning, and Relationships in Schools* (2005). This is a remarkably concise work that contains 25 strategies people can employ to refine their leadership skills. Sparks's visionary *and* practical strategies include a variety of ways to clarify and achieve your goals, several suggestions for developing clear thinking, skills for improving authentic listening and encouraging dialogue, and other strategies leaders can employ to walk the talk as they lead.

Henry Cloud's *Integrity: The Courage to Meet the Demands of Reality* (2006) is a very readable but wise and useful book that describes six qualities that determine leadership success in business (I believe his suggestions also apply to the social sector). The six qualities are establishing trust, oriented toward truth, getting results, embracing the negative, oriented toward increase, and oriented toward transcendence.

Marcus Buckingham and Curt Coffman's *First, Break All the Rules: What the World's Greatest Managers Do Differently* (1999) introduces the Big Six Questions included in this chapter. Based on over 80,000 interviews conducted by the Gallup Organization, the book describes three basic strategies used by outstanding managers. First, in managing, leading, and "sustained individual success," the most productive leaders find the talents of people they work with and do not dwell on their negative aspects. Second, managers shape jobs to fit people, rather than shape people to fit jobs. Third, they are crystal clear in expectations and goals. Fourth, leaders choose employees for the talent they have, not just their expertise.

TO SUM UP

- Leadership is an unavoidable part of instructional coaching.
- There are eight tactics ICs can use to increase their effectiveness as leaders:
- *Stay detached:* Find ways to take the long view and keep yourself from being overly invested in each component of your coaching program.
- *Walk on solid ground:* Know what you stand for if you want others to stand with you.
- *Clarify your message:* Develop a deep understanding and clear way of communicating the ideas you have to share with others.
- *Be ambitious and humble:* Embody a paradoxical mix of ambition for students and personal humility.
- *Confront reality:* Ask questions that help you focus on the real situation in teachers' classrooms and in your school.
- *Understand school culture:* Recognize that behavior is often as much a product of organizational culture as it is of each individual's characteristics.
- *Manage change effectively:* Do all you can to ensure that your teachers know what is expected of them and have what they need to implement the teaching practices you share with them.
- *Take care of yourself:* If you want to lead change, you must protect and nourish yourself.

NOTE

1. At the end of Jean's second year, Bohemia Manor again showed more growth than any other middle school in Cecil County.

Instructional Coach's Tool Kit

Instructional Coaching
Progress through Partnership

ACTION PLANNING
LEVERAGE POINT FORM

		1	2	3	4	5	
ISSUE # ____	Very Difficult	☐	☐	☐	☐	☐	Very Easy
	Little Impact	☐	☐	☐	☐	☐	Significant Impact
ISSUE # ____	Very Difficult	☐	☐	☐	☐	☐	Very Easy
	Little Impact	☐	☐	☐	☐	☐	Significant Impact
ISSUE # ____	Very Difficult	☐	☐	☐	☐	☐	Very Easy
	Little Impact	☐	☐	☐	☐	☐	Significant Impact
ISSUE # ____	Very Difficult	☐	☐	☐	☐	☐	Very Easy
	Little Impact	☐	☐	☐	☐	☐	Significant Impact
		1	2	3	4	5	

TEACHER MEETING
L O G

Date: ___ / ___ / ___   Time / Mod: _____

Teacher: _____

Purpose/Strategy: _____

Teacher Plan / To Do: Date Completed

• _____   ___ / ___

• _____   ___ / ___

• _____   ___ / ___

• _____   ___ / ___

• _____   ___ / ___

IC Plan / To Do: Date Completed

• _____   ___ / ___

• _____   ___ / ___

• _____   ___ / ___

• _____   ___ / ___

• _____   ___ / ___

Follow-up on: ___ / ___ / ___ @ ___ : ___ (Mod ___)

Instructional Coaching
Progress through Partnership

ARE YOU INTERESTED?

NAME: _____

DATE: _____

I am most interested in:

_____
_____
_____
_____
_____
_____
_____
_____
_____

☐ Times good for me:

_____
_____

☐ Maybe some other time

KU CENTER FOR RESEARCH ON LEARNING The University of Kansas | Instructional Coaching
Progress through Partnership

AFTER-ACTION
R E P O R T

School: _____   Strategy/Routine: _____
Teacher: _____   Unit/Content: _____

What was supposed to happen?

_____
_____
_____
_____
_____

What happened?

_____
_____
_____
_____
_____

What accounts for the differences?

_____
_____
_____
_____
_____

What should be done differently next time?

_____
_____
_____
_____
_____

Additional Comments? (Please use back of form)

TIME CHART

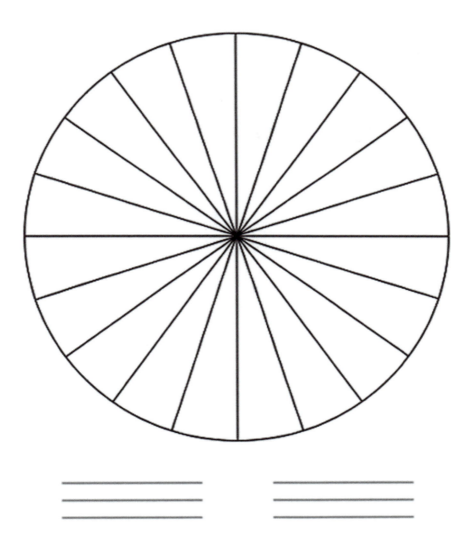

OBSERVATION FORM

Teacher: _____   School: _____

Unit/Content: _____   Module: _____

Date: _____

TEACHING PRACTICE	OBS.	COMMENTS

Abrahamson, E. (2004). *Change without pain: How managers can overcome initiative overload, organizational chaos, and employee burnout.* Boston: Harvard Business School.

Allen, D. (2001). *Getting things done: The art of stress-free productivity.* New York: Penguin.

Argyris, C., Putnam, R., & Smith, D. M. (1985). *Action science.* San Francisco: Jossey-Bass.

Bernstein, R. J. (1983). *Beyond objectivism and relativism: Science, hermeneutics, and praxis.* Philadelphia: University of Pennsylvania Press.

Bishop, C. H., Jr. (2001). *Making change happen one person at a time: Assessing your change capacity within your organization.* New York: AMACOM.

Black, P., Harrison, C., Lee, C., Marshall, B., & Wiliam, D. (2003). *Assessment for learning: Putting it into practice.* Berkshire, England: McGraw-Hill.

Block, P. (1993). *Stewardship: Choosing service over self-interest.* San Francisco: Berrett-Koehler.

Block, P. (2001). *The answer to how is yes: Acting on what matters.* San Francisco: Berrett-Koehler.

Bloom, B. S., Englehart, M. D., Furst, E. J., Hill, W. H., & Krathwohl, D. R. (1956). *Taxonomy of educational objectives. Handbook 1: Cognitive Domain.* New York: Longman, Green.

Bloom, G. S., Castagna, C. L., Moir, E., & Warren, B. (2005). *Blended coaching: Skills and strategies to support principal development.* Thousand Oaks, CA: Corwin Press.

Bohm, D. (2000). *On dialogue.* New York: Routledge.

Bossidy, L., & Charan, R. (2004). *Confronting reality: Doing what matters to get things right.* New York: Random.

Brubaker, J. W., Case, C. W., & Reagan, J. G. (1994). *Becoming a reflective educator: How to build a culture of inquiry in the schools.* Thousand Oaks, CA: Corwin Press.

Buckingham, M., & Coffman, C. (1999). *First, break all the rules: What the world's greatest managers do differently.* New York: Simon & Schuster.

Bulgren, J. A., Deshler, D. D., & Schumaker, J. B. (1993). *The concept mastery routine.* Lawrence, KS: Edge Enterprises.

Bulgren, J. A., & Lenz, B. K. (1996). Strategic instruction in the content areas. In D. D. Deshler, E. S. Ellis, & B. K. Lenz (Eds.), *Teaching adolescents with learning disabilities: Strategies and methods* (2nd ed., pp. 409–473). Denver, CO: Love Publishing.

Bulgren, J. A., Lenz, B. K., Deshler, D. D., & Schumaker, J. B. (2001). *Question exploration routine.* Lawrence, KS: Edge Enterprises.

Bush, R. N. (1984). *Effective staff developments in making our schools more effective: Proceedings of three state conferences.* San Francisco: Far West Laboratories.

Carnegie, D. (1936). *How to win friends and influence people.* New York: Simon & Schuster.

Collins, J. (2001). *Good to great: Why some companies make the leap . . . and others don't.* New York: HarperCollins.

Collins, J. (2005). *Good to great and the social sector: A monograph to accompany Good to Great.* Boulder, CO: Collins.

Costa, A. L., & Garmston, R. J. (2002). *Cognitive coaching: A foundation for renaissance schools* (2nd ed.). Norwood, MA: Christopher-Gordon.

Covey, S. (1989). *The 7 habits of highly effective people: Powerful lessons in personal change.* New York: Simon & Schuster.

Covey, S. (2004). *The eighth habit: From effectiveness to greatness.* New York: Simon & Schuster.

Cloud, H. (2006). *Integrity: The courage to meet the demands of reality.* New York: HarperCollins.

Csikszentmihalyi, M. (1990). *Flow: The psychology of optimal experience.* New York: Harper & Row.

Csikszentmihalyi, M. (1994). *The evolving self: A psychology for the third millennium.* New York: HarperCollins.

Danielson, C. (1996). *Enhancing professional practice: A framework for teaching.* Alexandria, VA: Association for Supervision and Curriculum Development.

Davenport, T. H. (2005). *Thinking for a living: How to get better performance and results from knowledge workers.* Boston: Harvard Business School Press.

DuFour, R. (1998). Why look elsewhere? Improving schools from within. *The School Administrator, 2*(55), 24–28.

DuFour, R., & Eaker, R. E. (1998). *Professional learning communities at work: Best practices for enhancing student achievement.* Bloomington, IN: National Education Service.

Duke Corporate Education. (2006). *Coaching and feedback for performance.* Chicago: Dearborn Trade Publishing.

Eisler, R. (1988). *Chalice and the blade: Our history, our future.* New York: HarperCollins.

Eisler, R. (2000). *Tomorrow's children: A blueprint for partnership education for the 21st century.* Boulder, CO: Westview.

Ekman, P. (2003). *Emotions revealed: Recognizing faces and feelings to improve communication and emotional life.* New York: Henry Holt.

Ellis, E. S. (1998). *The framing routine.* Lawrence, KS: Edge Enterprises.

Evertson, C. M. (1995). Classroom management in the learning centered classroom. In A. Ornstein (Ed.), *Teaching: Theory and practice.* Boston: Allyn & Bacon.

Evertson, C. M., & Harris, A. H. (1999). Support for managing learning centered classrooms: The Classroom Organization and Management Program. In H. J. Freiberg (Ed.), *Beyond behaviorism: Changing the classroom management paradigm* (pp. 57–73). Boston: Allyn & Bacon.

Fisher, R., & Brown, S. (1988). *Getting together: Building relationships as we negotiate.* New York: Penguin.

Fisher, R., & Shapiro, D. (2005). *Beyond reason: Using emotions as you negotiate.* New York: Viking Press.

Fisher, R., & Sharp, A. (1998). *Getting it done: How to lead when you're not in charge.* New York: HarperCollins.

Fisher, R., Ury, W., & Patton, B. (1991). *Getting to yes: Negotiating agreement without giving in* (2nd ed.). New York: Penguin.

Flaherty, J. (1999). *Coaching: Evoking excellence in others*. Boston: Butterworth.

Freire, P. (1970). *Pedagogy of the oppressed*. New York: Continuum.

Fullan, M. (1993). *Change forces: Probing the depths of educational reform*. New York: Falmer Press.

Fullan, M. (1999). *Change forces: The sequel*. Philadelphia: Falmer Press.

Fullan, M. (2001). *Leading in a culture of change: Being effective in complex times*. San Francisco: Jossey-Bass.

Fullan, M. (2003). *Change forces with a vengeance*. New York: RoutledgeFalmer.

Fullan, M. (2005). *Leadership and sustainability: System thinkers in action*. Thousand Oaks, CA: Corwin Press.

Fullan, M. (2001). *The new meaning of education change* (3rd ed.). New York: Teachers College Press.

Fullan, M., & Hargreaves, A. (1996). *What's worth fighting for in your school* (2nd ed.). New York: Teachers College Press.

Gadotti, M. (1996). *Pedagogy of praxis: A dialectical philosophy of education*. Albany: State University of New York Press.

Gladwell, M. (2000). *The tipping point: How little things can make a big difference*. Boston: Little, Brown.

Gladwell, M. (2005). *Blink: The power of thinking without thinking*. Boston: Little, Brown.

Gleick, J. (1999). *Faster: The acceleration of just about everything*. New York: Pantheon Books.

Godin, S. (2002). *Unleashing the ideavirus*. New York: Hyperion.

Goldsmith, M., Lyons, L., & Freas, A. (2000). *Coaching for leadership: How the world's greatest coaches help leaders learn*. San Francisco: Jossey-Bass.

Goleman, D., Boyatzis, R., & McKee, A. (2002). *Primal leadership:Learning tolead with emotional intelligence*. Boston: Harvard Business School Press

Gottman, J. M. (2001). *The relationship cure: A five-step guide for building better connections with family, friends, and lovers*. New York: Crown.

Gottman, J. M., & Silver, N. (1999). *The seven principles for making marriage work*. New York: Crown.

Greenleaf, R. K. (1998). *The power of servant-leadership*. San Francisco: Berrett-Koehler.

Hall, G. E., & Hord, S. M. (2005). *Implementing change: Patterns, principles, and potholes*. Boston: Allyn & Bacon.

Heifetz, R., A., & Linsky, M. (2002). *Leadership on the line: Staying alive through the dangers of leading*. Boston: Harvard Business School Press.

Hunter, M. (1994). *Mastery teaching: Increasing instructional effectiveness in elementary, secondary schools, and colleges and universities*. Thousand Oaks, CA: Corwin Press.

International Reading Association. (2006). *Standards for middle and high school literacy coaches*. Newark, DE: Author.

Isaacs, W. (1999). *Dialogue and the art of thinking together*. New York: Doubleday.

Jacobs, H. H. (1997). *Mapping the big picture: Integrating curriculum and assessment, K–12*. Alexandria, VA: Association for Supervision and Curriculum Development.

Jacobs, H. H. (2004). *Getting results with curriculum mapping*. Alexandria, VA: Association for Supervision and Curriculum Development.

Jeary, T. (2004). *Life is a series of presentations: 8 ways to inspire, inform, and influence anyone, anywhere, anytime*. New York: Fireside.

Jensen, B. (2000). *Simplicity: The new competitive advantage in a world of more, better, faster*. New York: HarperCollins.

Jensen, B. (2005). *What is your life's work? Answer the big questions about what really matters . . . and reawaken the passion for what you do*. New York: HarperCollins.

Joyce, B., & Showers, B. (2002). *Student achievement through staff development* (3rd ed.). Alexandria, VA: Association for Supervision and Curriculum Development.

Kegan, R., & Lahey, L. (2001). *How the way we talk can change the way we learn*. San Francisco: Jossey-Bass.

Kegan, R., & Lahey, L. (2002). *How the way we talk can change the way we work: Seven languages for transformation*. San Francisco: Jossey-Bass.

Killion, J. P., & Todnem, G. R. (1991). A process of personal theory building. *Educational Leadership, 48*(2), 14–16.

Killion, J., Harrison, C. (2006). *Taking the lead: New roles for teachers and school-based coaches*. Oxford, OH: National Staff Development Council.

Kise, J. (2006). *Differentiated coaching: A framework for helping teachers change*. Thousand Oaks, CA: Corwin Press.

Kleiner, A. (2003). *Who really matters: The Core Group Theory of power, privilege, and success*. New York: Doubleday.

Kline, F. M., Schumaker, J. B., & Deshler, D. D. (1991). The development and validation of feedback routines for instructing students with learning disabilities. *LD Forum, 14*, 191–207.

Knight, J. (1994). *Personal vision: A study of the role of personal vision and teacher efficacy*. Unpublished manuscript.

Knight, J. (1998). *The effectiveness of partnership learning: A dialogical methodology for staff development*. Lawrence: University of Kansas Center for Research on Learning.

Knight, J. (2000, April). *Another damn thing we've got to do: Teacher perceptions of professional development*. Paper presented at the meeting of the American Educational Research Association, New Orleans, LA.

Knight, J. (December, 2002). Crossing boundaries: What constructivists can teach intensive-explicit instructors and vice versa. *Focus on Exceptional Children*.

Knight, J. (2004). Instructional coaches make progress through partnership. *Journal of Staff Development, 25*(2), 32–37.

Knight, J. (2006). Instructional coaching: Eight factors for realizing better classroom teaching through support, feedback and intensive, individualized professional learning. *The School Administrator, 63*(4), 36–40.

Kolb, D. M., & Williams, J. (2000). *The shadow negotiator: How women can master the hidden agendas that determine bargaining success*. New York: Simon & Schuster.

Kuhn, T. S. (1970). *The structure of scientific revolutions* (2nd ed.). Chicago: University of Chicago Press.

Lawrence-Lightfoot, S. (2000). *Respect: An exploration*. New York: HarperCollins.

Lenz, B. K., Alley, G. R., & Schumaker, J. B. (1987). Activating the inactive learner: Advance organizers in the secondary content classroom. *Learning Disability Quarterly, 10*(1), 53–67.

Lenz, B. K., Bulgren, J. A., Kissam, B. R., & Taymans, J. (2004). SMARTER planning for academic diversity. In B. K. Lenz & D. D. Deshler with B. R. Kissam (Eds.), *Teaching content to all: Evidence-based inclusive practices in middle and secondary schools* (pp. 47–77). Boston: Pearson Education.

Lenz, B. K., Bulgren, J., Schumaker, J., Deshler, D. D., & Boudah, D. (1994). *The unit organizer routine.* Lawrence, KS: Edge Enterprises.

Lenz, B. K., & Deshler, D. D. (2004). Adolescents with learning disabilities: Revisiting "The educator's enigma." In B. Y. L. Wong (Ed.), *Learning about learning disabilities* (3rd ed., pp. 535–564). New York: Academic Press.

Lenz, B. K., Deshler, D. D., & Kissam, B. R. (2004). *The course organizer routine.* Lawrence, KS: Edge Enterprises.

Lenz, B. K., Marrs, R. W., Schumaker, J., & Deshler, D. D. (1993). *The lesson organizer routine.* Lawrence, KS: Edge Enterprises.

Lenz, B. K., Schumaker, J. B., Deshler, D. D., & Bulgren, J. A. (1998). *The course organizer routine.* Lawrence, KS: Edge Enterprises.

Lewin, K. (1951). *Field theory in social science: Selected theoretical papers.* New York: Harper & Row.

Loehr, J. S., & Schwartz, T. (2003). *The power of full engagement: Managing energy, not time, is the key to high performance and personal renewal.* New York: Free Press.

Marzano, R. J., Pickering, D., & Pollock, J. E. (2001). *Classroom management that works: Research based strategies for increasing student achievement.* Alexandria, VA: Association for Supervision and Curriculum Development.

McMillan, J. H. (2001). *Essential assessment concepts for teachers and administrators.* Thousand Oaks, CA: Corwin Press.

McTighe, J., & O'Connor, K. (2006). Seven practices for effective learning. *Education Leadership, 63*(3), 10–17.

Meyerson, D. E. (2001). *Tempered radicals: How people use difference to inspire change at work.* Boston: Harvard Business School Press.

National Staff Development Council. (2001). *NSDC's standards for staff development* (Rev.). Oxford, OH: Author.

Nonanka, I., & Takeuchi, H. (1995). *The knowledge creating company: How Japanese companies create the dynamics of innovation.* New York: Oxford University Press.

Palmer, P. (1998). *The courage to teach: Exploring the inner landscape of a teacher's life.* San Francisco: Jossey-Bass.

Patterson, K., Grenny, J., McMillan, R., & Switzler, A. (2002). *Crucial conversations: Tools for talking when stakes are high.* New York: McGraw-Hill.

Polanyi, M. (1958). *Personal knowledge.* Chicago: University of Chicago Press.

Polanyi, M. (1983). *The tacit dimension.* Gloucester, MA: Peter Smith.

Prochaska, J. O., Norcross, J. C., & DiClemente, C. C. (1994). *Changing for good.* New York: Avon Books.

Rademacher, J., Deshler, D. D., Schumaker J. B., & Lenz, B. K. (1998). *Quality assignment routine.* Lawrence, KS: Edge Enterprises.

Reinke, W. (2005). *The classroom check-up: A brief intervention to reduce current and future student problem behaviors through classroom teaching practices.* Unpublished dissertation, University of Oregon, Eugene.

Rosenholtz, S. J. (1991). *Teacher's workplace: The social organization of schools.* New York: Teachers College Press.

Scanlon, D., Deshler, D. D., & Schumaker, J. B. (2004). *The order routine.* Lawrence, KS: Edge Enterprises.

Schein, E. H. (1992). *Organizational culture and leadership* (2nd ed.). San Francisco: Jossey-Bass.

Schön, D. A. (1987). *Educating the reflective practitioner.* San Francisco: Jossey-Bass.

Schumaker, J. B. (2002a). *The paragraph writing strategy.* Lawrence, KS: Edge Enterprises.

Schumaker, J. B. (2002b). *The theme writing strategy.* Lawrence, KS: Edge Enterprises.

Schumaker, J. B., Deshler, D. D., & McKnight, P. C. (1991). Teaching routines for content areas at the secondary level. In G. Stover, M. R. Shinn, & H. M. Walker (Eds.), *Interventions for achievement and behavior problems* (pp. 473–494). Washington, DC: National Association of School Psychologists.

Schumaker, J. B., & Sheldon, J. (1985). *The sentence writing strategy.* Lawrence, KS: Edge Enterprises.

Scott, S. (2002). *Fierce conversations: Achieving success at work and in life, one conversation at a time.* New York: Penguin.

Seligman, M. E. P. (1998). *Learned optimism: How to change your mind and your life.* New York: Simon & Schuster.

Senge, P. M. (1990). *The fifth discipline: The art and practice of the learning organization.* London: Random House.

Senge, P. M., Kleiner, A., Roberts, C., Ross, R., & Smith, B. (1994). *The fifth discipline fieldbook.* New York: A Currency Book.

Sparks, D. (2005). *Leading for results: Transforming teaching, learning, and relationships in schools.* Thousand Oaks, CA: Corwin Press.

Sprick, R., Garrison, M., & Howard, L. (1998). *CHAMPs: A proactive and positive approach to classroom management.* Longmont, CO: Sopris West.

Sprick, R., Knight, J., Reinke, W., & McKale, T. (2007). *Coaching classroom management: A toolkit for coaches and administrators.* Eugene, OR: Pacific Northwest Publishing.

Stiggins, R. J. (2004). *Student-involved assessment for learning* (4th ed.). Upper Saddle River, NJ: Pearson Prentice Hall.

Stiggins, R. J., Arter, J. A., Chappuis, J., & Chappuis, S. (2004). *Classroom assessment* for *student learning: Doing it right—using it well.* Portland, OR: ETS Assessment Training Institute.

Stone, D., Patton, B., & Heen, S. (1999). *Difficult conversations: How to discuss what matters most.* New York: Penguin.

Sturtevant, E. G. (2005). *The literacy coach: A key to improving teaching and learning in schools.* Washington, DC: The Alliance for Excellent Education.

Tichy, N. M., & Cardwell, N. (2002). *The cycle of leadership: How great leaders teach their companies to win.* New York: HarperBusiness.

Tomlinson, C. A., & McTighe, J. (2006). *Integrating differentiated instruction and understanding by design: Connecting content and kids.* Alexandria, VA: Association for Supervision of Curriculum Development.

Ury, W. (1991). *Getting past no: Negotiating your way from confrontation to cooperation.* New York: Bantam.

U.S. Army. (2004). *The U.S. Army leadership field manual.* New York: McGraw-Hill.

Vella, J. (1995). *Training through dialogue: Promoting effective learning and change with adults*. San Francisco: Jossey-Bass.

Vernon, S., Deshler, D. D., & Schumaker, J. B. (2000). *Talking together*. Lawrence, KS: Edge Enterprises.

Walberg, H. J. (1984). Improving the productivity of America's schools. *Educational Leadership*, *41*(8), 19–27.

Wheatley, M. (2002). *Turning to one another: Simple conversations to restore hope to the future*. San Francisco: Berrett-Koehler.

Whitemore, J. (1999). *Coaching for performance*. Naperville, IL: Nicholas Brealey.

Whiteworth, L., Kimsey-Hourse, H., & Sandahl, P. (1998). *Co-active coaching: New skills for coaching people toward success in work and life*. Palo Alto, CA: Davies-Black.

Wiggins, G., & McTighe, J. (2005). *Understanding by design* (2nd ed.). Alexandria, VA: Association for Supervision and Curriculum Development.

Yankelovich, D. (1999). *The magic of dialogue: Transforming conflict into cooperation*. New York: Simon & Schuster.

Abrahamson, Eric, "initiative overload" and, 4
Action, stages of change and, 86
Action stage, teachers and, 88
advance and post organizers, 162–163
Advocacy, overview of, 128
After-Action Report, diagram of, 131
Albright, Madeleine, dancing at United
    Nations and, 181
Allen, David, productivity and, 105
Allen, Woody, attentiveness and, 62
Annual Yearly Progress (AYP), overview of, 1
Archer, Anita, "I Do It, We Do It,
    You Do It" approach, 163
Argyris, Chris, external commitments and, 186
Assessment Training Institute, training
    materials and, 177
The Attempt, Attack, Abandon Cycle,
    200–203
Attentiveness, 62
Authenticity, listening techniques, 63

Balance, goal of, 10
Barnes, Lynn:
    asking questions and, 67
    background of, 58
    collaboration with, 75
    emotional bids and, 76
    empowering students and, 27
    group presentations and, 68
    interference and, 72
    learning conversations and, 57, 60
    quick fixes and, 1
    reading body language and, 74
    setting goals and, 204
Beckhard, Richard, reciprocity and, 50
Behavior:
    classroom management and, 100
    content and, 149–150
    creating respect and, 148
    effective corrective comments and, 144–145
    "Opportunities to respond" and, 146–148
    overview of, 23
    Time on Task and, 145–146
Behavior Coaching and Data Measures, 149
Bernstein, Richard, partnership and, 39
Bernstein, Richard J., praxis and, 50
Big Four:
    Disclaimer 1: The Big Four Is Not Just for
        Weaker Teachers, 140
    Disclaimer 2: This Is Just an Introduction,
        140–141
    overview of, 141–142
Bishop, Jr., Charles, path to organizational
    change, 22

Block, Peter:
    collaborative problem solving and, 28
    partnership and, 39
    Stewardship, 42, 52
Bloom, Benjamin:
    six levels of educational objectives, 166
    Taxonomy of Educational Objectives, 165
Bohm, David:
    listening and, 61
    On Dialogue, 135–136
    true dialogue and, 46
Bolejack, Shelly:
    background of, 181
    Core Group Theory and, 192
    empowering students and, 27
    infectious personality and, 189
    instructional coach, 179
    Paragraph Strategy and, 184
    spreading ideas and, 180
    Writing Strategies and, 194
Books:
    coaching and, 16
    Dialogue and, 135–136
    Harvard Negotiation Project and, 135
Brasseur, Irma, Strategic Advantage project, 14
Breaking it down, tactics for translating
    research into practice, 105
Brieck, Mary, 71
Buckingham, Marcus, outstanding managers
    and, 218
Buckley, Joe, 216
Bulgren, Jan:
    Concept Mastery Routine, 31
    defining concepts and, 159

Carnegie, Dale, *How to Win Friends
    and Influence People*, 79
Center for Research on Learning, Web sites, 177
*Chalice and the Blade: Our History,
    Our Future*, 53
CHAMPs approach, 31
    areas of behavior and, 143
China, Hopei province and, 179
Choice:
    definition of, 53
    partnership and, 24–25, 41–43
Claflin, Susan, conversations about teaching
    and, 28
Clarify, tactics for translating research
    into practice, 103
Clark, Jean:
    background of, 198
    final word on, 216–217
    finding confidants and, 214

follow-up and dialogue and, 207
   instructional coach, 197
   partnership approach and, 211
   walking on solid ground and, 203
Classroom Academic Engagement Form, 147
Classroom Organization and Management
   Program, Web sites, 142
Cloud, Henry:
   importance of being clear and, 203
   leadership and, 217–218
CNN, "Macarena fever" and, 181
Coaching:
   books on, 16
   Coaching in Schools, 16
   coactive coaching and, 9–10
   cognitive coaching and, 10–11
   common forms of, 9–14
   components of, 89–94
   executive coaching and, 9
   final word about and, 15–16
   literacy coaching, 11–12
   reading coaching, 11–12
Coaching and Feedback for
   Performance, 16
Coaching for Leadership, 16
Coaching Instruction, advance and post
   organizers, 162–163
Coaching: Evoking Excellence in Others, 16
Coactive coaching, overview of, 9–10
Coffman, Curt, outstanding managers and, 218
Cognitive coaching, 10–11
Coherence-building practices, 185–186
Collaboration:
   exploration of data and, 122–132
   instructional coaching and, 27–28
   "language of ongoing regard" and, 125–126
   top-down feedback, 123–124
Collins, Jim, leadership and, 213
Communication:
   partnership principles and, 60
   six aspects of, 57
Communication process:
   building emotional connections and, 75–77
   components of, 59–60
   empathy and respect, 63–64
   employing authentic listening and, 60–65
   facial expressions and, 73–75
   interference and, 60
   recognizing and overcoming interference,
     69–73
   self-awareness and, 62
   understanding of, 59–60
   understanding our audience and, 65–69
Concept Diagram, 161
Concept Mastery Routine, 6, 31, 159, 205
Contemplation, stages of change and, 85
Contemplative stage, teachers and, 87
Content, teaching and, 101

Content Coaching:
   Critical Questions Checklist, 153
   developing essential questions and, 151–153
   direct instruction and, 160
   Example Compare-and-Contrast Organizer, 156
   Example Descriptive Organizer, 157
   Example Problem-Solution Organizer, 157
   Example Sequential Organizer as a
     Timeline, 156
   Identifying, Defining, and Teaching
     Concepts, 158–160
   mapping content and, 152–158
   modeling and, 163–165
   Unit Organizer, 154
Content Coaching, 151–162
Content Enhancement, 150, 203, 205
Content Enhancement Routine, 47, 158, 172, 176
   overview of, 8, 121
Content knowledge, overview of, 23
Content Structures, 158
   contracting, Getting Teachers on Board and,
     94–95, 94
Core Group Theory, 192
Course Organizers, praxis and, 49
Covey, Stephen:
   The 7 Habits of Highly Effective People, 79
   *The Eighth Habit: From Effectiveness to
     Greatness*, 53
   empathy in the act of listening, 63
   listening strategies and, 65
   living a fulfilled life, 45
Critical Questions Checklist, 153
Csikszentmihalyi, Mihaly:
   competition and, 182
   evolution of ideas and, 181
   flow experiences and, 169
   key to happiness and, 169
   student learning and, 168
"Cue, Do, Review" teaching routine, 121

Danielson, Charlotte, Direct instruction and, 23
Davenport, Thomas, need for autonomy and,
   133–134
Dawkins, Richard, memes and, 181
DeClaire, Joan, emotional connections and, 24
Deshler, Don, Strategic Advantage project, 14
Dialogue:
   books and, 135–136
   collaborative exploration of data and, 126–129
   definition of, 54
   partnership and, 25, 46–47
   strategies for promoting and, 127–129
Differentiated Coaching, 68
*Differentiated Coaching: A Framework for
   Helping Teachers Change*, 67
*Difficult Conversations: How to Discuss What
   Matters Most*, 69
Direct instruction, overview of, 23

Dunekack, Devona:
   biography of, 20
   caring and, 207
   collaboration and, 28
   enrolling teachers and, 22
   modeling and, 29
   Pathways to Success and, 19
   support and, 32

Edmiston, Jim, emotional connections and, 75
Eichinger, Sherry, finding confidants and, 214
*The Eighth Habit: From Effectiveness to
   Greatness*, 53
Eisler, Riane:
   *Chalice and the Blade: Our History, Our
     Future,* 53
   partnership and, 39, 52
Ekman, Paul:
   Emotions Revealed, 79
   Facial Action Coding System, 74
Ellis, Ed, "I Do It, We Do It, You Do It"
   approach, 165
   emotional bids, 76–77
   emotional connections, building and, 24–26
Emotions Revealed, facial expressions and, 74
Empathy, listening and, 63–64
Enrico, Roger, PepsiCo and, 205
   enrollment, Getting Teachers on Board, 90
Equality:
   definition of, 53
   partnership and, 24
   partnership and, 40–41
Evertson, Carolyn, collaboration and, 142
Example Compare-and-Contrast Organizer, 156
Example Descriptive Organizer, 157
Example Problem-Solution Organizer, 157
Example Sequential Organizer as a Timeline, 156
Executive coaching, overview of, 9
Expectations:
   developing and teaching, 143–151
   ratio of interactions and, 143–144
Exploring, collaborative exploration of data
   and, 122–132
Extraversion and Introversion, energy and, 67

Facial Action Coding System, 74
Facial expressions, 73–75
Faith, 215
Fear, overcoming fear and, 20–22
Feedback:
   instructional variables and, 174
   observing and providing feedback and, 29–31
Five Tactics for Translating Research Into
   Practice, 103–106
Flow experiences, 169
Formative assessment, 168–176
   Developing Course and Unit Questions,
     171–172

developing high-quality assessments,
   172–173
involving students and, 175–176
overview of, 23
teaching and, 102
Framing Routine, 82, 88
Freire, Paulo:
   partnership and, 39
   Pedagogy of the Oppressed, 52
Fulfillment, goal of, 10
Fullan, Michael:
   change in schools and, 195
   direct approach and, 185
   moral purpose and, 204
   partnership and, 39
   personality and, 188
   "pressing immediacy" and, 4

Gadotti, Moacir, praxis and, 49
Gallup Organization, outstanding managers
   and, 218
Gau, Tom, persuasive people and, 188
GEAR UP program, 13
Getting Results With Curriculum Mapping, 23
Getting Teachers on Board:
   "The Big Four" and, 100–102
   building relationships during interviews, 94–96
   contracting and, 94–95
   enrollment and, 90
   explaining the teaching practice, 102–103
   identify and, 99
   interview questions and, 93–94
   Large-Group Presentations, 97–98
   One-to-One Informal Meetings, 98
   One-to-One Interviews, 90–91
   overview of, 81–83
   Principal Referrals, 98–99
   professional learning in schools and, 87–89
   scheduling interviews and, 91–92
   small-group meetings and, 95–96
   spiral model of change and, 87
   stages of change and, 85–87
   the first meeting and, 99–100
   translating research into practice and,
     103–106
Gladwell, Malcolm:
   Blink, 78
   law of the few and, 191
   sharing ideas and, 188
   spreading ideas and, 180, 194
Gleick, John, fast times and, 28
Godin, Seth, spreading ideas and, 180, 193–194
Goleman, Daniel, leadership and, 217
Gottman, John:
   emotional connections and, 24
   The Relationship Cure, 78
Greenleaf, Robert K., servant leadership and, 61
Gregorio, Vince, model lessons and, 119

Gronquist, Paul, model lessons and, 117
Guskey, Tom, knowledge of processes and
  procedures, 171

HALO effect, addressing student needs and, 167
Hargreaves, Andy, "pressing immediacy" and, 4
Harvard Negotiation Project, 132, 135
Heen, Sheila, listening skills and, 61
Heifetz, Ronald, resistance and personal
  attacks, 199
High-Level Questions, 165–166
Hirsch, Stephanie, coaching programs and, 185
Holmgren, LaVonne:
  advance organizers and, 163
  "assessment literacy" and, 170
  background of, 141
  CHAMPs and, 143
  collaboration and, 142
  Content Enhancement, 150
  correcting inappropriate behavior and, 145
  developing essential questions and, 151–153
  instructional coach, 139
  interviews and, 91
  involving students and, 175
  modeling and, 164–165
  teaching for understanding and, 162
Honesty, listening techniques, 63
*Hope and Hopelessness When Leading
  Change*, 214
Hunter, Madeline, Direct instruction and, 23

"I Do It, We Do It, You Do It," format, 110,
  163, 165
  identity conversation, overview of, 69
Inquiry, overview of, 128
Instruction, teaching practices and, 101–102
Instructional Coaches, questions for
  collaborating teachers and, 66–67
Instructional Coaches and Implementation,
  graph for, 3
Instructional Coaches Professional Learning
  Community, 104
Instructional coaching:
  as leaders of change and, 197
  The Attempt, Attack, Abandon Cycle,
    200–203
  Big Four issues and, 22–23
  building emotional connections and, 24–26
  coherence-building practices and, 185–186
  Creating Answers for Unit Questions, 172
  Developing Course and Unit Questions,
    171–172
  developing high-quality assessments, 172–173
  encouraging implementation and, 26–27
  following the law of the few and, 191–194
  formative assessment and, 170–176
  getting teachers on board and, 81–84
  infectious personality and, 187–189

Observation Form, 113
  observing and providing feedback and, 29–31
  overcoming fear and, 20–22
  partnering with principal and, 32–33, 189–191
  starting points and, 22
  support and, 31–32, 31
  Tactic 1: Staying Detached, 198–203
  Tactic 2: Walk On Solid Ground, 203–204
  Tactic 3: Clarifying Your Message, 204–205
  Tactic 4: Managing Change Effectively,
    205–208
  Tactic 5: Confronting Reality, 208–210
  Tactic 6: Understanding School Culture,
    210–211
  Tactic 7: Being Ambitious and Humble,
    211–213
  Tactic 8: Taking Care of Yourself, 213–216
Instructional Coach's Tool Kit, 219–223
Interference, recognizing and overcoming,
  69–73
International Reading Association, literacy and
  reading coaches, 12
Interventions, 184
Interviews:
  building relationships during, 94–96
  during the interviews and, 92
  interview questions and, 93–94
  scheduling interviews and, 91–92
  teacher interviews and, 117–118
Isaacs, William:
  advocacy of, 128
  Dialogue and the Art of Thinking Together,
    126, 136
  listening and, 61
  respect and, 64
  role of theory and, 39
  self-awareness and, 62

Jacobs, Heidi Hayes, *Getting Results With
  Curriculum Mapping*, 23
Jeary, Tony, Life Is a Series of Presentations, 79
Jensen, Bill, Simplicity, 106
Judging and Perceiving, approaching life and, 67

Kansas University Center for Research on
  Learning:
  Big Four overview and, 100, 139
  components of coaching and, 89
  instructional practices and, 23
  Pathways to Success and, 13
  Strategic Instruction Model and, 5
Kanter, Rosabeth Moss, "stuck" and "moving"
  institutions, 210
Kise, Jane, *Differentiated Coaching: A
  Framework for Helping Teachers
  Change*, 67
Kleiner, Art, Core Group Theory and, 192
Kline, Frank, feedback and, 175

Kolb, Deborah, responsive turns and, 211
Kuhn, Thomas, understanding the world and, 70

LaFrance, Dee:
    infectious personality and, 187
    teaching practices of, 194
Laing, R. D., listening and, 61
Lake, Linda, model lessons and, 118
Lancaster, Paula, Strategic Advantage project, 14
Large-Group Presentations, 97–98
Lawrence-Lightfoot, Sarah, *Respect*, 44
Learning conversations:
    creation of, 57–58, 57
    empathy and respect, 63–64
    employing authentic listening and, 60–65
    recognizing and overcoming interference, 69–73
    understanding our audience and, 65–69
Learning Teams, 192–193
Lenz, Keith:
    Course, 23
    Course Organizer, 152
Lewin, Kurt, pioneers of social psychology and, 37
Linsky, Marty, resistance and personal attacks, 199
Listening:
    misconceptions and, 61–62
    self-awareness and, 62
Listening Strategies:
    building emotional connections and, 75–77
    clarifying and, 65
    communicating our understanding, 65
    developing inner silence, 64
    facial expressions and, 73–75
    listening for what contradicts our assumptions, 65
    practicing every day and, 65
    practicing with terrible listeners and, 65
    understanding our audience and, 65–69
Literacy coaching, 11–12

Maintenance:
    stages of change and, 86
    supporting a teacher and, 88
Mapping content, 152–158
Maryland State Department of Special Education, Passport to Success and, 14
Marzano, Robert, *Classroom Management That Works*, 142
McKale, Tricia:
    background of, 112
    collaboration and, 110, 142
    collaborative exploration of data, 124
    dialogue and, 126
    instructional coach, 109
    model lessons and, 114–116
    observing lessons and, 121

open-ended questions and, 129
    reflection and, 132
McTighe, Jay, diagnostic assessments and, 170
Memes, understanding memes and, 181–182
Meyerson, Debra, tempered radicals and, 211
Model lessons:
    survey results and, 116–117
    "tacit" knowledge and, 119–120
Modeling, 29, 163–165
    The Observation Form, 111–112
    overview of, 109–110
    providing model lessons and, 114–116
    Ready-Made Checklists and, 112
    teacher interviews and, 117–118
Myers-Briggs Type Indicator tool (MBTI), overview of, 67

Negotiation, core concerns and, 132–135
No Child Left Behind (NCLB) legislation, 1, 184

O'Brien, Mike, simplicity and, 106
Observation Form, 113
Observing:
    "language of ongoing regard" and, 125–126
    model lessons and, 120–122
    top-down feedback, 123–124
O'Connor, Ken, diagnostic assessments and, 170
The October Session, 5–9
One-Shot Professional Development, impact on teacher practices and, 2
One-shot sessions, The October Session, 5–9
One-to-One Informal Meetings, 98
One-to-One Interviews, 90–91
"Opportunities to respond", 146–148

Palma, Ric:
    dialogue and, 47
    equality and, 41
    instructional coaching approach, 39
    listening and, 46
    partnership and, 37
    Pathways to Success project, 40
    praxis and, 50
    reciprocity and, 51
    reflection and, 48
Palmer, Parker:
    reflection and, 48
    teaching and vulnerability, 26
Paragraph Writing Strategy, 105, 182–183
Partnership:
    choice and, 41–43
    dialogue and, 46–47
    equality and, 40–41
    overview of, 37–38
    praxis and, 49–50
    reciprocity and, 50–51
    reflection and, 47–49
    voice and, 43–46

Partnership Learning, 14
  overview of, 39
Partnership Learning Structures
  large-group presentations and, 97
  overview of, 106
Partnership Mind-set, definition of, 24
Passport to Success program, 14
Pathways to Success, 104, 183, 189, 190,
    192, 194
  coaching term and, 15
  research and, 13–14
  teacher fidelity and, 34
Pedagogy of the Oppressed, 52
Pinchot, Elizabeth, comparing executive
    coaches to therapists, 140
Pinchot, Gifford, comparing executive coaches
    to therapists, 140
Planning conversation, cognitive coaching and, 11
Polanyi, Michel:
  tacit aspects of knowledge, 119
  understanding the world and, 70
Post organizers, 162–163
Praxis:
  definition of, 54
  partnership and, 25, 49–50
Preconference, first conversation and, 100
Precontemplation, stages of change and, 85
Precontemplative stage, teachers and, 87
Preparation:
  stages of change and, 86
  teachers and, 88
Principal, partnering with, 189–191
Principal Referrals, 98–99

Quality Assignment Routine, 166, 171
Quality Assignments, 166–168
Question Exploration Device, 172
Question Exploration Guide, 173
Questions:
  Critical Questions Checklist, 153
  developing essential questions and, 151–153
  High-Level Questions, 165–166

Rademacher, Joyce, Quality Assignment
    Routine, 166
Ratio of Interactions, 143–144
Reading coaching, 11–12
Reciprocity:
  definition of, 54
  partnership and, 26
  partnership and, 50–51
Reflecting conversation, cognitive coaching
    and, 11
Reflection:
  components of coaching and, 130
  definition of, 53
  partnership and, 25
  partnership and, 47–49

Reinke, Wendy
  collaboration and, 142
  Time on Task and, 146
The Relationship Cure, emotional bids and, 78
Research, overview of, 13–14
Respect:
  creating respect and, 148
  listening and, 63–64
Respect, 44
Responsive Turns:
  chart for, 212
  definition of, 211
Rosenholtz, Susan, reality and, 210

Safe and Civil Schools, Web sites, 176
Sanctuary, 215–216
Scanlon, David, The Order Routine, 158
Schön, Donald A., reflection and, 48
Schumaker, Jean, Strategic Advantage
    project, 14
Scott, Susan, attentiveness and, 62
Self-awareness, listening and, 62–63
Seligman, Martin
  "learned helplessness" and, 194
  optimism and, 188
Senge, Peter:
  partnership and, 39
  understanding the world and, 70
Sensing and Intuition, gathering information
    and, 68
The Sentence Writing Strategy, 52
*Seven Principles for Making Marriage
    Work,* 78
Sheritts, Hannah, model lessons and, 118
Simplify, tactics for translating research
    into practice, 106
Small-Group Meetings, 95–96
Sparks, Dennis, leadership and, 217
spiral model of change, getting teachers
    on board, 87
Spreading knowledge:
  coherence-building practices and, 185–186
  following the law of the few and, 191–194
  infectious personality and, 187–189
  intellectual evolution and, 194
  interventions and, 184
  overview and, 179–180
  partnering with principal, 189–191
  understanding memes and, 181–182
Sprick, Randy:
  CHAMPs approach, 31
  CHAMPs: A Proactive and Positive
      Approach to Class, 142
  correcting rule violations, 145
*Standards for Middle and High School Literacy
    Coaches,* 33
Standards for Staff Development, 33
Status, definition of, 134

Stewardship, 42, 52
Stiggins, Richard:
    formative assessment and, 168
    state assessments and, 171
    student motivation and, 169
    Student-Involved Assessment for Learning, 23
Strategic Advantage project, 14
Strategic Instruction Model, 194, 205
    learning strategies and, 175
Student-Involved Assessment for Learning, 23
Sturtevant, Elizabeth, literacy coaches and, 12
Sue Woodruff, instructional coach, 81
Support:
    components of coaching and, 129
    instructional coaching and, 31–32
Synthesize, tactics for translating research into
        practice, 104

"Tacit" knowledge, model lessons and,
        119–120
Taxonomy of Educational Objectives, 165
Teachable Point of View (TPOV), building
        blocks of, 205
Teachers'/Students' Eyes, tactics for translating
        research into practice, 105
Teaching:
    and "The Job I Love", 26–27
    coherence-building practices and, 185–186
    content and, 149-150
    developing essential questions and, 151–153
    distinguish your role from your self, 214
    Do I have proper equipment?, 206–207
    Do I Know What Is Expected of Me?, 206
    effective corrective comments and, 144–145
    finding confidants and, 214–215
    finding sanctuary and, 215–216
    infectious personality and, 187–189
    interventions and, 184
    mapping content and, 152–158
    mastering new teaching practices and, 110–111
    "Opportunities to respond" and, 146–148
    partnering with principal, 189–191
    quality assignments and, 166–168
    "resisting change" and, 3
    survey results and, 116–117
    Time on Task and, 145–146
Tempered radicals, definition of, 211
Termination:
    stages of change and, 86
    teaching and, 88
Theme Writing Strategy, 82, 88
Theory, definition of, 39
Thinking and Feeling, making decisions
        and, 68
Thom, Ronald J., Trent University campus
        and, 185

Tichy, Noel, clarity and, 204–205
Time on Task, 145–146
*Tomorrow's Children: A Blueprint Education
        for Partnership for the 21st Century,* 53
Top-down feedback, 123–124
Traditional professional development
    failure and, 1–5
    "initiative overload" and, 4
    The October Session, 5–9
    "pressing immediacy" and, 4
*Turning to One Another: Simple Conversations
        to Restore Hope to the Future,* 57
Tutu, Desmond, 58

The U.S. Army Leadership Field Manual,
        reflection and, 130
U.S. Army: After-Action Review (AAR), 130
Understanding by Design, 23
    developing essential questions, 152
Unit Organizer Routine, 28, 154, 199, 205
Unit Organizers, 23

Virus, worm virus, 180
Voice:
    definition of, 53
    partnership and, 25
    partnership and, 43–46

Waldy, Hannah, model lessons and, 118
Web sites:
    Center for Research on Learning, 177
    Classroom Organization and Management
        Program, 142
    Safe and Civil Schools, 176
Wheatley, Margaret:
    listening and, 61
    *Turning to One Another: Simple
        Conversations to Restore Hope to
        the Future,* 57
Williams, Judith, responsive turns and, 211
Wilson, Kim, instructional coaching and, 81
Woodruff, Sue:
    background of, 84
    enrolling teachers and, 90
    interviews and, 91
    partnership approach and, 83
    seeing things through teachers' eyes, 105
    the Big Four and, 102
    the first meeting and, 99–100
Worm virus, 180

Yankelovich, Daniel
    dialogue and, 126
    *The Magic of Dialogue: Transforming
        Conflict Into Cooperation,* 136
Yersinia pestis, virus and, 179

**CORWIN
PRESS**

The Corwin Press logo—a raven striding across an open book—represents the union of courage and learning. Corwin Press is committed to improving education for all learners by publishing books and other professional development resources for those serving the field of PreK–12 education. By providing practical, hands-on materials, Corwin Press continues to carry out the promise of its motto: **"Helping Educators Do Their Work Better."**

NSDC's mission is to ensure success for all students by serving as the international network for those who improve schools and by advancing individual and organization development.